The Myth of Triumphalism

The Myth of Triumphalism

*Rethinking President Reagan's
Cold War Legacy*

BETH A. FISCHER

UNIVERSITY PRESS OF KENTUCKY

Scholarly publisher for the Commonwealth,
serving Bellarmine University, Berea College, Centre
College of Kentucky, Eastern Kentucky University,
The Filson Historical Society, Georgetown College,
Kentucky Historical Society, Kentucky State University,
Morehead State University, Murray State University,
Northern Kentucky University, Transylvania University,
University of Kentucky, University of Louisville,
and Western Kentucky University.

Editorial and Sales Offices: The University Press of Kentucky
663 South Limestone Street, Lexington, Kentucky 40508-4008
www.kentuckypress.com

Library of Congress Cataloging-in-Publication Data

Names: Fischer, Beth A., 1964– author.
Title: The myth of triumphalism : rethinking President Reagan's Cold War
    legacy / Beth A. Fischer.
Description: Lexington, Kentucky : University Press of Kentucky, [2020] |
    Series: Studies in conflict, diplomacy, and peace | Includes
    bibliographical references and index.
Identifiers: LCCN 2019030036 | ISBN 9780813178172 (hardcover) |
    ISBN 9780813178196 (pdf) | ISBN 9780813178202 (epub)
Subjects: LCSH: Reagan, Ronald. | Cold War. | United States—Foreign
    relations—Soviet Union. | Soviet Union—Foreign relations—United
    States. | United States—Foreign relations—1981–1989. | United
    States—Politics and government—1981–1989.
Classification: LCC E876 .F567 2020 | DDC 973.927092—dc23
LC record available at https://lccn.loc.gov/2019030036

For Gerard, Kate, Andrew, Jack, and—of course—Toby

Contents

Introduction

Triumphalism and President Reagan's Cold War Legacy

What role did the Reagan administration play in ending the Cold War? This is an important question because the ending of this conflict was arguably the biggest surprise of the twentieth century. The Cold War had divided much of the globe since 1947, and during the 1980s it was widely assumed that it would continue indefinitely. The Cold War was considered to be an enduring and fundamental feature of the international system. It simply did not occur to most Americans that it *could* end. Even the so-called experts failed to anticipate its demise. As Bruce Jentleson explains in his popular textbook on US foreign policy, "What we must acknowledge is how humbling the end was, or should have been, for 'experts.' It was not uncommon in the mid-1980s for professors to assume that any student who imagined a post–Cold War world was just young, naïve, and idealistic. The Cold War was with us, and, students were told, likely to have its ups and downs, its thaws and freezes, but it was not about to go away."[1]

It was widely assumed that if the Cold War were to end, it would end very badly indeed. Common scenarios envisioned a regional conflict escalating out of control, drawing the United States and the Soviet Union into direct confrontation, most likely in Europe. A large-scale conventional war would be fought and horrific losses would ensue. The war would end, it was feared, with the superpowers unleashing their nuclear weapons, resulting in Armageddon. A nuclear winter would then settle over Europe and North America.

After 1949, when the Soviets detonated their first nuclear bomb, the United States's primary objective had been to avoid all-out war with the

1

USSR. Virtually no one entertained the idea of actually *resolving* the Cold War—that is, solving the underlying disagreements that led to mistrust, arms races, and competing alliance systems. Resolving these fundamental disputes seemed too preposterous to consider seriously. As one Reagan administration official explained in 1983, "[N]o one man—indeed no group of men—can affect, except at the very margins, the fundamentally competitive nature of [the superpower] relationship. . . . And I must caution you that improvements, if they do come, are bound to be modest. We will not see the day of days with the Soviet Union. Our rivalry will, I fear, outlive all of us in this room."[2]

The great irony is that not only did the Cold War end, it ended peacefully. Despite widespread assumptions that the conflict was permanent and irresolvable, the superpowers resolved their differences and began to disarm. If we can understand how this happened, we can gain insight into how to peacefully conclude other seemingly intractable conflicts. Getting the story right is therefore a high-stakes proposition.

Views about President Reagan's Role in Ending the Cold War

When President Ronald Reagan left office in January 1989 the conventional view was that he had played at best a minor role in ending the Cold War.[3] From this perspective Soviet General Secretary Mikhail Gorbachev single-handedly ended the Cold War by introducing a series of revolutionary policies that ended the arms race and improved relations between East and West. Gorbachev came to power seeking to revitalize the Soviet economy. Consequently, he sought to reduce defense expenditures and to invest instead in consumer goods, technology, and infrastructure. In order to reduce defense spending, Gorbachev needed to end the costly arms race and improve relations with the United States and its allies. He therefore introduced his policy of "New Thinking," which entailed a more conciliatory posture toward the West and a series of unilateral gestures intended to build trust, such as unilaterally reducing Soviet arsenals and instituting moratoriums on the deployment of new intermediate-range nuclear missiles and on nuclear weapons tests. Rather than focusing on superpower rivalries, Gorbachev emphasized common interests, such as the need to end the threat of nuclear annihilation, stem environmental degradation, and address global disparities in wealth.[4]

From this perspective, it was Gorbachev's desire to reform the Soviet system that led to the end of the Cold War. His decision to end the arms race led first to improved relations between Moscow and Europe and ultimately to an end of the hostility between the superpowers. President Reagan played a largely passive role in these events. He was simply the lucky beneficiary of Soviet initiatives to conclude the Cold War.

This school of thought was common in the United States during the late 1980s and 1990s. At the time, scholars and journalists were taken aback by the momentous changes within the USSR and the Eastern bloc and were consequently fixated on Soviet policy. The result was a "Gorby-centered" view of the world. Moreover, it was fashionable in some quarters to dismiss Reagan as an unsophisticated thinker who was largely detached from the policy-making process. The idea that the president played virtually no role in ending the Cold War was based in part upon assumptions that he played a secondary role in his own administration.

This perspective was eventually eclipsed by another school of thought, known as "triumphalism."[5] Triumphalism contends that President Reagan won the Cold War by building up US military power and threatening the Soviet Union. In this view, Reagan's unprecedented military buildup combined with his belligerent rhetoric and refusal to negotiate compelled Moscow to agree to arms reductions, adopt democratic reforms, withdraw from its war in Afghanistan, and ultimately collapse. In short, Reagan's hawkish policies enabled the United States to triumph over the Soviet Union.

In this perspective, the Reagan administration was keenly aware of the fragile state of the Soviet economy during the 1980s and intended to force the country to collapse. Reagan introduced the largest peacetime military buildup in US history so as to lure the Kremlin into an arms race it could not afford. Likewise, he initiated the costly Strategic Defense Initiative (SDI) not because he thought a nuclear defensive system was desirable or feasible, but rather because he wanted to goad Moscow into investing in an SDI program of its own. Faced with a costly arms race and technology they could not master, the Soviets increased their defense spending until they were on the brink of bankruptcy. Ultimately, they had no option other than to surrender. Reagan's policies compelled Gorbachev to become more conciliatory toward the United States and to acquiesce to American demands for arms reductions and democratic reforms. From this perspective, Gorbachev's moratoriums and unilateral efforts at disarmament were acts of desperation, not determination.

Reagan's hard-line policies compelled the Soviet Union to surrender the arms race and then collapse.

Triumphalism emerged in the 1990s and has since gained widespread credibility and influence. After leaving office Reagan administration officials began publishing their memoirs, and some argued that the administration's policies had forced Moscow to agree to arms reductions. For example, Defense Secretary Caspar Weinberger maintained that the Kremlin could not match the Reagan military buildup and was therefore compelled to accept American demands for disarmament.[6]

Triumphalism was then popularized by Peter Schweizer in his 1994 book *Victory: The Reagan Administration's Secret Strategy That Hastened the Collapse of the Soviet Union*. Schweizer argued that the administration had a secret plan to bankrupt the Soviet Union and force it to implode. The president launched a military buildup and introduced SDI so as to entice Moscow into an arms race it could not afford. According to Schweizer, Reagan's buildup and resolve ultimately forced the USSR to succumb.[7]

Since the 1990s, triumphalism has been promoted by scholars, pundits, and politicians.[8] The triumphalist description of the ending of the Cold War has not only become conventional wisdom, it has taken on near-mythic proportions. For example, much of the media coverage of the president's carefully orchestrated 2004 funeral portrayed Reagan as a superhero who brought the United States to soaring new heights of strength, forced the evil communists to surrender, and single-handedly bestowed peace upon the world. "On June 5, 2004 a great and gallant leader passed from our midst and the whole world is diminished by his loss," read one typical commentary. "Ronald Reagan stood against the darkness of communism. He won the fight for freedom and brought down what he rightly termed 'the Evil Empire.'"[9] Likewise, shortly after Reagan's death the influential newsweekly the *Economist* ran a cover photo of the president with the banner headline "The Man Who Beat Communism." Even though CNN was careful to say that the president "hastened" the end of the Cold War, the overall effect of the reporting left viewers to believe that Reagan had forced the Soviets to collapse. A CNN.com "Quick Poll" on the day of Reagan's death asked, "What will President Reagan be most remembered for?" A striking 78 percent of the nearly 100,000 respondents answered, "End of the Cold War."[10] On television, film clips of Reagan's June 1987 speech in front of the Berlin Wall declaring "Mr. Gorbachev! Tear down this wall!" were juxtaposed with images of East Germans streaming through the breech in November 1989. The impression was that Reagan's determination had opened the gates in a manner akin to Moses parting the Red Sea. Mikhail Gorbachev had nearly become a historical footnote. At most he was Robin to Reagan's Batman.

Triumphalism and Post–Cold War Foreign Policy

Triumphalism claims to explain how the Cold War ended. It also stipulates how to cope with current and future conflicts: President Reagan's hawkish policies forced the Soviet Union to acquiesce to American demands and collapse, therefore contemporary leaders should compel adversaries into submission. Like Reagan, they should threaten others with military buildups, avoid negotiations, and seek regime change abroad.

Triumphalists assert that the Reagan administration's military buildup was crucial in compelling the Soviets to agree to arms reductions and democratic reforms. Consequently, the United States should continue to pursue overwhelming military power. As Joshua Muravchik argued in 1992, defense spending purchases "peace and security."

> Our bloodless victory in the Cold War has just given eloquent answer to those who asked so insistently why we were "wasting" so many billions on weapons "that will never be used." . . . Had we heeded them in the first place the Cold War might not have been won, for if the United States had not chosen in the 1980s to hold up its end of the arms race, Soviet rulers might have sought to remedy their economic crisis by means of extortion rather than through the radical reforms that doomed their system.[11]

In this view, defense spending has multiple payoffs. Most obviously, it increases the capability to protect one's territory and project one's power. The United States was both safer and stronger owing to its renewed military strength under the Reagan administration.

Moreover, defense spending can lead to important new technological innovations. Such advances place the adversary at an important disadvantage. A good case in point is the Strategic Defense Initiative. In the triumphalist view the Soviets were deeply afraid of SDI not only because they did not have the financial resources to mount their own SDI program, but also because they were unable to master the technology involved in constructing such a system. In addition, the Soviets feared that spin-offs from SDI research might lead to a new generation of technologies that would render Soviet weapons systems obsolete.[12]

Defense spending can also be a psychological weapon. Triumphalists maintain that Reagan's military buildup—and SDI in particular—were effective simply because of the alarm they generated within Moscow. Soviet officials feared that they could not keep pace with the United States and that they could not counter SDI. These fears led them to surrender the arms race, withdraw from Afghanistan, and adopt democratic reforms.

The implication of all these arguments is that military threats resolve conflicts. The United States should seek military superiority so as to prevail over adversaries and compel the resolution of disputes.

Triumphalists also contend that negotiating with adversaries is counterproductive. During the détente of the 1970s Washington sought to engage Moscow through a series of arms control talks and summit meetings. In the triumphalist view, détente was a complete failure. The Soviet Union was able to attain parity with the United States and was emboldened to invade Afghanistan in December 1979. The Soviets embarked on this quest to expand their empire because American military strength had been allowed to decline and the Carter administration had appeared weak. The United States simply did not have the strength or resolve to deter Soviet expansionism.

President Reagan, by contrast, refused to meet with his Soviet counterparts during his first term in office and instead delivered stinging denunciations about the immorality of their system. It was this refusal to negotiate, combined with renewed American strength, that compelled the Soviet Union to make concessions. Triumphalists therefore conclude that contemporary leaders should avoid negotiations with adversaries.

Triumphalists also advocate regime change. In this view, President Reagan's military buildup, combined with his tough talk and refusal to negotiate, compelled Moscow to agree to democratic reforms and eventually to abandon communism altogether. As Republican presidential hopeful John McCain explained in 2007:

Many argued for reconciliation with our global adversary. But [President Reagan] held firm. . . . He called for resolve and firmness in dealing with the Soviet Union. And he refused to condemn millions

to perpetual Communist tyranny in the false hope that accommo-
dating the Soviet Union would contribute to America's security. . . .
Thanks to his leadership, the Soviet Union dissolved and the Cold
War was won on our terms.[13]

Like Reagan, post–Cold War presidents should pursue regime change via
military threats and demonstrations of resolve.

Triumphalist Myths

This book demonstrates that despite its popularity, the triumphalist description of the ending of the Cold War is a myth, and a dangerous one at that.
Triumphalism not only overlooks the ways in which Reagan's hard-line policies undermined US interests and brought the superpowers to the brink of
war, it also ignores the pivotal role that diplomacy played in bringing about
the peaceful conclusion of the conflict. Triumphalism is a series of fallacies
about President Reagan's intentions, his policies, and the impact his administration had on the Soviet Union.

Fundamentally, triumphalism rests on flawed logic. Triumphalists argue
that the Reagan administration wanted the Soviet Union to disarm and collapse; the Soviet Union did disarm and collapse; therefore Reagan *caused* the
Soviets to disarm and collapse. This is a gross error in causal logic; the argument confuses correlation with causation. In order to understand why the
Soviets acted the way they did—and, therefore, the impact that US policies
had on Moscow—it is necessary to examine Soviet sources and Soviet decision making. Yet triumphalists focus exclusively on American policies and
American perceptions of how the Cold War concluded. They make no effort
to understand the causes of Soviet behavior. They consistently fail to ask,
"Why did the Soviet Union reduce its arsenals, reform, withdraw from its
war in Afghanistan, and collapse?" They simply assume the Reagan administration caused these events.

In the late 1980s and 1990s such errors were understandable because
credible information about Soviet policy making was limited. During the
Reagan years the United States had few human or technical intelligence
sources in the Kremlin, and information about Soviet policy discussions was
therefore sparse.[14] No one really knew with certainty why the Soviets adopted
the policies they did. Trying to discern Soviet motivations and intentions

was largely guesswork. One could observe inputs (American proposals to reduce nuclear arms) and outputs (reductions in the Soviet arsenal), but the decision-making process inside the Kremlin was largely a black box. US officials assumed that Moscow tried and failed to match the American military buildup and therefore had no option but to acquiesce to US demands for arms reductions. Others speculated that the mere prospect of an enhanced arms race with the United States compelled Moscow to disarm.[15] But the reality was that few outside the Politburo knew for certain why the Soviets behaved the way they did.

But we now have much information about Soviet decision making during the 1980s and are therefore better able to assess the impact of Reagan's policies on Moscow. Soviet archives opened after the USSR collapsed in December 1991, there have been a host of oral history conferences in which Soviet officials have shared their recollections of their time in office, and Gorbachev and many of his colleagues have published memoirs.[16] Moreover, there is a robust literature about Soviet policy making during the 1980s by Soviet scholars and others.[17]

This book addresses this fundamental flaw in triumphalism. Drawing upon Soviet sources it seeks to understand the causes of Soviet behavior during the 1980s. In doing so, it finds that triumphalist claims are largely unsupported by evidence. Reagan's policies did not compel Moscow to disarm, adopt democratic reforms, withdraw from its war in Afghanistan, and collapse. Rather, the hard-line policies of Reagan's first term brought the superpowers to the brink of war in 1983. Moreover, the high-tech SDI research program did not cause the Soviets to be so fearful that they acquiesced to American demands to disarm. In fact, military scientists concluded that SDI could be easily countered and in all likelihood would never be built. Perhaps most importantly, the increases in US defense spending did not compel the Kremlin to invest in a buildup of its own. Reagan's policies had a negligible impact on Soviet defense spending and thus on the Soviet collapse. Finally, Reagan's belligerence during his first term undermined US interests by weakening the position of Soviet reformers who sought to improve relations with the West and reduce arsenals.

Triumphalists not only fail to accurately understand the impact that Reagan's policies had on the Soviet Union, they also mischaracterize the president's intentions and objectives. President Reagan had revolutionary ideas about global security and sought to eliminate nuclear weapons. These views caused rifts within the administration, and the president encountered resistance from his advisers, allies, and fellow Republicans. But Reagan's pursuit of a nuclear-free world was the foundation upon which the Cold War concluded. The conflict began to subside once the president began engaging in talks with Moscow during his second term. These negotiations enabled the superpowers to build trust, identify common goals, and work together toward nuclear disarmament. Thus, the ending of the Cold War was a triumph of diplomacy and disarmament, not force and compellence. This is the legacy that should guide contemporary American leaders.

In addition, triumphalists often conflate the ending of the Cold War with the collapse of the Soviet Union. These are two separate events, and this book treats them as such. The conclusion of the Cold War entailed an end to the hostility between the communist East and the democratic West. The dissolution of the USSR, however, entailed the collapse of a system of government. The Soviet Union collapsed on December 31, 1991, when the Soviets lowered their flag for the last time. But the Cold War had largely concluded years earlier. Superpower relations had begun to improve in the wake of Reagan and Gorbachev's first meeting in Geneva in November 1985. After Geneva there were signs that Cold War hostilities were beginning to abate, although not everyone acknowledged or accepted them.[18] By 1987, however, the Cold War was unraveling at a rapid pace. "From late 1987, . . . we began to register significant results in all parts of the US-Soviet agenda," former ambassador to the Soviet Union Jack Matlock has recalled. "The speed of change was dizzying for those of us who had worked for decades on what had long seemed the intractable problems of dealing with the USSR."[19] In December 1987 Gorbachev visited the United States for the first time and joined President Reagan in signing the Intermediate-Range Nuclear Forces (INF) Treaty, the first treaty to eliminate an entire class of nuclear weapons. Captivated by the revolutionary changes in the Soviet Union, "Gorby mania" swept through the United States. By the time Reagan strolled through Red Square in May 1988 he declared that the USSR was no longer the "evil empire." That had been "another time, another era," Reagan explained.[20] Many Americans agreed. A majority of Americans polled in the spring of 1988 believed that the Soviet Union posed only a minor threat, if any at all.[21] By the spring of 1989 leading American newspapers were running editorials with titles such as "Beyond the Cold War" and "The Cold War Is Over." In May the new president, George H. W. Bush, declared it was time for the

United States to "move beyond containment."[22] In November 1989 democratic revolutions swept through Eastern Europe and the Berlin Wall was breached. The Soviet Union stood aside and watched. There could be little doubt that a new era had begun. At a joint press conference concluding the Malta summit that December President Gorbachev declared, "The world is leaving one epoch and entering another. We are at the beginning of a long road to a lasting, peaceful era. The threat of force, mistrust, psychological and ideological struggle should all be things of the past." President Bush agreed. "We can realize a lasting peace and transform the East-West relationship to one of enduring cooperation," he replied. Gennadi Gerasimov, the Soviet Foreign Ministry spokesman, added, "We [have] buried the Cold War at the bottom of the Mediterranean Sea."[23] It would be two years before the Soviet Union would expire. Had it not collapsed, it is conceivable—indeed, likely—that the superpowers *together* would have presided over the transition to a more peaceful post–Cold War era.

Organization and Scope of the Book

This book has two sections. The first focuses on President Reagan's policies and intentions, while the second focuses on Soviet decision making, seeking to understand the impact that the Reagan administration's policies had on the USSR. Each chapter focuses on a different fallacy, debunking its claims.

The first section begins by debunking triumphalist claims that President Reagan employed hard-line policies toward Moscow throughout his eight years in office and avoided summit meetings with his Soviet counterparts. Chapter 1 demonstrates that by 1984 the president was actively seeking dialogue and cooperation, and by the time he left office he had met with Soviet leaders more frequently than any of his predecessors. His ultimate goal was nuclear disarmament, which was a revolutionary idea at the time and caused deep disagreements between the president and his advisers.

The first section of the book also challenges the claim that President Reagan launched a military buildup and SDI so as to entice the Soviets into an expensive arms race that would bankrupt their country. As Chapter 2 details, US government documents demonstrate that the buildup was intended to persuade Moscow to engage in arms reduction talks. Administration officials mistakenly believed that the Soviets would not agree to reductions unless they were confronted by a strong and menacing adversary. Paradoxically, the military buildup was intended to bring about arms reductions. Moreover, as Chapter 3 explains, Reagan launched SDI in the hope that the system would be able to protect civilians from nuclear attack. Much to his advisers' chagrin, the president repeatedly offered to share SDI technology with the Soviet Union so that citizens around the world could be protected from nuclear annihilation. Reagan also reasoned that if both sides had defenses, nuclear weapons would become obsolete and could therefore be eliminated. Thus, SDI was a critical component of the president's quest to eliminate nuclear weapons.

The second section of the book is told from Moscow's perspective and debunks triumphalist claims that the Reagan administration forced the Kremlin to withdraw from its war in Afghanistan, adopt democratic reforms, agree to arms reductions, and collapse. Chapter 4 demonstrates that within four weeks of the 1979 invasion of Afghanistan Soviet leaders believed they had made a mistake and had begun looking for a face-saving way out. In addition, for decades before Reagan took office a reform movement had been growing in the USSR. These reformers sought to decrease defense expenditures and invest instead in consumer goods and technology. They sought to end the arms race, adopt democratic reforms, and improve relations with the West. Thus, these policy changes were not examples of Moscow "knuckling under" American pressure; rather, they were rooted in decades-long domestic discussions.

This section also debunks the triumphalist claim that the US military buildup and SDI enticed the Soviets into a costly arms race that bankrupted their country. Chapter 5 explores Soviet perceptions of SDI and crucial reforms in Soviet military doctrine. Although Soviet military officials were initially concerned about SDI, after careful review they concluded that it could easily be countered and in all likelihood would never be built. Thus, they urged Gorbachev to ignore it. Moreover, for a variety of strategic and financial reasons Moscow never sought to match the increases in American defense spending. Thus, Reagan's buildup played a negligible role in the financial collapse of the Soviet Union.

In sum, despite its popularity, triumphalism is a series of fallacies about President Reagan's policies and the influence his administration had on the Soviet Union. It ignores the ways in which Reagan's initially hard-line approach undermined US interests and overlooks the pivotal role that diplomacy and antinuclearism played in bringing about the peaceful conclusion of the Cold War.

A note about the scope of the book is in order. This volume is not meant to be a comprehensive history of the ending of the Cold War. Rather, it is tightly focused on the myth of triumphalism. In doing so it necessarily summarizes some literature and refers only briefly to tangential debates and events. Where appropriate, the endnotes refer the reader to other, more detailed sources about these issues.

One final point is needed. Triumphalists often speak of Reagan "winning" the Cold War. "Winning" is a vague term that can mean anything from destroying the Soviet Union to peacefully concluding the Cold War. Thus, this book avoids using this term. Instead, it focuses on understanding how the superpower conflict was resolved as well as the causes of specific changes in Soviet policy, such as Moscow's decision to reduce its arsenals, adopt democratic reforms, and withdraw from its war in Afghanistan.

1

Engaging the Enemy

I didn't have much faith in Communists or put much stock in their word. Still, it was dangerous to continue the East-West nuclear standoff forever, and I decided that if the Russians wouldn't take the first step, I would.

Ronald Reagan

The fact that neither of us likes the other's system is no reason to refuse to talk. . . . We will never retreat from negotiations.

Ronald Reagan

In the triumphalist view, President Reagan was the ultimate hard-liner: he talked tough, he built up US military power, and he refused to engage with Moscow until it complied with his demands for change. He employed threats and shunned negotiations. These hawkish policies compelled the Kremlin to acquiesce to American demands for reform and disarmament and ultimately to collapse. Reagan's hawkish posture enabled the United States to triumph over its enemy.

Triumphalists believe that President Reagan demonstrated the effectiveness of compelling adversaries into submission. Engaging with the enemy through diplomacy and negotiations is a sign of weakness, they say, while threats and diplomatic isolation force enemies to cooperate. Post–Cold War leaders should follow Reagan's example.

This caricature of President Reagan is misguided. It focuses exclusively on Reagan's earliest years in the White House and overlooks the bulk of his presidency. Reagan started out by rattling his saber, but this hawkish posture brought the superpowers to the brink of war, as this chapter demonstrates. By 1983 the president was actively seeking to engage Moscow in negotiations so as to improve superpower relations and reduce nuclear arsenals. By the time he left office Reagan had met with his Soviet counterpart more frequently than any of his predecessors. This quest for dialogue, cooperation, and arms reduction was pivotal in concluding the Cold War. Engaging the enemy is an integral part of Reagan's legacy.

This chapter considers the broad strokes of the Reagan administration's policies toward the Soviet Union, debunking the triumphalist claim that the president was a hard-liner who refused to engage with adversaries. Chapter 2 focuses more narrowly on the motives behind President Reagan's military buildup, while Chapter 3 considers the president's objectives in launching the Strategic Defense Initiative.

Schoolboy Scuffles: Disorganization and Turf Battles within the Administration

Ronald Reagan was sworn in as the fortieth president of the United States on January 20, 1981, an unseasonably mild, albeit cloudy, day. A few months earlier, Reagan had defeated President Jimmy Carter in a landslide. Carter's presidency had been marred by one tragedy after another, leading many voters to conclude that American strength had weakened dangerously on his watch. In November 1979 fifty-two Americans had been taken hostage by Islamic revolutionaries in Iran. The attack was not only horrifying, it was insulting. The Americans were being held by a ragtag bunch of students in a Third World country, and the Carter administration had proven incapable of extricating them. An attempt to rescue the hostages by helicopter in April 1980 had been marred by a series of embarrassing technical failures, resulting in a crash that took the lives of eight US servicemen. The Americans languished in captivity for 444 days, each day another humiliation for the president and the country.[1]

In addition, on December 24, 1979, the Soviet Union had invaded Afghanistan. Although this rural country was on Moscow's doorstep, it had not traditionally been part of the Soviet Union's sphere of influence. The incursion was therefore both unexpected and unprecedented, leading many Americans to perceive it as a direct challenge to the United States. Soviet power was on the rise, it seemed, and Moscow had calculated that Washington was too weak to prevent the USSR from expanding its influence.

The American economy was also in a prolonged slump. There had been a series of energy crises during the 1970s, and the economy was growing at an anemic rate. Inflation ran into the double digits, unemployment was high, and by November 1979 the prime interest rate had reached 15.5 percent.[2]

During the presidential campaign Reagan had pledged to renew American strength. His supply-side economic plan would reinvigorate the economy, and increased defense expenditures would restore American power abroad. These pledges resonated with voters. On Election Day the former governor of California carried forty-four states and received the highest number of electoral votes ever won by a nonincumbent presidential candidate. Americans clearly wanted a change.

Once in office, President Reagan focused on spurring an economic recovery. "Nothing was more important than getting the tax and spending cuts through Congress," he explained in his memoirs.[3] Over time, however, these budget cuts led to a ballooning deficit, which created increasing opposition to his economic plan. During his first three years in office, Reagan recalls, he "was under almost constant pressure to abandon the economic program. . . . [I]t was largely a tug of war on this issue that dominated my first term in the White House."[4]

Given these pressing economic concerns, foreign policy took a back seat. The administration was slow off the mark in formulating a coherent policy toward Moscow. Despite the president's campaign promises to stand up to the Soviet Union, the administration was unable to develop a definitive statement of its goals and strategies toward the USSR until January 1983.[5] This was due in part to Reagan's fixation on the economy, but there were other difficulties as well. For one thing, the administration suffered from serious organizational problems. Policy goals were not clearly delineated, and lines of authority and responsibility were unclear. Edwin Meese, counselor to the president, was in charge of policy coordination, but his poor organizational skills rendered him particularly ill suited to the job. Secretary of the Treasury Donald T. Regan referred to this disarray as "the guesswork presidency." In March 1981 he complained in his diary, "Never has [the president] or anyone else sat down in private to explain to me what is expected of me, what goals he would like to see me accomplish, what results he wants. . . . How can one do a job if the job is not defined?" Years later Regan reflected, "From the first day to last at the Treasury, I was flying by the seat of my pants."[6]

This problem was particularly acute in foreign policy making. "[T]here was no description of duty, no rules, no expression of the essential authority of the president to guide his subordinates in their task," Secretary of State Alexander Haig lamented in his memoirs.

In the absence of such a charter, there can be no other result than confusion. The grand purposes of the nation to keep the peace . . . and to admonish our enemies fall victim to schoolboy scuffles for personal advantage in the corridors of the White House. What begins in uncertainty nearly always ends in chaos.[7]

This confusion led to bureaucratic battles between the State Department, the National Security Council (NSC), the Defense Department, and the Central Intelligence Agency (CIA).

These organizational troubles were exacerbated by ideological rifts. Broadly speaking, the administration was composed of two types of foreign policy advisers. The first group was comprised of conservative ideologues who were passionately anticommunist. These "fire-eaters," as one observer called them, repeatedly denounced the Soviet Union for seeking military superiority and world domination, and engaging in unethical conduct both at home and abroad.[8] In their view, détente had been a complete failure, resulting in American military inferiority and emboldening the Soviet Union to the extent that it felt it could invade Afghanistan with impunity. The United States should build up its military strength and refuse to negotiate with Moscow, they believed. This group, which included Meese, Secretary of Defense Caspar Weinberger, CIA Director William Casey, and the Soviet and East European affairs specialist on the NSC, Richard Pipes, favored a hard-line policy toward Moscow: lots of pressure, no negotiations, and no concessions on arms control. Pipes—the most zealous of the group—had to be reined in at times. In one instance he was publicly reprimanded by the White House and the State Department for saying that the "Soviet leaders would have to choose between peacefully changing their Communist system in the direction followed by the West, or going to war. There is no other alternative, and it could go either way."[9]

The second group was less ideological and more focused on problem solving. While they believed the Soviet Union was a threat, they also believed that it would not change its ways unless the United States engaged. Certain areas of the superpower relationship were amenable to improvement, they believed, but threats and mutual recriminations were counterproductive. Negotiation was necessary. This group, which included Reagan's second secretary of state, George P. Shultz, National Security Adviser Robert "Bud" McFarlane, and Soviet expert Jack F. Matlock Jr. (who replaced Pipes in

1983), favored pragmatic engagement on specific issues, such as regional conflicts, human rights, and arms reduction. "I felt we had to turn the relationship around: away from confrontation and toward real problem solving," Shultz explained in his memoirs.[10]

Personality clashes were superimposed over these ideological disputes and organizational difficulties. A career military officer, Secretary Haig sought an orderly, structured foreign policy making system, with himself at the pinnacle of power. His brusque manner and frustration over the administration's disorganization—combined with his desire for control—only deepened the discord during the first eighteen months of the administration. When the president was shot in March 1981 Haig immediately stepped forward and asserted that he was in charge, a claim that had no legal foundation and that further irritated his cabinet colleagues.[11] Haig's opponents took to leaking unflattering information about him to the press, which added to the secretary's anxieties.[12] As Pipes recalled, "The entire first year and a half of the administration passed in an atmosphere of unremitting tension between the NSC and the State [Department]."[13] The hostility between Haig and the Defense Department was even more acute. As Secretary Weinberger described it, Haig "seemed to be constitutionally unable to present an argument without an enormous amount of passion and intensity, heavily overlaid with a deep suspicion of the competence and motives of anyone who did not share his opinions."[14] Although the president sought to stay above the fray, he too eventually became frustrated with Haig's "turf battles" and "paranoid attitude."[15] Thus, in June 1982 Haig was replaced by George P. Shultz.

Shultz could not have been more different from his intensely emotional and ambitious predecessor. A former academic and labor mediator, Shultz was mild-mannered, cautious, and technocratic. He preferred to keep his views to himself and was scrupulously respectful of the president's authority. Shultz viewed himself as a "gardener" of diplomacy: his job was to plant the president's ideas and tend them carefully over the long term.[16] Composed, tight-lipped, and businesslike, his aides in the State Department referred to him as "Buddhalike," while the Soviet ambassador to the United States branded him "the Sphinx."[17]

Despite the fact that Shultz was far less abrasive than Haig, he encountered many of the same frustrations over policy making and often found himself at odds with the CIA, the Defense Department, and the NSC. Shultz soon discovered that the "staffs of [these] organizations, supposedly following the same administration policy, waged perpetual battle on behalf of—and often without the knowledge of—their principals. . . . [A] cult of secrecy verging on deception had taken root in the White House and NSC staffs."[18]

Shultz particularly butted heads with Caspar Weinberger. A native Californian, Weinberger had been Governor Reagan's director of finance. He went on to become director of the Office of Management and Budget under President Richard Nixon, where he was known as "Cap the Knife" for his ruthless ability to slash spending. As defense secretary, however, he favored massive increases in military spending, earning the nickname "Cap the Ladle."[19] A lawyer by training, Weinberger was notoriously stubborn and took pride in his ability to stonewall those who disagreed with him. His preferred negotiating strategy was to filibuster, thus preventing his interlocutors from getting a word in edgewise. He was not inclined to compromise with his own Cabinet colleagues, much less with the Kremlin. Clashes between Shultz and Weinberger became one of the defining features of the Reagan years.[20]

President Reagan was uncomfortable with these conflicts among his advisers. When his officials could not agree, Reagan avoided choosing sides, preferring instead to dispel the tension with humorous anecdotes. Indeed, he contributed to the problem by making remarks that seemed to support each group. Advisers were frequently left to divine the president's wishes, and they often came into conflict with each other, each claiming to represent the "true" Reagan.[21] As Haig described it at the time, "Because of his habitual cheery courtesy, it is at times difficult to know when [President Reagan] is agreeing or disagreeing, approving or disapproving."[22] The president's mixed signals undermined his administration's ability to craft a coherent policy toward the USSR.

The feuding within the administration led to a high turnover rate among key foreign policy advisers. During the first term alone, the administration went through two secretaries of state and three national security advisers.[23] By 1983, however, a degree of stability was emerging. Shultz had settled into his position at the State Department, and McFarlane became national security adviser in October and remained in that post for over two years. And in June 1983 Matlock replaced Pipes as the Soviet expert on the NSC. More important, the changes in personnel also brought a shift in the balance of power within the administration. Like Shultz, McFarlane and Matlock favored pragmatic engagement with the Kremlin. While some hard-liners such as Weinberger and Casey remained, others, such as Richard Allen, William Clark, Haig, and Pipes, had moved on.

A final reason why the Reagan administration was slow to develop a coherent policy toward the Soviet Union was that there was no sense of urgency on the matter. Under its aged general secretary Leonid Brezhnev, the Soviet Union continued to plod along, spewing out the same ideological dogma that it had for nearly a decade. Given Brezhnev's poor health, US officials suspected it was unlikely that the Kremlin would engage in a summit meeting for fear the general secretary would embarrass himself. Among foreign policy experts there was a sense that little could be achieved until Brezhnev passed the torch to a successor.[24] However, after Brezhnev died in November 1982, he was succeeded by two equally infirm leaders, Yuri Andropov and Konstantin Chernenko. The Soviet Union did not have a stable leader capable of engaging with the United States until Mikhail Gorbachev came to power in March 1985.

The Hard-Line Years, 1981–1983

Owing to the disorganization and turf battles, the Reagan administration's initial policy toward the USSR was little more than a military buildup combined with a series of hawkish public statements. The focus—to the extent that there was one—was on building military strength and demonstrating American resolve.

During these early years Reagan officials repeatedly denounced the Soviet Union. "Moscow is the greatest source of international insecurity today," Secretary Haig proclaimed in April 1981. "Soviet promotion of violence as the instrument of change constitutes the greatest danger to world peace."[25] The Kremlin promoted revolution and global terrorism and engaged in weapons proliferation, Haig insisted.[26]

Throughout 1981 and 1982 Reagan officials routinely accused Moscow of seeking military superiority. The president asserted that the Soviet Union had been engaging in "the greatest military buildup in the history of man" and that it was "plainly . . . offensive in nature."[27] At the same time, the United States had allowed its military capabilities to deteriorate, he claimed. The result was a dangerous imbalance in which the United States could not match Soviet military power. "The truth of the matter is that on balance the Soviet Union does have a definite margin of superiority," he insisted in 1982, "enough so that there is risk and there is what I have called . . . 'a window of vulnerability.'"[28]

Reagan called on the Soviet Union to disarm. "The defense needs of the Soviet Union hardly call for maintaining more combat divisions in East Germany today than were in the whole Allied invasion force that landed in Normandy on D-Day," the president reasoned. "The Soviet Union could make no more convincing contribution to peace in Europe, and in the world, than by agreeing to reduce its conventional forces significantly and constrain the potential for sudden aggression."[29]

Meanwhile, President Reagan sought to build up American military power. Although he slashed government spending across the board, Reagan increased defense expenditures substantially. The president introduced the largest peacetime military budget in US history, increasing defense spending more than 10 percent per year between 1981 and 1985. In six years this amounted to a 160 percent increase over the last Carter budget, which in itself had represented a significant increase in military outlays. The administration allocated $1.46 trillion to defense over five years.[30] These expenditures consumed more than 30 percent of the federal budget.[31]

Given this commitment to building up military strength, the administration initially placed little emphasis on arms control negotiations. "Arms control is no longer the centerpiece of US-Soviet relations," Haig declared in July 1981.[32] It would serve "no useful purpose," he explained, to engage in arms talks with the Kremlin while it continued its "imperialist activities abroad."[33]

There were other components to this policy of strength. For instance, in 1981 the Reagan administration decided to forge ahead with a planned deployment of US intermediate-range nuclear missiles (or "INF," intermediate-range nuclear forces) to Western Europe. NATO had devised this "Euromissile" plan in 1979 as a way to counter the Soviet deployment of SS-20 missiles that targeted Western Europe. By the early 1980s, however, such a deployment seemed overly provocative to many. Nonetheless, the Reagan administration believed a show of allied strength and unity was necessary so as to check Soviet military power and aspirations. Consequently, it announced that it would deploy Pershing II and cruise missiles to Western Europe beginning in November 1983.

This decision prompted public protests throughout Europe and generated an increasingly vocal peace movement. As opposition to the planned deployment of US nuclear missiles to Europe grew, pressure mounted for arms reduction talks. In response, in the fall of 1981 the administration proposed that the United States would forego its planned deployment if the Soviets would dismantle the SS-20s they had already deployed in the region. This proposal became known as the "Zero Option" because its aim was to reduce to zero the number of intermediate-range nuclear weapons in Europe.[34]

Initially, West European allies welcomed the proposal because they saw it as a way to placate the growing nuclear freeze movement in the region.[35] In addition, many were relieved that the administration was finally showing signs of engaging in substantive matters. As one observer put it, the president got credit "for finally having moved to rebut the European contention that he is presiding over an erratic, divided, bellicose administration [that is] less dedicated to arms control than the Kremlin."[36]

Others dismissed the Zero Option as a cynical move, since it required far more of the Soviet Union than it did of the United States. Interestingly, Secretary Haig was among this group. "The fatal flaw in the Zero Option as a basis for negotiations was that it was not negotiable," Haig fumed in his memoirs. "It was absurd to expect the Soviets to dismantle an existing force of 1,100 warheads, which they had already put into the field at a cost of billions of rubles in exchange for a promise from the United States not to deploy a missile force that we had not yet begun to build and that had aroused such violent controversy in Western Europe."[37] Suspicions arose that the proposal was simply a public relations maneuver rather than a sincere attempt to limit nuclear proliferation. Critics noted that the plan was supported most enthusiastically by the hard-liners within the administration, such as Defense Secretary Weinberger, who had no personal or institutional interest in arms reduction. In fact, behind closed doors the plan's supporters believed the Soviets would reject it out of hand, thus handing the administration a public relations victory. As was widely expected, the Kremlin immediately dismissed the Zero Option as a "propaganda ploy."[38]

The Reagan administration also rejected the unratified Strategic Arms Limitation Treaty (SALT II), claiming that it institutionalized the military imbalance.[39] Instead, it proposed a new series of negotiations—the Strategic Arms Reduction Talks (START). Unlike previous arms talks, START's aim would be to reduce nuclear stockpiles rather than to simply limit the rate at which they could grow. At first glance, the START proposal appeared to be a significant step toward reining in the arms race. The devil was in the details, however. The proposal called for a cap on land-based warheads that would have required the Soviets to destroy more than half of their arsenal, while allowing the United States to build up.[40] Since these weapons were the foundation of

Soviet nuclear strength, reducing them by half would have assuredly weakened its position vis-à-vis the West. Consequently, the Soviets dismissed the proposal as disingenuous.

The Reagan administration's approach to regional disputes was also confrontational. The White House sought to check Soviet influence throughout the globe and to place "maximum pressure" on them throughout the Third World. It wanted to insure that Soviet costs would remain high in these regions and thus sought to assist those fighting them "to the maximum degree possible."[41] In Afghanistan the Reagan administration beefed up US support to the mujahedin fighting the Soviets, while simultaneously demanding that the Kremlin withdraw.

1983: Descent toward War?

By 1983 the Reagan administration's bristling polemics and military buildup were causing growing concern that the world was sliding toward superpower confrontation. Peace movements had sprung up in Europe and the United States, and the European nuclear freeze movement had become increasingly strident. President Reagan repeatedly rejected the idea of freezing nuclear arsenals at their current level, however, stating that such a move would institutionalize the military imbalance and leave the West in a permanently vulnerable position.

The drumbeat toward war appeared to boom louder as the year progressed. In March President Reagan delivered a speech to the National Association of Evangelicals in which he excoriated the Soviet Union. "[L]et us pray for the salvation of those who live in that totalitarian darkness," he intoned. "[T]hey are the focus of evil in the modern world. . . . [We cannot] ignore the forces of history and the aggressive impulses of an evil empire."[42]

Two weeks after this blistering denunciation, President Reagan delivered another speech in which he unveiled the Strategic Defense Initiative (SDI), a research program that sought to develop a space-based system of lasers that would defend the United States against a nuclear attack.[43] As was custom during these years, Reagan devoted much of his address to the Soviet threat. "The final fact is that the Soviet Union is acquiring what can only be considered an offensive military force," he asserted.

As soon as it was unveiled, SDI unleashed a storm of opposition. Given Reagan's strident denunciations of the Soviet Union, many perceived SDI to be offensive in nature. The perception was that the United States was starting an arms race in space. Although Reagan had called for a reduction in armaments and declared that he did not think war was inevitable, these statements faded into the background as observers focused on the potentially threatening implications of a space-based defensive system.[44]

Relations between the superpowers grew increasingly tense in the fall of 1983. On September 1 a Soviet Su-15 jet fighter intercepted and shot down a Korean Air Lines passenger jet, KAL 007, killing all 269 passengers on board, including 61 Americans. The disaster stemmed from a tragedy of errors. The Boeing 747's automatic pilot system had been set incorrectly, allowing it to stray more than 300 miles into Soviet airspace, toward a militarily sensitive region. Incredibly, the inattentive Korean pilots had not noticed the transgression. The Soviets considered such a violation to be a provocation of the highest order. Moreover, they were on edge owing to an American military campaign in which aircraft would fly straight at the Soviet border, sending Soviet radar stations onto alert, before peeling off at the last moment. The purpose of the American operation had been both to test Soviet early warning systems and to harass Soviet military personnel.[45] In this instance Soviet pilots had mistakenly identified KAL 007 as one of these American reconnaissance planes. Although they attempted to contact the Korean pilots, their efforts had failed. The Soviet pilots had also fired warning flares, but they were launched at such an angle that they were imperceptible to the Korean crew. Ultimately, the Soviet pilot fired on flight KAL 007 without a positive visual identification of the plane, defying his commander's orders.[46]

Although the American intelligence community had evidence indicating the incident had been a mistake, Reagan administration officials seized on the tragedy as yet another instance of Soviet "barbarism." President Reagan expressed his "revulsion at this horrifying act of violence" and asserted that it underscored the Soviets' immorality.[47]

The Soviets made the situation worse by at first denying that the accident had happened and then, when it was clear that such a falsehood was unsustainable, charging that the plane had been on a spy mission for the United States. Their refusal to accept responsibility, and the shrill manner in which they asserted American culpability, plunged relations to a new low. On September 28 General Secretary Andropov condemned the United States for its "sophisticated provocation" and its "militarist course that poses a grave threat to peace." The Kremlin was through dealing with such "dangerous, inhuman policies," Andropov declared. The KAL incident dispelled any illusions that superpower relations could evolve for the better.[48]

In November the "Euromissile" crisis reached its climax. Once the Soviets had rejected the Zero Option, the Reagan administration remained committed to deploying US intermediate-range nuclear missiles to Europe, despite growing opposition in both the USSR and Western Europe. In mid-November the first ground-launched cruise missiles began to arrive in Great Britain, followed by the arrival of Pershing II missiles in West Germany on November 23. The Soviets responded by immediately withdrawing their delegation from arms control talks in Geneva. The following day Andropov announced countermeasures, which included the deployment of additional Soviet missiles to East Germany and Czechoslovakia as well as the redeployment of nuclear-armed submarines to a position closer to the US coast.[49] And on December 8 Soviet officials stormed out of strategic arms reduction talks.

Behind the scenes, relations became alarmingly hostile. Between November 7 and 11 NATO conducted a large-scale military exercise in Europe called "Able Archer 83."[50] The purpose of the drill was to rehearse a nuclear attack on the Soviet Union. NATO had conducted similar exercises in the past, but none had been as massive—or as realistic—as this one.

As was customary, the Soviets eavesdropped on the NATO exercise through listening posts in Eastern Europe. As they did so, they grew increasingly alarmed. During World War II, Adolf Hitler had launched a devastating surprise attack against the Soviet Union's western border, which had left an indelible scar on the Soviet psyche, known as "1941 syndrome." An entire generation became obsessed with identifying and preventing another such invasion. By the mid-1970s the Soviet strategy was "launch on warning": upon detecting the initial signs of an attack, Moscow would unleash its nuclear forces in a massive attack on US cities.[51] The Soviet strike would be instantaneous and overwhelming. Such a plan depended upon both good intelligence collection and forces that were on hair-trigger alert.

General Secretary Andropov had long believed that President Reagan was actively preparing for war. In May 1981, when he was still director of the KGB, Andropov had declared at a closed meeting for high-level intelligence officers that the United States was planning a nuclear attack. Consequently, he ordered the Soviet intelligence community to search for evidence of the impending strike. This mission—code-named Operation RYAN, for the Russian acronym

"Nuclear Missile Attack"—became the most comprehensive peacetime intelligence operation in Soviet history and was the intelligence community's foremost priority. For the first time, the KGB joined with the military intelligence agency, the GRU, in a global intelligence-gathering operation aimed at detecting the first signs of a nuclear attack against the USSR and its allies.[52]

By the time Andropov became general secretary in November 1982 he had become even more alarmed. From his perspective, the probability of an attack was increasing rapidly. Reagan had failed to rein in his vitriolic rhetoric, and the US military buildup was continuing. The Soviets rejected as ludicrous the Reagan administration's charges that the Soviet Union had military superiority; they believed the American buildup to be an attempt to dominate the USSR. The planned deployment of US Pershing II missiles to Europe—from which the West could strike Soviet territory in less than six minutes—only heightened these anxieties.[53] Thus, throughout 1983 Moscow demanded increasing amounts of information from its KGB agents in Europe about the impending attack. The Kremlin's insistence that an attack was imminent, combined with its demand that agents look for signs of such a strike, became a self-fulfilling prophecy. "Because the political leadership was expecting to hear that the West was becoming more aggressive, more threatening, better armed, the KGB was obedient and reported: yes, the West was arming. . . . [I]t may signify something sinister," Oleg Gordievsky, the deputy chief of the London KGB office, recalls. "Residencies were, in effect, required to report alarming information even if they themselves were skeptical of it. The Centre was duly alarmed by what they reported and demanded more."[54]

The KAL 007 tragedy heightened Soviet concerns about its security. Andropov and Marshal Nikolai Ogarkov, the chief of staff of the armed forces, both believed the Korean plane had, in fact, been on an American intelligence mission. They feared the plane had gained precious information about Soviet early warning systems and defense procedures, and might even have photographed Soviet defense facilities. The affair also highlighted the deficiencies of Soviet air defense. Eight of the eleven early warning stations on the Soviet perimeter had failed to detect the airliner. The plane had been in Soviet airspace for over two hours and had traveled hundreds of miles toward sensitive military installations before Soviet air defense forces had even approached it, and once they had, communications between the Soviet pilots and the ground commanders had been chaotic. The KAL 007 tragedy had underscored Soviet vulnerability.

Able Archer 83 appeared to be the nuclear attack Moscow had been both fearing and searching for. Soviet defense plans envisioned launching a surprise attack on the West under the guise of a planned exercise, and Soviet officials reasoned that NATO had similar plans. Soviet anxiety was palpable. "Perhaps never before in the postwar decades has the situation in the world arena been as tense as it is now," declared Grigory Vasilyevich Romanov, a Politburo member regarded as a potential successor to General Secretary Andropov, to the Kremlin Palace of Congresses on November 7. "Comrades! The international situation is white hot! Thoroughly white hot!"[55]

Thus, in the midst of the NATO exercise, the Soviets began to prepare for a nuclear strike against the West. Moscow raised the alert status of its nuclear capable aircraft in Poland, and in East Germany the Group of Soviet Air Forces began loading tactical nuclear weapons onto Sukhoi-17 long-range strike aircraft. Warsaw Pact forces prepared to bomb West Germany with nuclear weapons.[56]

As it happened, Able Archer 83 ended on November 11, 1983, before the crisis could become full-blown. For reasons that remain unclear, the Soviet Union did not launch its nuclear missiles.[57]

Thus, 1983 ended on a note of fear and loathing. "The second cold war has begun," warned the Italian newsweekly *Panorama*. The French president, François Mitterrand, believed that the situation was as grave as the Cuban Missile Crisis of 1962.[58] The influential Soviet weekly *Literaturnaya Gazeta* ran a fictionalized account of that crisis on November 23, 1983, suggesting that Moscow, too, perceived the situation to be comparable.[59] Alarmed by the arrival of the American missiles in Europe and the subsequent collapse of nuclear arms talks, the Vatican tried to mediate the growing rift between the superpowers. After a visit to Washington, however, the Vatican Secretary of State, Cardinal Agostino Casaroli, was pessimistic. "I do not believe that reaching very conciliatory results is possible," he concluded solemnly.[60]

In the United States, *Time* magazine declared that the apparent descent toward war had been the defining feature of 1983.

> [T]here is grave danger: if not of war tomorrow, then of a long period
> of angry immobility in superpower relations; of an escalating arms
> race bringing into US and Soviet arsenals weapons ever more expen-
> sive and difficult to control; of rising tension that might make every

world trouble spot a potential flash point for the clash both sides fear. The deterioration of US-Soviet relations to [this] frozen impasse overshadowed all other events of 1983.[61]

1984: Turning the Tide

Beginning in January 1984 the White House adopted a strikingly different tone toward the Soviet Union. The administration began repeatedly calling for dialogue, cooperation, and disarmament. Reagan insisted that the United States did not threaten the security of the USSR and called for meetings so that the superpowers could discuss their differences and build trust.

The president unveiled these changes during an address on January 16.[62] Reagan and his advisers had been working on the speech for months and had devoted more time and effort to this address than any other speech except the State of the Union. In an attempt to underscore its importance, Reagan officials had hand-delivered advance copies to Soviet Ambassador to the US Anatoly Dobrynin and Soviet Foreign Minister Andrei Gromyko. In addition, they wrote to Soviet officials calling attention to the upcoming address and reiterating its themes.[63] In a departure from custom, Reagan officials held several press briefings in advance of the address, discussing its main themes. This speech was to be a "watershed," McFarlane explained.[64]

"I believe that 1984 finds the United States in its strongest position in years to establish a constructive and realistic working relationship with the Soviet Union," the president began. "Our working relationship with the Soviet Union is not what it must be. . . . [W]e want more than deterrence; we seek genuine cooperation; we seek progress for peace."

The United States sought "cooperation, dialogue and understanding," Reagan explained. His primary objective was to avoid war and reduce arsenals. "Neither we nor the Soviet Union can wish away the differences between our two societies and our philosophies," he reasoned. "But we should always remember that we do have common interests. And the foremost among them is to avoid war and reduce the level of arms." Reagan underscored his desire for peace. "[T]he people of our two countries share with all mankind the dream of eliminating the risks of nuclear war. . . . Today our common enemies are poverty, disease, and above all, war."

In a marked change in tone, President Reagan sought to reassure Moscow of Washington's benign intentions. "Our challenge is peaceful. We do not threaten the Soviet Union," he explained. "Our countries have never fought each other; there is no reason why we ever should."

After three years without a superpower summit, Reagan proclaimed such meetings to be a necessity. "We must and will engage the Soviets in a dialogue as serious and constructive as possible, a dialogue that will serve to promote peace in the troubled regions of the world, reduce the level of arms, and build a constructive working relationship," he stated. "We seek genuine cooperation, [and] cooperation begins with communication," the president reasoned. "The fact that neither of us likes the other's system is no reason not to talk. Living in the nuclear age makes it imperative that we do talk."

The superpowers' primary task would be to "find ways to reduce the vast stockpiles of armaments in the world. . . . [R]educing the risk of war—and especially nuclear war—is priority number one." In a radical departure from the accepted wisdom about international security, Reagan called for the abolition of nuclear weapons. "[M]y dream is to see the day when nuclear weapons will be banished from the face of the Earth," he declared.

The president also sought to resolve regional conflicts in places such as Afghanistan, southern Africa, and Central America. Rather than denouncing the Soviets' "expansionist" activities, as was custom in the past, Reagan stated that the superpowers "should jointly examine concrete actions that we can both take to reduce US-Soviet confrontation" throughout the world.

President Reagan's address was noteworthy for the new cooperative tone, the desire for dialogue, and the call for the elimination of nuclear weapons. It was also noteworthy for what it did *not* say. There was no name-calling, no paternalistic demands for behavioral change, no sermons about the immorality of the communist system, and, most conspicuously, no lengthy oration about the threat posed by the ever-growing Soviet arsenal. In a striking departure from the past, the tone was collegial rather than accusatory.

President Reagan's aim was to improve superpower relations and usher in an era of nuclear disarmament. Jack Matlock, the Director of Soviet Affairs on the National Security Council (NSC) staff explained, "[T]he president's speech of January 16, 1984 set forward the parameters on which the Cold War was eventually eliminated. What we envisioned at that time was a process which we hoped conceivably could end in the end of the Cold War, but we couldn't be confident that it would."[65] Matlock, who wrote the bulk of the January 16 address, has recollected that the administration thought an improvement in superpower relations might be years in the making.

At the time [January 1984] I said, "I don't see any way the present Soviet leadership is going to be able to respond, but we need to be on the record. At least when there are changes [in Soviet leadership] and they are prepared to engage, we should have a policy that is ready and which is directed at not doing them in. . . . Now, did we think they would say, "Hoorah, that's right, we're gonna do it"? Of course not. We were very aware of all of the suspicions and of the real problems. My own estimate at the time was that nothing would happen for a year or even two, but if we could keep steadily reiterating our [new policy] we would eventually engage the Soviets on it."[66]

As McFarlane explained in a background briefing to reporters just before Reagan delivered the speech, "The fundamental purpose of the president's address will be to present in a clear and comprehensive manner his objective, which is to solve problems with the Soviet Union and to improve the state of this crucial relationship."[67] Matlock later explained, "Ending the Cold War seemed too utopian to offer as an explicit objective, though that was Reagan's goal."[68]

Why did the Reagan administration shift to this more cooperative approach? There were a number of factors. The rapid deterioration in superpower relations certainly played a role. The White House had intended to convey American strength, but by the fall of 1983 some officials grew concerned that it had gone too far. They were disturbed to realize that Moscow seemed to believe President Reagan was preparing for war. The president in particular was troubled by Moscow's reaction to Able Archer 83. Reagan had long been concerned about the possibility of an accidental nuclear Armageddon, and the KAL 007 tragedy and the war scare surrounding Able Archer heightened these anxieties.[69] According to McFarlane, the president was "genuinely anxious" about the war scare, and it had a "big influence" on his subsequent approach to the Kremlin.[70] A week after Able Archer ended, Reagan wrote in his diary, "I feel the Soviets are so defense minded, so paranoid about being attacked that without any way being soft on them we ought to tell them that no one here has any intention of doing anything like that." He then added, "What the h—l have they got that anyone would want?"[71]

Douglas MacEachin, the director of the CIA's Office of Soviet Analysis (SOVA) from 1984 through March 1989, recalled in 1998 that there were "concerns that maybe we had ratcheted the rhetoric up too high, and that, frankly, some of the actions of our defense organizations were too aggressive."

> [T]he president was [originally] supposed to have been a participant [in Able Archer]. All you can think now is thank heaven he wasn't. Because then it really would have looked real. Many of us [in the CIA] did not know that this was going on so we were asking naively, "I wonder why the Soviets are so upset," only to find out later that we were . . . throwing mudballs over the fence.[72]

"[This was] the reason for the January 16, 1984 speech," Matlock added. "[W]e were shocked that the Soviet leaders could think that they were on the brink of war. . . . To us, that was inconceivable. We said, 'Gee, we've got to look at what we're doing because we don't mean to upset them.'"[73] The "January 16th speech was deliberately intended to try to ratchet [things] back," MacEachin explained.[74] As Reagan confided to his diary after meeting with his speechwriters, "We want [this address] to be a level headed approach to peace to reassure the eggheads and our European friends I don't plan to blow up the world."[75] In his memoirs, President Reagan reflected:

> Three years had taught me something surprising about the Russians. Many people at the top of the Soviet hierarchy were genuinely afraid of America. . . . Perhaps this shouldn't have surprised me, but it did. . . . During my first three years in Washington, I think many of us in the administration took it for granted that the Russians, like ourselves, considered it unthinkable that the United States would launch a first strike against them. But the more experience I had . . . the more I began to realize that many Soviet officials feared us not only as adversaries, but as potential aggressors who might hurl nuclear weapons at them in a first strike. . . . Well, if that was the case, I was even more anxious to get a top leader in a room alone and try to convince him we had no designs on the Soviet Union and the Russians had nothing to fear from us.[76]

Reagan's assertions in his January 16 address that "our challenge is peaceful" and "we do not threaten the Soviet Union" were specifically intended to placate Soviet fears surrounding the war scare.[77]

But the January 16 speech did not come from out of the blue. President Reagan had envisioned a two-stage approach to the Soviet Union. During the first stage, the United States would build up its military capabilities and demonstrate its determination to stand firm against Soviet expansionism. The second stage, however, would focus upon improving superpower relations and reducing nuclear arms. President Reagan abhorred nuclear weapons, and his ultimate objective was to reduce—if not eliminate—superpower arsenals. Reagan believed the Soviets would only agree to such reductions if they were confronted by an adversary of equal strength and resolve. Administration officials referred to this two-part policy as "peace through strength."[78]

Reagan explained his "peace through strength" strategy during an address to the nation in 1982. "The United States wants deep cuts in the world's arsenal of weapons, but unless we demonstrate the will to rebuild our strength and restore the military balance, the Soviets, since they're so far ahead, have little incentive to negotiate with us," he reasoned.[79] As the president reflected in his memoirs, "[R]ecognizing the futility of the arms race and the hair-trigger risk of annihilation it posed to the world, I tried to send signals to Moscow indicating we were prepared to negotiate a winding down of the arms race if the Soviets were also sincere about it—and proved it with *deeds*. That's why 'peace through strength' became one of the mottoes of our administration."[80]

According to Matlock, the "shift occurred [in January 1984] because it represented Reagan's aspirations for his record as president. In his mind, the larger defense budget and his criticism of Soviet actions were only a prelude to a period of intense negotiation that would set the world on a course of arms reduction."[81]

The fact is, President Reagan had been trying to lay the groundwork for such negotiations since April 1981. Shortly after he was shot, the president had penned a letter to Soviet leader Leonid Brezhnev in the hopes of improving relations between the two capitals and reducing the threat of nuclear war. "I didn't have much faith in Communists, or put much stock in their word. Still it was dangerous to continue the East-West nuclear standoff forever, and I decided that if the Russians wouldn't take the first step, I would," Reagan explained in his memoirs. "Perhaps having come so close to death made me feel I should do whatever I could in the years God had given me to reduce the threat of nuclear war; perhaps there was a reason I was spared."[82]

Throughout 1983 President Reagan and some of his closest foreign policy advisers were working behind the scenes to try to develop a more coherent policy aimed at improving superpower relations and drawing down nuclear arsenals. Officials reasoned that by 1984 the United States would be in a much stronger position than it had been when the president took office.[83] The military buildup was taking hold, US nuclear missiles would be deployed to Europe, the American economy was recovering, and the Western alliance appeared to be unified.[84] The time had come to negotiate a lasting peace.

As early as January 1983 Secretary Shultz had sent a memo to the president outlining his vision of US policy for the year ahead.[85] In the memo Shultz called for "an intensified dialogue with Moscow to test whether an improvement in the US-Soviet relationship is possible." Shultz acknowledged that superpower competition was deep-rooted and cautioned that "there is no realistic scenario for a breakthrough to amicable relations." But he maintained that such efforts were critical. "If this dialogue does not result in improved US-Soviet relations, the onus will rest clearly on Moscow; if it leads to actual improvement, all the better." The goal of the dialogue would be to reduce nuclear arsenals, resolve regional conflicts in places such as Afghanistan and Angola, promote human rights, and improve economic relations.

Shultz was initially uncertain as to whether his proposals were in keeping with the president's aims. His uncertainty was soon dispelled, however. The president authorized Shultz to open "a careful dialogue" with the Soviet ambassador to the United States, Anatoly Dobrynin, along the principles that Shultz had outlined in his earlier memo. A few weeks later, during a private dinner one snowy February evening, Reagan explicitly discussed with Shultz his desire to improve relations with both the Soviet Union and China. He also expressed his frustration over obstacles coming from within his own administration. The directness of Reagan's remarks and the clarity of his vision came as a surprise to Shultz, and the evening proved to be pivotal. From that point on, the secretary understood that Reagan personally sought to engage the Soviets.[86]

Shultz and Reagan began to quietly put together a new agenda for improving relations with Moscow. On March 25 the president gave the "green light" to implement the new policy, which Shultz believed had "the potential for a real reversal in US-Soviet relations."[87] In May Soviet expert Jack Matlock was recruited to join the NSC to help with the plan. "Bud McFarlane and John Poindexter . . . were very frank," Matlock recalls. "They told me that the president entered office hoping he would build American strength so we would be able to negotiate with the Soviet Union. Our defense buildup was moving along, but we had not yet put together a negotiating plan. . . . They said they wanted me to come back to Washington and put together a negotiating plan."[88]

Throughout 1983 the president, Shultz, McFarlane, and Matlock all worked—sporadically and erratically—on developing a plan to improve superpower relations. Even as the president was calling the Soviet Union "the evil empire" and unveiling SDI, he was seeking to establish a meaningful dialogue aimed at reducing nuclear weapons and improving superpower relations.[89] Such seeming contradiction reflected the discord and disarray within the administration.

Matlock recalls that by the end of 1983 "it was apparent to all of us, except possibly to Reagan himself, that [the administration] had to do more to get both the American public and the Soviet leaders to understand just what our policy was. While Reagan had from the beginning of his administration spoken of the need to negotiate and of the prospects of cooperation if Soviet policy made it possible, the media had focused on his criticism of the Soviet Union. . . . [T]he US approach needed a more reasoned explanation than the piecemeal comments of the past had offered."[90] The January 16 speech was intended to clearly convey the president's desire for peace. "In Reagan's mind the [speech] contained nothing more than what he had been saying all along," Matlock has noted. "What he didn't understand was the degree to which his intentions had been misinterpreted and misunderstood by much of the public."[91]

Other factors played a role in the shift as well. European allies had become anxious about the state of superpower relations and had been quietly appealing for the administration to be "less shrill."[92] Such messages found a receptive audience within some quarters of the administration. The president's domestic advisers, Michael Deaver and James Baker, had an eye on the 1984 presidential election and believed a less confrontational approach would score points with voters. In addition, Vice President Bush, who met Reagan for a private lunch each Thursday, believed it would be irresponsible for the president not to engage with the Soviets. Mrs. Reagan also urged the president to consider his legacy and his responsibility to leave behind something more enduring than a military buildup.[93] In McFarlane's view, Nancy Reagan was particularly influential. "[Mrs. Reagan] was relentless, especially in 1983, about trying to get the president to be less confrontational," McFarlane has recollected. "Many times I heard her say that 'Ronnie' needed to tone it down because he was scaring the voters, and I'm sure she repeated that message frequently out of my earshot as well. I don't think he changed his approach *because* of Nancy, but he did have a lot of respect for her."[94]

President Reagan continued to seek cooperation and nuclear disarmament throughout the rest of his years in office. The administration toned down its rhetoric—with some notable exceptions—and sought to focus on building a more collegial relationship with Moscow. However, movement toward this end was slow. The new policy had difficulty gaining traction. In part, this was due to ongoing dissension within the administration. Both Secretary Weinberger and CIA Director Casey opposed the new emphasis on dialogue and arms reduction. The president's distaste for dealing with internal conflict also played a role. In his memoirs Shultz paints a picture of a president who sought to engage the Soviets, but who also allowed himself to be routinely undermined by the ideologues within his own administration. Matlock concurs. "Despite his impatience to get relations with Moscow on a constructive track, Reagan did not seem to be focusing on the substantive issues," he noted. "Decisions were stalled by squabbles among the various agencies."[95]

In addition, the Kremlin was going through a period of unprecedented turmoil with the death of three leaders in less than two and a half years. Soviet officials were preoccupied with their own internal politics, and they were simply not in a position to engage.

Although Reagan officials saw disarmament and improved relations as a long-term project, they grew frustrated at the way in which both Americans and Soviets ignored the new message. Matlock was dismayed that the American press did not pick up on the new approach and attributed this oversight to the 1984 presidential election. "We told [the press] beforehand that this was serious and important, and we even briefed them beforehand, but this was a partisan time," he lamented. "The new approach kept going long after the election was over, but many journalists didn't do their job. And then in 1987–1988 the journalists were surprised and asking, 'How did we get to this point?' And I said, 'We told you in 1984 we were doing this!'"[96]

1985–1988: Ending the Cold War

"General Secretary Gorbachev," Secretary Shultz began, as he met the new Soviet leader during Chernenko's funeral in March 1985, "President Reagan told me to look you squarely in the eyes and tell you: Ronald Reagan believes this is a very special moment in the history of mankind. . . . Over the past year we have found solutions to some problems, though not to the great problems, and if it is at all possible, we must establish a more constructive relationship between the United States and the USSR. . . . President Reagan is ready to work with you and . . . is inviting you to visit the United States at the earliest convenient time." Gorbachev replied, "[T]his is a unique moment; I am ready to return US-Soviet relations to a normal channel. It is necessary to know each other, to find time for meetings to discuss outstanding problems, and to seek ways to bring the two countries closer together."[97]

For more than two years the Reagan administration had been seeking to engage the Kremlin in a dialogue so as to build trust, reduce nuclear arms, and address regional conflicts. Little had come of these efforts, in part because of the rapid turnover in Soviet leadership. By March 1985, however, the Soviet Union had a stable, capable leader in Mikhail Gorbachev.

To President Reagan's delight, Gorbachev quickly accepted his invitation for a summit meeting. Reagan had sought the meeting in the hopes of establishing a personal rapport with his Soviet counterpart in order to "break down the barriers of mistrust that divided our countries," he explained. "During the previous five years I had come to realize there were people in the Kremlin who had a genuine fear of the United States. I wanted to convince Gorbachev that we wanted peace and they had nothing to fear from us."[98]

The summit took place in Geneva in November 1985. President Reagan's foremost priority at the meeting was to begin to establish trust between the two countries. "We are divided by suspicions," the president explained to the general secretary.[99] In his view, if the superpowers could eliminate mutual suspicions the resolution of other issues, such as arms reduction, would follow naturally. "We don't fear each other because we're armed," Reagan was fond of saying; "we're armed because we fear each other."[100] Eliminate the fear, Reagan reasoned, and the arms would take care of themselves.

The administration had adopted this position years earlier. Reagan officials believed that too much emphasis had been placed on arms reduction in the past, with the result being that the entire superpower relationship was being judged by whether there was progress in arms control. The administration sought to broaden the agenda—and to create other avenues for progress—by focusing on issues other than armaments. This so-called four-part agenda included arms reduction, but also focused on human rights, regional conflicts, and efforts to increase bilateral cooperation.[101] The hope was that discussions on this broader range of issues would foster mutual understanding.[102]

In fact, the bulk of the president's preparations for the Geneva summit meeting consisted not of briefings on weapons systems, but on a series of over twenty papers that Matlock commissioned about Soviet history, culture, and social issues. The president had requested these studies so that he could better understand Gorbachev's perspective.[103] These papers were extremely influential, McFarlane recalled. During the first sessions of the Geneva meeting the president's "focus was not on arms control, not on SDI, but on why Gorbachev mistrusted us and why he should not mistrust us, and on why Reagan mistrusted Gorbachev."[104]

Gorbachev had different priorities for the Geneva summit, however. The Soviet leader's foremost goal was to end the arms race.[105] President Reagan proposed a 50 percent reduction in strategic offensive arms and the eventual elimination of intermediate-range missiles in Europe, which Gorbachev readily accepted. However, he would not consent to these proposals until the president agreed to abandon SDI.[106] Reagan was not inclined to bargain away his pet project, though, and the meeting concluded without an arms agreement.

Nevertheless, the Geneva meetings were a success. Reagan officials described them as "very worthwhile" and noted the "friendly mood and good atmosphere." The president believed Geneva had been "a good start at improving relations the Soviets" and was hopeful for the future. Gorbachev had indicated his desire to withdraw from Afghanistan, the two leaders had agreed in principle on the need to reduce nuclear arms, and they had established something of a rapport. Although no substantive agreements were reached, Reagan and Gorbachev had agreed to two additional summit meetings, first in Washington and then in Moscow. "I can't claim that we had a meeting of the minds on such fundamentals as ideology or national purpose," Reagan reported to a joint session of Congress upon his return, "but we understand each other better and that is a key to peace."[107] In his memoirs Gorbachev recalls the summit as being "constructive, intensive, and sometimes even emotional. But more important, it was frank, and increasingly friendly the more we got to know each other. Tempers became heated when we touched upon topics such as human rights, regional conflicts and the notorious SDI. Nonetheless, I realized by the end of our two-day meeting that Ronald Reagan was a man you could do business with."[108] Gorbachev told the press, "Because of the Geneva summit the world has become a more secure place."[109]

Superpower relations improved after the Geneva summit, albeit slowly. For years the administration had engaged in vitriolic denunciations of Soviet communism, and this rhetoric continued to reverberate more loudly than did the new, more conciliatory language. Furthermore, old habits die hard, and from time to time the president and the secretary of state could still be accusatory in their private dealings with the Soviets, lecturing them on human rights and free markets. The Reagan administration's decision to focus on topics other than arms reduction also frustrated Gorbachev and his aides, who continued to regard arms control as the defining feature of superpower relations.[110]

Moreover, there were aspects of the Reagan administration's policy that seemed to be at odds with its desire for peace and disarmament. In particular, President Reagan's devotion to SDI made his calls for the elimination of nuclear weapons appear insincere. Additionally, in February 1985 Secretary Shultz unveiled a policy of promoting and supporting democratic opposition to communist influence throughout the world, an approach that came to be known as the Reagan Doctrine.[111] In reality, this promise of interventionism was nothing new. Many previous administrations had sought to check Soviet expansionism. Shultz's speech, however, and the publicity surrounding it seemed entirely at odds with the new calls for cooperative solutions to regional conflicts. Indeed, Soviet officials found this policy of "neoglobalism," as they called it, irritating and inconsistent with the administration's overtures toward peace.[112]

Washington also stepped up its assistance to the mujahedin fighting Soviet forces in Afghanistan while simultaneously demanding that Moscow withdraw.[113] The United States funneled untold amounts of weapons and approximately $3.2 billion to the "freedom fighters" through Pakistan. In 1986 it began sending Stinger antiaircraft missiles to the Soviet resistors. These shoulder-fired missiles ended Soviet dominance of the air and were critical in defeating the Soviet Union. Gorbachev had indicated his desire to withdraw Soviet forces from Afghanistan, but the White House did nothing to facilitate the process.[114]

The seed of a friendship that Ronald Reagan and Mikhail Gorbachev planted in Geneva continued to grow throughout the next three years. Momentum ebbed and flowed, but the two leaders were able to build trust, decrease superpower hostility, and reduce nuclear arms in a manner that few could have foreseen. Over the years Gorbachev, Reagan, and their advisers forged friendships borne out of their mutual desire for peace.[115] When Gorbachev visited Washington in 1987 the superpowers signed the landmark Intermediate-Range Nuclear Forces (INF) Treaty, which eliminated all medium-range nuclear weapons, such as the Soviet SS-20s and the US Pershing II missiles. Based on Reagan's earlier Zero Option, the treaty was a stunning accomplishment. Prior to this treaty, the superpowers had never even agreed to reduce their nuclear arsenals, much less eliminate an entire class of weapons. Americans treated the Soviet leader like a rock star, mobbing him as he traveled through the capital. The American press was captivated, and warmth and good humor infused the meetings.[116]

By the time President Reagan's plane touched down in Moscow for the May 1988 summit meeting it was apparent to many—though not all—that the Cold War was drawing to a close.[117] The superpowers were in close and constant talks. They were near to an agreement to slash strategic nuclear arsenals by 50 percent. The Soviet Union would soon begin withdrawing from Afghanistan. Democratic reforms were sweeping through the Soviet Union and beyond. As the general secretary strolled through the Kremlin grounds with the president they were surrounded by excited journalists from all over the globe. "After all these meetings are you now old friends?" one reporter shouted. "Da, da," Gorbachev immediately replied. "Yes!" declared the president, beaming. "And what has become of the 'evil empire'?" another journalist asked Reagan. "I was talking about another time, another era," the American leader explained. Gorbachev smiled.[118]

Engagement, Reassurance, and Disarmament

In the triumphalist view, President Reagan was a hawk who eschewed negotiations with Moscow, built up American strength, and compelled the Soviet Union to concede the Cold War. His greatest legacy is his military buildup and the collapse of the USSR.

But this caricature is a myth. President Reagan's early threat-based approach to the Kremlin led to a rapid deterioration in relations, culminating in the autumn of 1983. His initial hard-line policy did not end the Cold War—it exacerbated it. The Soviets did not surrender, nor did they collapse. Rather, they hurled insults of their own, walked out of arms talks, and prepared for a retaliatory nuclear strike against the West.

By 1984 the administration shifted gears; it sought to reassure Moscow that Washington posed no threat to its security, and it embarked on negotiations in an attempt to build trust and reduce arsenals. The White House aimed for constructive cooperation on a range of issues, the most important of which was the elimination of nuclear weapons. It was this strategy of reassurance that opened the door to a gradual improvement in relations and the drawing down of nuclear arsenals.

Triumphalists also suggest that President Reagan refused to engage with the Soviets until they changed their behavior. Reagan stood firm until Moscow complied, the story goes. This is also a fallacy. Reagan did not wait for his adversary to reform before engaging in peace talks. The president began seeking dialogue and disarmament *before* the Soviet Union began to reform. The administration was plotting a path toward improved relations in 1983, while Andropov was leader. It continued to seek a rapprochement with Chernenko. The president invited Gorbachev to a summit meeting the day he became leader of the USSR—before there was any indication of the revolution Gorbachev would usher in—and the meeting took place before major policy changes had begun. And although the president had avoided summit meetings during his first term, beginning in 1985 Reagan and Gorbachev engaged in an unprecedented five meetings in a little more than three years.[119]

President Reagan believed that dialogue with adversaries was essential and that refusing to engage was irresponsible. "I have openly expressed my view of the Soviet system," he noted in 1984. "But this doesn't mean we can't deal with each other. . . . The fact that neither of us likes the other's system is no reason to refuse to talk. . . . We will never retreat from negotiations."[120]

2

Reagan's Military Buildup

"Busting the Soviet Union"?

We are not trying to spend the Soviet economy into the ground. . . . Our effort to maintain a stable military balance is entirely consistent with our goal of improved relations with the Soviet Union. In fact, the one is clearly necessary for the other—a reality that some, of late, seem to have forgotten.

Undersecretary of State Lawrence Eagleburger, February 1983

None of the key players [in foreign policy making] were operating from the assumption that we were going to do the Soviet Union in, or . . . bring them down. . . . That's all thinking after the fact. Our goal was always to give the Soviets incentives to bring the Cold War to an end.

Jack F. Matlock Jr., US ambassador to the Soviet Union, 1987–1991

The previous chapter debunked triumphalist claims that President Reagan employed hard-line policies and avoided negotiations with the Soviets throughout his eight years in office. Rather, Reagan engaged in negotiations and trust building, particularly during his second term. This diplomacy was pivotal in bringing about the peaceful conclusion of the Cold War.

Chapter 2 focuses more specifically on the Reagan administration's military buildup. In March 1981 the president announced the largest peacetime military buildup in US history. Although President Carter had significantly increased defense spending before leaving office, President Reagan proposed to spend an additional 7 percent per year between 1981 and 1985. Defense expenditures would cost $1.5 trillion and consume more than 30 percent of the federal budget over that four-year period. The administration planned to use these resources to strengthen forces, improve combat readiness, and enhance force mobility.[1]

Did the president launch this military buildup so as force the collapse of the Soviet Union, as triumphalists claim? In this view, Reagan sought to entice Moscow into an arms race that it could not afford, thus forcing it into bankruptcy. The buildup was intended to be the straw to break the back of the USSR.[2]

This argument rests on two assumptions. The first is that, upon taking office, Reagan officials believed the Soviet Union to be so fragile that it was close to collapse or could be nudged to collapse. The second assumption is that Reagan and his advisers intended to force the USSR to implode. This chapter considers both of these assumptions and finds them wanting. The first half examines American perceptions of Soviet strength during the late 1970s and early 1980s and finds that, although the president believed the USSR was unsustainable in the long run, virtually all of his advisers strongly disagreed with this view. They saw Moscow as a formidable adversary that would continue to challenge the West for the foreseeable future. The second half of the chapter examines the administration's statements about the objectives of the buildup. Not only did officials repeatedly affirm that its purpose was to get the Soviets to agree to arms reductions, they explicitly rejected the notion that the goal was to force the collapse of the USSR. Both of Reagan's defense secretaries and both of his secretaries of state, along with other foreign policy and defense officials, have dismissed the idea that their aim was to "bust the Soviet Union." Their aim, they insist, was to bring about a reduction in superpower arsenals.

Reagan's Views on the Strength of the Soviet Union

Like most myths, the myth that Reagan sought to destroy the Soviet Union contains a kernel of truth. In 1977 Ronald Reagan famously quipped to Richard Allen, "My idea of American policy toward the Soviet Union is simple, and some would say, simplistic. It is this: We win and they lose."[3] In fact, Reagan's views were more complex than this witticism let on. They also evolved considerably during his two terms in office.[4]

Ronald Reagan had long believed that the Soviet system was not sustainable. A government that systematically suppressed human freedom carried the seeds of its own demise, he reasoned. Ultimately, Soviet citizens would rebel against economic, political, and social repression. While Reagan did not indicate that the collapse of the Soviet system was imminent, throughout the

1970s and 1980s he was thinking about such a geopolitical earthquake more than most foreign policy experts.[5] "Communism is neither an economic nor a political system—it is a form of insanity," he asserted during a May 1975 radio address that he wrote himself. "[It is] a temporary aberration which will one day disappear from the earth because it is contrary to human nature."[6]

In another address that year, Reagan contended that the Achilles heel of the Soviet system was its economy and questioned whether the sale of American grain to the USSR was in the best interest of the West. "If we believe the Soviet Union is hostile to the free world . . . then are we not adding to our own danger by helping the troubled Soviet economy?" he asked. "Are we not helping a Godless tyranny maintain its hold on millions of helpless people? Wouldn't those helpless victims have a better chance of becoming free if their slave masters' regime collapsed economically?" Reagan concluded, "Maybe there is an answer. We simply do what's morally right. Stop doing business with them. Let their system collapse but in the meantime buy our farmers' wheat ourselves and have it on hand to feed the Russian people when they finally become free."[7]

Two years later Reagan reiterated his view that the USSR could fall from within. "The Soviet Union is building the most massive military machine the world has ever seen and is denying its people all kinds of consumer products to do it," he explained. "We might have an unexpected ally if citizen Ivan is becoming discontented enough to start talking back. Maybe we should drop a few million typical mail order catalogues on Minsk and Pinsk and Moscow to whet their appetites."[8]

Reagan also believed that the Soviets could not keep pace with American technological progress. In a September 1979 radio address condemning the second Strategic Arms Limitation Treaty (SALT II), Reagan asked, "[W]hich is worse? . . . An unrestrained arms race which the US could not possibly lose given our industrial superiority, or a treaty [SALT II] which says that the arms race is over and that we have lost it."[9]

Reagan's personal views about the weakness of the Soviet system found their way into policy statements, particularly during his first term as president. "The West won't contain communism, it will transcend communism," he proclaimed in 1981. "It will dismiss [communism] as some bizarre chapter in human history whose last pages are even now being written."[10] When asked by reporters to clarify these remarks, Reagan said, "I just think that it is impossible . . . for any form of government to completely deny freedom to people and have that go on interminably. There eventually comes an end to it. And I think the things we're seeing, not only in Poland, but the reports that are beginning to come out of Russia itself about the younger generation and its resistance to longtime government controls, is an indication that communism is an aberration. It's not a normal way of living for human beings, and I think we are seeing the first, beginning cracks, the beginning of the end."[11]

In March 1982 President Reagan received intelligence reports about Soviet military capabilities. He recalled,

> I had been given a briefing on the astonishing Soviet arms buildup, which left me amazed at its scale, cost, and breadth and the danger it posed to our country. The output of missiles alone was staggering. Several days later, I had another briefing, this time on the Soviet economy. The latest figures provided additional evidence that it was a basket case, and even if I hadn't majored in economics in college, it would have been plain to me that Communism was doomed as a failed economic system. The situation was so bad that if Western countries got together and cut off credits to it, we could bring it to its knees. How could the Soviets afford their huge arms build up?[12]

Shortly thereafter, the president proclaimed to the British Parliament that the Soviet Union was in "deep economic difficulty" and predicted that "the march of freedom and democracy . . . will leave Marxism-Leninism on the ashheap of history."[13]

In short, Reagan considered the Soviet Union to be a formidable military adversary, but its political and economic system was its soft underbelly. "President Reagan just had an innate sense that the Soviet Union would not, or could not survive," recalled Secretary of State George Shultz after leaving office. "That feeling was not based on a detailed learned knowledge of the Soviet Union; it was just instinct."[14]

Divisions within the CIA

The president's instincts were remarkably similar to the conclusions drawn by the Soviet experts within the Central Intelligence Agency (CIA). During the 1970s intelligence estimates portrayed the Soviet Union as a superpower whose military capabilities were steadily increasing. Its intentions, however, were more difficult to discern. Intelligence experts debated whether the Kremlin was seeking military superiority over the United States, or whether it would accept a roughly equal balance of power. Regardless, there was general consensus that Soviet military power was mounting.[15]

The Soviet economy, however, was a different story. The CIA detected a steady deterioration in the growth rate of the Soviet economy after 1975, attributing the decline to ongoing structural issues.[16] As Douglas MacEachin, the director of the Office of Soviet Analysis (SOVA) from 1984 through March 1989, recalled, "From the mid-1970s to the eve of Gorbachev's assumption of party leadership in the spring of 1985, the CIA portrayed a Soviet Union plagued by a deteriorating economy and intensifying societal problems. CIA products described the growing political tensions resulting from these failures, the prospect that sooner or later a Soviet leadership would be forced to confront these issues, and the uncertainty over what form this confrontation would take."[17] The problem—as Reagan intuited—was the Soviet system. Resources were not allocated efficiently, resulting in unsustainably large investments in heavy industry and defense and paltry financing for consumer goods and technological innovation. "The basic problem is [that] the formula for maintaining their high level of growth over the past 25 years, which has been to increase the inputs of labor and capital to make up for the inefficiency of the way they utilize them, does not appear to have long term prospects," CIA Director Stansfield Turner told members of Congress in June 1977. "They are not going to be able to continue this during the next ten years or so."[18] The declining growth rate would continue for the foreseeable future, the Agency believed.

The USSR's deteriorating economy could constrain defense spending, CIA analysts believed. Therefore, they did not expect the Soviet Union to match increases in American defense expenditures; rather, economic constraints would force spending levels to plateau or decline. In 1977 analysts observed that "powerful remedies" for Soviet economic problems were "either not readily available or not politically feasible. . . . The slowdown in economic growth could trigger intense debate in Moscow over the future levels and pattern of military expenditures."[19] At the time, CIA experts believed Soviet defense spending to be increasing 4–5 percent per year, increases that did not appear sustainable given the declining economic growth rate.[20] In September 1980 CIA Director Turner noted that the Soviet economy was "losing its momentum while military programs continued to be pursued with vigor and determination. . . . [T]he combination of slowing economic growth and rising military outlays [will] pose difficult choices for the Soviet leadership over the next several years."[21]

In December 1982 the CIA reported that "Soviet officials recognize that the Soviet Union now faces a wide array of social, economic, and political ills, including general social malaise, ethnic tensions, consumer frustrations, and political dissent. Precisely how these internal problems will ultimately challenge and affect the regime, however, is open to debate and considerable uncertainty. Some observers believe the regime will have little trouble coping. . . . Others believe that economic mismanagement will aggravate internal problems and ultimately erode the regime's credibility, increasing the long-term prospects for fundamental change."[22]

In June 1983 the Agency reported that the Soviet Union's "industrial growth, which had been declining since WW II, slowed unusually sharply during 1976–1982. . . . Even more dramatic was the slump in productivity." It continued, "The slow pace of industrial growth that we project for the 1980s (about 2 percent per year) will seriously limit growth in other sectors and in the economy as a whole, since industry accounts for nearly half of Soviet GNP. . . . It will limit the USSR's ability to boost living standards substantially and to accelerate military production. The report concluded that "[p]rospects for turning the situation around in the rest of the 1980s are not good."[23]

By the time Mikhail Gorbachev came to power in March 1985 the pressing question for Soviet experts in the CIA was not whether the Soviet Union was facing economic difficulty, but rather how the Kremlin would deal with these challenges and what the repercussions of any reforms might be.[24] In September 1985 they summed up the Kremlin's dilemma: "Although economic performance has improved in recent years from the low levels of 1979–1982, Gorbachev still faces an economy that cannot simultaneously maintain growth rates in defense spending, satisfy demand for greater quantity and variety of consumer goods and services, invest amounts required for economic modernization and expansion, and continue to support client-state economies."[25] The Agency predicted that Gorbachev would confront both mounting financial pressure to restrain defense spending and vested interests who would oppose such measures.[26]

The political appointees leading the CIA did not welcome these dire reports about the Soviet Union's economy. They were unable (or perhaps unwilling) to entertain the notion of a superpower on the brink of crisis, much less reform. Consequently, they sought to ignore, reject, or bury such assessments. Discussing Soviet new thinking was "counter-cultural," McEachin lamented in 1998. "Therefore it ended up at the bottom of somebody's in-box."[27]

CIA Director William Casey was a strident anticommunist who took it as an article of faith that Moscow would continue to be a formidable and enduring adversary. He enthusiastically supported the US military buildup and believed Washington should isolate and denounce Moscow. He also had little respect for the Soviet experts within the Agency. Nor did he have a high opinion of congressional authority, the law, or anyone who disagreed with him. Moreover, Casey took perverse delight in bending rules to the breaking point. "Casey was guilty of contempt of Congress from the day he was sworn in," CIA Deputy Director Robert Gates observed.[28] "Working for Casey was a trial for everybody, partly because of his growing erraticism and partly because of his own right-wing tendencies," long-time CIA analyst Dick Lehman recalled. "He was amenable to argument, but it took a hell of a lot of argument."[29] Casey's demeanor and tactics undermined morale throughout the Agency, prompting Lehman and other long-serving Soviet experts to leave. "[T]he atmosphere in the mid-1980s was poisoned," Douglas MacEachin recalled. "I hated this and was prepared to resign in the mid-1980s because of this."[30] The normally tactful Vice President Bush—himself a former DCI—lamented that Casey was "an inappropriate choice" for CIA director.[31]

Casey's deputy, Bob Gates, was more mindful of the law, but was equally polarizing. Although only in his mid-thirties when Reagan took office, he was contemptuous of the talent in the Agency. Gates alienated intelligence analysts from the moment he was promoted to deputy director, telling them they were "close-minded, smug, [and] arrogant." Their assessments, he claimed, "were irrelevant, uninteresting, too late to be of value, too narrow, too unimaginative, and too often just flat out wrong." They were novices "pretending to be experts."[32]

Casey and Gates's strong views and forceful personalities alienated many of the Soviet experts within the Agency. Intelligence analysts felt pressure to play up the Soviet threat so as to justify the administration's military buildup. Casey would try to bury assessments with which he disagreed. His preferred method was to drown unpalatable reports in a prolonged bureaucratic process.

If the DCI disliked conclusions drawn by CIA analysts he would call for a National Intelligence Estimate (NIE) to be written on the topic. During such a process all the major intelligence agencies within the US government study an issue and render a joint opinion. The final product of this laborious and time-consuming effort is a consensus document that effectively waters down any one agency's view.[33]

Casey and Gates frequently rejected the advice of Soviet experts in the Agency, preferring instead to cling to their personal beliefs. "Senior people [in the CIA] who held different opinions than what [Soviet analysts] were describing stated their opinion, and their view was the view given to the public," MacEachin explained in 1998.[34] For example, in early 1985 the CIA was trying to learn more about potential successors to Konstantin Chernenko, whom they knew to be ill. Drawing on information from Gorbachev's previous visits to Canada and Britain, CIA Soviet analysts portrayed Gorbachev as a welcome departure from his geriatric predecessors, with real potential to bring change. Gates pushed back. "I don't much care for the way we are writing about Gorbachev," he wrote to the CIA's top Soviet experts in February 1985. "We are losing the thread of what toughness and skill brought him to where he is. This is not some Gary Hart or even Lee Iacocca. We have to give the policymakers a clearer view of the kind of person they may be facing." He can "not be all sweetness and light," Gates insisted. Politburo members would not tolerate a "wimp."[35]

Several months later Casey employed similar tactics. In June 1985 the CIA sent to President Reagan its first official assessment of General Secretary Gorbachev, which was cautiously optimistic. The report depicted Gorbachev as "the most aggressive and activist Soviet leader since Khrushchev" and noted that he was intent on fighting social malaise and corruption at home. Casey, however, attempted to neutralize this hopeful assessment. As the paper was sent to the president he attached a covering letter which largely refuted the body of the report. Casey wrote that Gorbachev and his cohorts "are not reformers and liberalizers either in Soviet domestic or foreign policy." In this case even Gates thought Casey had crossed the line.[36]

The most divisive—and potentially explosive—intelligence issue arose shortly after President Reagan took office, when Soviet analysts within the CIA discovered that their earlier assessments about a Soviet military buildup had been wrong. New information indicated that Moscow had not been acquiring new weapons at an increasingly faster pace during the 1970s, as previously believed. In fact, the growth rate in Soviet military expenditures had peaked in the mid-1970s and was unlikely to increase in the near future.[37] In short, the Soviet military threat had been overstated.

Senior officials were "sour" about these revised estimates, CIA analysts recall.[38] The Reagan administration had justified its military buildup based on CIA assessments that Moscow had been engaging in a military buildup of its own during the 1970s. The administration would have a hard time convincing Congress and the American public of the need for additional defense funding if the CIA was reporting that the Soviet Union had, in effect, dropped out of the arms race. Hawkish policy makers were not amused. Agency officials had attempted to alert Defense Secretary Caspar Weinberger to their revised estimates in 1982, informing him that Soviet defense spending had "slowed substantially" and in all likelihood would not increase significantly any time soon.[39] The United States was acquiring new weapons at a faster clip than were the Soviets, they noted. The secretary knew this information would do nothing to bolster the administration's plan to seek further increases in defense spending. Thus, the Pentagon largely ignored the reassessments and continued to exaggerate the threat posed by Soviet defenses.[40]

Despite their revised estimates, CIA analysts felt pressured to continue overstating Soviet military spending. The "one issue on which I took the most . . . heat [was] the CIA estimate in the early and mid-1980s about the sad state of the economy in the Soviet Union, and [the conclusion] that this meant that there was not going to be an increase in defense spending, and that there had not been, in fact, too much growth in defense spending since at least the late 1970s," MacEachin recalled. "At one meeting I had given a draft assessment of the Soviet economic situation to a person who was supposed to read it to Congress. That person threw the draft [across the room]."[41] MacEachin recalled that, "in order to develop and sustain political support for building SDI," the CIA's Soviet analysts "had to continue to be showing an even greater Soviet buildup than the one we had been projecting in the 1970s—*which had never been realized in the first place.* So the numbers for the future projections [of Soviet forces] went even higher and they became part of the received wisdom. Dissenting from that view was pretty much a waste of time."[42]

Casey and Gates attempted to manage the fallout from these revised estimates. Gates persuaded Casey and Weinberger that estimates of Soviet defense spending should no longer be made public, while the NIE process was employed to water down the revised information.[43] The final document concluded that economic considerations would not "lead the Soviets to abandon major strategic weapons programs, to forsake force modernization goals, or to make substantial concessions in arms control."[44] This directly contradicted what CIA Soviet experts believed to be true.

Gates continued to advise policy makers that the Soviet Union was a strong and threatening adversary after he took over from Casey in December 1986. For example, in 1987—a rather late date—he sent a memorandum to Weinberger insisting that "the Soviet economy, despite some ugly warts that make its operation costly and inefficient, is vested with great crude strength from the enormous resource base, and remains a viable system, capable of producing large quantities of goods and services annually, especially for industrial and military applications." Moscow had the capacity and the willpower to increase defense spending, the memo continued, with manageable effects on living standards and industrial modernization. Such increases "would not cause economic collapse or social upheaval," the memo concluded.[45]

Such practices undermined the credibility of the entire CIA. Secretary Shultz grew increasingly distrustful of DCI Casey and his information on the USSR. Shultz suspected Casey manipulated intelligence so as to support the need for a hard-line policy toward Moscow. Casey's "intelligence" was little more than his personal opinion on CIA letterhead, the secretary believed. "The CIA and Bill Casey were as independent as a hog on ice and could be as confident as they were wrong," he recalled.[46] The DCI had "too much of an agenda," Shultz insisted. "It's a mistake for the CIA to have an agenda. They're supposed to produce intelligence. If they have an agenda, the intelligence can get slanted."[47] Soviet analysts within the CIA concurred with the secretary of state. Intelligence "analyses in the Gorbachev period were often not . . . disseminated to senior policymakers by DDCI [Deputy Director of Central Intelligence] Gates because he held a different view," CIA Soviet expert Raymond Garthoff recalled. "That was his right. But it was regrettable because the CIA analysis was far more correct than the view he held."[48] As Douglas MacEachin noted, "This acrimonious atmosphere was flourishing at a critical time in history.[49]

Perceptions of Soviet Strength in the Administration

Casey and Gates were not the only administration officials who considered the Soviet Union to be a strong and enduring adversary. In the early 1980s most of Reagan's advisers shared this view. For them, it was unfathomable

that the Soviet Union—the great superpower—would not be able to overcome its economic problems. "[T]he principal figures [in the Reagan admin-
istration]—Al Haig notably—had cut their teeth at a time when the
prevailing view in the United States was that even if the Soviet Union had a
dysfunctional economy, it still had sufficient capital resources to waste them
forever and still be quite powerful," National Security Adviser Robert McFarlane explained in 1998. "And so, even in the beginning of the 1980s national
security thinking was quite driven by the view that it didn't matter if the
Soviet Union was totally chaotic, that it was so wealthy that it could go on
forever. . . . Reagan had a very different view," McFarlane explained. "He
didn't subscribe to that notion and instead believed that a more aggressive—
well, that's the wrong word—a more energetic competition could impose
such burdens as to bring down the Soviet Union. . . . [H]owever, many in his
own Cabinet at the time didn't agree with him."[50]

The president's advisers simply did not share his view that the Soviet system was unsustainable. As a national security document stated in May 1982,
"The key military threats to US national security during the 1980s will continue to be posed by the Soviet Union and its allies and clients. Despite increasing pressures on its economy and the growing vulnerabilities of its empire, the
Soviet military will continue to expand and modernize."[51] The Soviet Union is
"beset by serious weaknesses," Secretary Shultz acknowledged in a letter to
President Reagan on January 19, 1983. "But it would be a mistake to assume
that the Soviet capacity for competition with us will diminish at any time during your presidency."[52] The following month, Under Secretary of State for
Political Affairs Lawrence Eagleburger declared in a speech:

> Let me not overstate the difficulties the Soviets face. The economy is
> not about to collapse. The Soviet government has a well-developed
> capacity for forcing the people it rules to bear hardships. . . . The
> regime and the people have faced far worse times than these and sur-
> vived. There is no sign that their economic difficulties will force the
> Soviet leaders to reduce their military spending. Nor are their trou-
> bles compelling them to pull back from the military adventures they
> have undertaken or sponsored beyond their borders.

Eagleburger concluded, "The next Russian revolution is not just around the
corner."[53]

In short, during the early 1980s Reagan administration officials disagreed about the strength of the Soviet Union. The president and the Soviet experts in the CIA suspected that economic constraints might someday force Moscow to reduce its military expenditures and reform its system. When that day of reckoning might be, however, was unknowable, as was the outcome of any future reforms. But most members of the administration considered the Soviet Union to be a formidable adversary with the capability to threaten American security indefinitely. Its collapse was simply unfathomable. And the notion that the United States might force such a disintegration seemed fanciful at best.[54]

Seeking Peace through Strength

The Reagan administration's military buildup was not intended to force the collapse of the USSR. Rather, its objective was "peace through strength," as officials repeatedly stated. This policy had three components.[55] The short-term goal was to catch up with the Soviet Union. Reagan officials (erroneously) believed Moscow had been building up its military capabilities throughout the 1970s, while the United States had let its forces languish. The United States had fallen behind in the arms race, they concluded, resulting in dangerous vulnerability.[56]

The second objective was to deter Soviet expansionism. Officials assumed (mistakenly) that Moscow had invaded Afghanistan in 1979 because America appeared weak and the Kremlin believed it could invade with impunity. Renewed American strength would prevent future adventurism.

The ultimate objective of the buildup, however, was to persuade the Soviet Union to agree to arms reductions. Reagan officials assumed that Moscow would not agree to draw down its forces until it was confronted by an adversary of equal strength. Their strategy was to build up military power so as to convince the Soviets to enter into arms reduction talks. They assumed—wrongly, as it turned out—that Moscow would not agree to disarmament unless it was pressured to do so. President Reagan's ultimate objective was to usher in an era of dialogue and disarmament.

Reagan explained his reasoning in 1982. "Some may question what modernizing our military has to do with peace," he acknowledged.

> [A] secure force keeps others from threatening us, and that keeps the peace. And just as important, it also increases the prospects of

reaching significant arms reductions with the Soviets, and that's what we really want. The United States wants deep cuts in the world's arsenal of weapons, but unless we demonstrate the will to rebuild our strength and restore the military balance, the Soviets, since they're so far ahead, have little incentive to negotiate with us. Let me repeat the point because it goes to the heart of our policies. Unless we demonstrate the will to rebuild our strength, the Soviets have little incentive to negotiate.[57]

As the president explained, "Our strength is necessary to deter war and to facilitate negotiated solutions. Soviet leaders know it makes sense to compromise only if they can get something in return. America can now offer something in return."[58] Although it seemed paradoxical, Reagan hoped the buildup would ultimately lead to arms reduction.

Shultz explained the strategy to the Senate Foreign Relations Committee in June 1983. "In the past 2 years this nation . . . has made a fundamental commitment to restoring its military and economic power and moral and spiritual strength," he began. "And having begun to rebuild our strength we now seek to engage the Soviet leaders in a constructive dialog—a dialog through which we hope to find political solutions to outstanding issues. This is the central goal we have pursued since the outset of this administration. We do not want to—and need not—accept as inevitable the prospect of endless, dangerous confrontation with the Soviet Union. . . . We can—and must—do better."[59]

Reagan clarified his policy of peace through strength in January 1984. "History teaches that wars begin when governments believe the price of aggression is cheap," he explained. "Strength is essential to negotiate successfully and protect our interests. . . . Our strength is necessary to deter war and to facilitate negotiated solutions. Strength and dialogue go hand in hand."[60] The United States had regained its strength, Reagan believed; the time had come for serious negotiations.

"Deterrence is necessary but not sufficient [for achieving peace]," President Reagan told the United Nations General Assembly in September 1984. "America has repaired its strength. We have invigorated our alliances and friendships. We are ready for constructive negotiations with the Soviet Union."[61] Secretary Shultz explained, "Strength and realism can deter war, but only direct dialogue and negotiation can open the path toward lasting peace."[62]

"What we were doing was laying out a game plan for ending at least the more serious aspects of the Cold War," Matlock explained in 1998. "It was not directed at undermining the Soviet system, though we were quite aware that they were going to be facing a difficult situation that they would have to manage. . . . I know at that point, in the president's mind, perhaps very vaguely, he was thinking of coming to terms with the Soviet Union in the sense of regularizing the relationship and, as we say now, ending the Cold War."[63]

"Busting the Soviet Union"?

Reagan officials have repeatedly rejected the notion that the aim of US policy was to force the USSR to collapse. "I understand [the idea that the Reagan administration sought to bankrupt the Soviet Union] is getting wide readership, but I cannot understand why, because I will go on record saying it belongs in the dust bin," Douglas MacEachin, the director of the Soviet Analysis division of the CIA during the 1980s, has asserted. "There may have been people who thought they were running some kind of a plot to break the bank in the Soviet Union . . . [but that] is utter nonsense. . . . It is absolutely dead wrong." Jack Matlock concurs. It is "absolute nonsense," he insists.[64]

Administration officials recall that they recognized Moscow's economic difficulties and sought to place pressure on these weaknesses, but the intent was to improve superpower relations and reduce nuclear arms. President Reagan discussed this in his memoirs. "I intended to let [the Kremlin] know that we were going to spend whatever it took to stay ahead of them in the arms race. . . . The Russians could never win the arms race; we could outspend them forever," he reflected. "But I wanted to let them know that the nuclear standoff was futile and dangerous for all of us and that we had no designs on their territories. They had nothing to fear from us if they behaved themselves. We wanted to reduce the tensions that had led us to the threshold of a nuclear standoff."[65]

"I think we recognized the difficulties with the Soviet economy," Matlock recalled in 1998.

> If you're going to negotiate, any rational negotiator tries to position things so your negotiating position will be advantageous. . . . There was no contradiction whatsoever in bringing pressure to bear on the

Soviet system, particularly since we knew they needed to end the arms race [for domestic reasons]. . . . [But] I would say that none of the key players [in foreign policy making] were operating from the assumption that we were going to do the Soviet Union in, or that the purpose of the pressure was to bring them down. . . . [T]hat's all thinking after the fact. Our goal was always to give the Soviets incentives to bring the Cold War to an end. [66]

The administration's first definitive statement of its policy toward the Soviet Union called for placing pressure on the USSR, but the aim was to avoid further strengthening the adversary and to encourage democratic reform. The 1983 National Security Decision Directive entitled "US Relations with the USSR" began by stating that "US policy toward the Soviet Union will consist of three elements: external resistance to Soviet imperialism; internal pressure on the USSR to weaken the sources of Soviet imperialism; and negotiations to eliminate, on the basis of strict reciprocity, outstanding disagreements." The document explained that the administration's aim was to "promote, within the narrow limits available to us, the process of change in the Soviet Union toward a more pluralistic political and economic system. . . . The US recognizes that Soviet aggressiveness has deep roots in the internal system, and that relations with the USSR should therefore take into account whether or not they help to strengthen this system and its capacity to engage in aggression."[67] The Soviet expert on the National Security Council at the time, Richard Pipes, recalls that the document reflected Reagan's views about the potential to promote evolutionary change in the USSR rather than an effort or desire to force it to collapse. Before the document was finalized, the president intervened so as to delete some of its more aggressive aspects. "Reagan specifically emphasized the importance of compromise with the Soviet leadership," Pipes recalled.[68]

The administration sought to pressure the USSR in a variety of ways. For example, Washington aided the mujahedin fighting the Soviet Union in Afghanistan, and the Defense Department invested in areas of comparative advantage in an attempt to capitalize upon American technological prowess.[69] The White House also sought to restrict Soviet revenues from its natural gas pipeline.[70] National Security Decision Directive 66, issued in late 1982, called upon the United States and its allies to limit their dependence upon Soviet gas and to search for Western alternatives. The document also sought to prevent the transfer of oil and gas technology to the USSR. But it concluded, "[I]t is not the purpose [of the United States and its allies] to engage in economic warfare against the Soviet Union. To be consistent with our broad security interests, trade with the USSR must proceed *inter alia* on the basis of a strict balance of advantages."[71]

Defense Secretary Weinberger, one of the more hawkish members of the administration, has recalled that the military buildup was not intended to force the collapse of the USSR. "There were some people who said that the whole thing was just an attempt to run the Soviet Union into bankruptcy," he observed in 2002. "Actually, it was not, in my view. What . . . we needed— and we were in full agreement on it—was to restore our military deterrent capability—to get a capability that would make it quite clear to the Soviets that they couldn't win a war against us—in such black and white terms as that."[72] The second aim of the buildup was to place the United States in a stronger position so as to negotiate arms reductions. "In order for a negotiation to succeed you have to have something to give up," Weinberger explained in 1995, "and when the president entered office we had nothing to give up."[73]

Frank Carlucci, Reagan's national security adviser who replaced Weinberger as secretary of defense in January 1987, also rejects the notion that the president's aim was to destroy the USSR. "I don't think [the president] ever thought of it in terms of bankrupting the Soviet Union or forcing it to collapse," he recalled. "He just saw it as a lousy system, and if we could negotiate them into some common sense, they'd change their system."[74]

Secretary of State Alexander Haig was not seeking to force the collapse of the USSR either. Haig did not think that a policy of "trying to exploit and exacerbate internal Soviet weaknesses was either viable or wise." While he believed the Soviet system had serious flaws, he did not share Reagan's view that it was bound to fail or that it might do so in response to American pressure. Like many others within the administration, Haig believed the superpower would be able to overcome any economic or political difficulties.[75]

Haig's successor, George Shultz, agreed. The USSR had its weaknesses, Shultz knew, but its capacity to compete with the United States was not about to diminish.[76] It was absurd to think that the United States could exhaust its adversary. Twenty years after leaving office Shultz reflected, "I've heard a lot of people say that [President Reagan's strategy was to bankrupt the Soviet Union], but I've never really bought that. That is, we felt that they couldn't keep up with us, but the idea of building up our military capability was not to outspend them, but to provide ourselves with adequate defenses. That was the justification for it."[77]

In February 1983 Undersecretary of State Eagleburger summed up the rationale behind the buildup: "Our efforts are designed to assure equality in the military relationship. . . . We are not trying to spend the Soviet economy into the ground. Indeed, we would not mind at all if the Soviets improved their economic condition by spending less on their military. . . . Our effort to maintain a stable military balance is entirely consistent with our goal of improved relations with the Soviet Union. In fact, the one is clearly necessary for the other—a reality that some, of late, seem to have forgotten."[78]

Shultz has expanded, "There are some people who want to have [military] strength and use the strength and not have any diplomacy connected with it. My idea always was strength and diplomacy go together. If you don't have any strength, your diplomacy is in the ashcan. You've got nothing to take to the table. And at the same time, if you don't have any diplomatic process going on, it erodes your strength. A good diplomatic process helps your strength."[79]

In November 1983 Secretary Shultz began chairing a series of Saturday morning meetings on Soviet policy for senior officials. The aim was to jump-start the process of improving relations with Moscow. After the first meeting Matlock jotted down notes summarizing the proceedings. "[T]here was general agreement on American goals," he wrote, but "sharp differences regarding the specific steps that should be taken to reach those goals." Notably, "[N]obody argued that the United States should try to bring the Soviet Union down. All recognized that the Soviet leaders faced mounting problems, but understood that US attempts to exploit them would strengthen Soviet resistance to change rather than diminish it. President Reagan was in favor of bringing pressure to bear on the Soviet Union, but his objective was to induce the Soviet leaders to negotiate reasonable agreements, not to break up the country."[80]

In a policy guidance that he drew up after the meeting Matlock noted that the group had agreed upon three objectives. First, the United States should seek to "reduce the use and threat of force in international relations." Second, Washington should seek to "lower high levels of armaments by equitable and verifiable agreements." Finally, it should "establish minimal trust" on a variety of issues. "Our policy should **not** include the following goals," the guidance stated. First, "challenging the legitimacy of the Soviet system." Second, seeking "military superiority"; and finally, "forcing the collapse of the Soviet system (as distinct from exerting pressure on Soviets to live up to agreements and abide by civilized standards of behavior)."[81]

Richard Pipes, Matlock's notoriously hard-line predecessor at the National Security Council, has explained that the administration was not interested in "busting the Soviet Union"; rather, it aimed to "creat[e] difficulties" for the Soviets, "pushing them" to reform. With this pressure, the administration hoped, the Soviets' economic condition would become "so aggravate[d] that they would undertake reforms." Pipes further stated that he "didn't expect these reforms to bring down the Soviet Union," but he did think that "they would lead to very far-reaching changes in the Soviet system and Soviet policy."[82]

Matlock concurs. "We wanted to use what influence we had to change the internal structure," he explained in 1998. "We wanted to change it the same way that Gorbachev himself had said he wanted to change it. But that was not because we wanted to make the Soviet Union weaker. We wanted to see someone there who could be a partner, and could be a healthy economy, meeting the needs of its people, and therefore not a threat to its neighbors. You know, that was really our goal. It sounds very idealistic, but that was what we really believed."[83] US officials understood very well that a weak Soviet regime with nuclear arsenals pointing at the United States was not in America's interests. "I would say that none of the key players [in foreign policy making] were operating from the assumption that we were going to do the Soviet Union in, or that the purpose of the pressure was to bring them down," Matlock explained. "[T]hat's all thinking after the fact. Our goal was always to give the Soviets incentives to bring the Cold War to an end."[84]

When President Reagan took office in 1981 administration officials mistakenly believed the United States was falling behind the Soviet Union in the arms race and US forces needed to be both modernized and expanded.[85] Thus, Reagan introduced a military buildup. The short-term objective was to catch up with the USSR, but the ultimate goal was to persuade Moscow to agree to arms reductions. Reagan officials reasoned that the Kremlin would not agree to reduce arsenals until it was confronted by an adversary of equal strength and resolve. Although it may seem paradoxical, the ultimate objective of the US military buildup was to bring about arms reductions. The administration sought "peace through strength," as the president was fond of saying.

Triumphalists suggest that Reagan was insincere. Although he claimed to be seeking peace and disarmament, his secret plan was to destroy the

USSR. The president sought to end the Cold War not by ushering in an era of dialogue and arms reductions, they argue, but rather by forcing the Soviet Union into bankruptcy.

The president and his chief foreign policy advisers categorically reject this notion. Both of Reagan's defense secretaries, both of his secretaries of state, the Soviet experts on the National Security Council, and other high-ranking officials have repeatedly stated that the administration was not seeking to force the Soviet Union to collapse. For one thing, during the early 1980s most officials considered the Soviet Union to be a formidable and enduring adversary. President Reagan believed that the Soviet system was unsustainable in the long run, but his advisers did not share his views. The Soviets had economic problems, it was acknowledged, but the idea that the superpower was on the verge of collapse seemed too fanciful to be considered seriously. Moreover, CIA Director Casey, Deputy Director Gates, and Secretary Weinberger were so wedded to their belief that the USSR was a strong and enduring foe that they rejected or ignored reports from experts within the Agency that highlighted Soviet weaknesses. Gates and Casey also pressured CIA analysts to overstate the strength of the Soviet Union.

More important, fatally undermining the Kremlin would have been a dangerous proposition. Moscow had tens of thousands of nuclear warheads targeting the United States. If the center were to fall, who would control these weapons? And what would happen to Soviet nuclear materials during the ensuing chaos? (The Bush administration later faced just such a conundrum, which prompted it to collaborate with Gorbachev in managing the process of change.)

The Reagan administration's objective was to persuade the Kremlin to improve relations and reduce its nuclear arsenals. It is worth recalling the president's January 16, 1984, address. "I believe that 1984 finds the United States in its strongest position in years to establish a constructive and realistic working relationship with the Soviet Union," Reagan began. "We must and will engage the Soviets in a dialogue as serious and constructive as possible, a dialogue that will serve to promote peace in the troubled regions of the world, reduce the level of arms, and build a constructive working relationship. . . . [W]e want more than deterrence; we seek genuine cooperation; we seek progress for peace."[86] As paradoxical as it may seem, the buildup was intended to lead to disarmament.

3

The Strategic Defense Initiative

Ending the MADness

> I know I speak for people everywhere when I say our dream is to see the
> day when nuclear weapons will be banished from the earth.
>   Ronald Reagan, November 11, 1983

On March 23, 1983, President Reagan unveiled a daring new research program, the Strategic Defense Initiative (SDI). Reagan was vague about the details, but the long-term objective was to develop a system that would defend Americans against a nuclear attack. SDI would use space-based lasers to obliterate nuclear warheads in flight, thus protecting civilians. The project had a science-fiction quality to it, prompting critics to dub the project "Star Wars."

SDI was a radical idea. The conventional approach to security was known as "Mutual Assured Destruction," or MAD. In this approach the United States deterred the Soviets from attacking by maintaining a large and resilient nuclear arsenal. If Moscow attacked, the United States would retaliate with its own nuclear weapons, and both countries would be obliterated. In order for this arrangement to work, both superpowers had to forego defenses. If one side was able to defend itself against a nuclear attack, it would be able to launch a first strike on the other without fear of a retaliatory attack. Thus, MAD depended upon enormous nuclear arsenals being on hair-trigger alert in countries without meaningful defenses. Experts insisted this arrangement had prevented the Cold War from becoming hot. The ever-present prospect of nuclear annihilation had deterred the superpowers from waging war.

SDI had been a closely guarded secret. In fact, few members of the administration knew about it before its public unveiling. Reagan's own secretary of state only found out about it two days before it was announced publicly.[1] Secretary of Defense Caspar Weinberger was not even allowed to have a full text of the address until it had been delivered.[2] Close allies, such as British Prime Minister Margaret Thatcher and Canadian Prime Minister Brian Mulroney, were not given advance notice. It was the president's pet project, his signature foreign policy initiative.

Reagan's announcement unleashed a storm of controversy. Most doubted that SDI was technologically feasible and considered it a pipe dream. Others thought it a bombshell that would aggravate both the Soviets and US allies who were already skittish over the president's strident anticommunism. Still others thought it would prove dangerously destabilizing because, if deployed, it would allow the United States to attack the USSR without fear of reprisal, thus undermining MAD. And these were just the reactions from *within* the Reagan administration.[3]

The Soviets were even more incensed. SDI violated the Anti-Ballistic Missile (ABM) Treaty, they charged. It would allow the United States to launch a first strike with impunity, they asserted. It threatened to unleash an arms race in space, they insisted. SDI plunged the superpowers into a colder Cold War. It would become the most contentious issue in superpower relations for the next four years. "[T]o say that there was 'opposition' to the plan does not really convey the torrent of fury and scorn that was released by the president's proposal," Weinberger observed.[4]

SDI remains controversial. Triumphalists insist that President Reagan introduced the program so as to drive Moscow to its knees. The president knew that the Soviets could not match US technology nor could they afford a system of their own. Thus, Reagan embarked on the project in order to force the Kremlin to surrender, if not collapse.

But this tale is jarringly at odds with the president's own accounts of what inspired him to pursue the Strategic Defense Initiative. Ronald Reagan despised MAD and sought to abolish nuclear weapons. SDI held out the promise of rendering nuclear weapons obsolete, he believed. The president reasoned that if both superpowers could defend themselves from a nuclear attack, maintaining such arsenals would be pointless. Thus, they could be eradicated. SDI was an integral part of Ronald Reagan's quest to abolish nuclear arsenals.

President Reagan's Opposition to Nuclear Weapons and MAD

Ronald Reagan abhorred nuclear weapons and sought to eliminate them. Nuclear arms symbolized a tragic loss of civility in modern times, he believed. At the beginning of the twentieth century soldiers fought soldiers; they did not intentionally target civilians as part of their battle strategy. However, as the president explained in his memoirs, "[b]y the time the 1980s rolled around we were placing our entire faith in a weapon whose *fundamental target was the civilian population. A nuclear war is aimed at people, no matter how often military men like to say, 'No, we only aim to hit other missiles.'"[5] Their destructive capacity made them morally repugnant. "For the first time in history, man had the power to destroy mankind itself," he reasoned. "A war between the superpowers would incinerate much of the world and leave what was left of it uninhabitable forever."[6] "No *one* could win a nuclear war," Reagan insisted. "Yet as long as nuclear weapons were in existence, there would always be risks they would be used, and once the first nuclear weapon was unleashed, who knew where it would end? My dream, then, became a world free of nuclear weapons. . . . [F]or the eight years I was president I never let my dream of a nuclear-free world fade from my mind. "[7]

As Martin Anderson, Reagan's longtime friend and adviser, recalls, "The concern about nuclear war and the challenge to diminish that war was always foremost in [Reagan's] mind. It was not something he talked about a lot in public. But he had strong feelings and strong convictions about what could and should be done."[8] Edwin Meese, another long-term adviser, recalls Reagan's "deep aversion to nuclear weapons and even the remotest prospect of nuclear war. [In this] he never wavered throughout his eight years at the White House."[9]

Reagan called for the reduction of nuclear arsenals from his earliest days in the Oval Office. "We should start negotiating [with the Soviets] on the basis of trying to effect an actual reduction in the number of nuclear arms," Reagan told reporters during his first press conference in 1981. "That would then be *real* strategic arms limitation."[10] By March 1982 he was calling for the complete elimination of such arsenals. In fact, President Reagan called for the abolition of nuclear weapons nearly 90 times before Mikhail Gorbachev took office, and approximately 150 times before he departed the White House.[11] "I believe there can only be one policy for preserving our precious civilization in this modern age: a nuclear war can never be won and must never be fought," the president said in November 1983. "I know I speak for people everywhere when I say our dream is to see the day when nuclear weapons will be banished from the earth."[12]

At the time, Reagan's desire to abolish nuclear weapons was radical, if not quixotic. The conventional view was that MAD required large arsenals. There would be "peace" as long as each superpower had the ability to withstand a nuclear attack and launch a devastating retaliatory strike in return. Few of the so-called experts were even calling for a *reduction* in nuclear arsenals, much less their elimination. Previous administrations had merely sought to limit the rate at which nuclear arsenals could continue to grow. Earlier treaties had allowed nuclear arsenals to increase, seeking to manage the arms race rather than end it. Reagan took office with a decided hostility against this tacit agreement and likened it to "two westerners standing in a saloon aiming their guns at each other's head—permanently."[13]

MAD drove the superpowers to develop arsenals large enough to withstand a first attack and still be able to retaliate. Redundancy and excess capacity were crucial. Not only did MAD result in vast stockpiles of weapons, it required them to be on hair-trigger alert. According to the logic of the doctrine, if an aggressor launched a nuclear attack, the target would have to respond quickly so as to be able to retaliate effectively. "MAD [was] madness," Reagan insisted. "It was the craziest thing I ever heard of." It rendered the world "a button push away from oblivion."[14]

Such a situation also increased the probability of a nuclear accident, the president reasoned. Humans were fallible. If there were a misunderstanding or a crisis, panic could ensue or communications could break down, leading to an unintentional launching of nuclear missiles. Systems can fail, Reagan knew. The Soviet attack on Korean Airliner 007 in September 1983 proved this. "If anything, the KAL incident demonstrated . . . how much we needed arms control. . . . If mistakes could be made by a [Soviet] fighter pilot, what about a similar miscalculation by the commander of a missile launch crew? Yet if somebody made that kind of mistake—or a madman got possession of a nuclear missile—we were defenseless against it. Once a nuclear missile was launched, no one could recall it, and until we got something like the Strategic Defense Initiative system in operation, the world was helpless against nuclear missiles."[15] The president repeatedly spoke to his advisers about his concerns regarding an unintended nuclear Armageddon. As National Security Adviser Robert "Bud"

McFarlane has recalled, President Reagan "was genuinely alarmed that the world could get out of control. . . . [H]e genuinely understood that systems can fail, and he saw a responsibility to think beyond established doctrine."[16]

There was also the possibility that terrorists could gain control of nuclear weapons. "We all know how to make nuclear weapons," Reagan pointed out. "One day a madman could come along and make the missiles and blackmail all of us—but not if we have a defense against them."[17] MAD was simply too fragile, the president believed. It depended upon "no slip-ups, no madmen, no unmanageable crises, no mistakes—forever."[18]

As mentioned earlier, Mutual Assured Destruction required the superpowers to forego defenses. Mutual vulnerability was crucial. A country would refrain from initiating a nuclear war if it was unable to defend itself against a retaliatory strike. To attack would prove suicidal. In 1972 the superpowers had codified this mutual vulnerability into law by signing the Anti-Ballistic Missile (ABM) Treaty. This treaty obligated both superpowers to forego defenses against a nuclear attack.[19] Both sides would be safe as long as both sides remained vulnerable.

Reagan thought foregoing defenses was both irrational and immoral. "Somehow this didn't seem to me to be something that would send you to bed feeling safe," he remarked. "There had to be a better way."[20] Reducing nuclear weapons would improve security, he reasoned, but this was not sufficient. Even if arsenals were reduced by 90 percent, security would still be achieved through a "balance of terror" in which both sides were vulnerable to nuclear annihilation. Defenses were necessary, regardless of what the experts advised. "Every offensive weapon ever invented by man has resulted in the creation of a defense against it," he observed. "[Wasn't] it possible in this age of technology that we could invent a defensive weapon that could intercept nuclear weapons and destroy them as they emerged from their silos?"[21]

Shortly after taking office President Reagan began to explore the possibility of building a system to defend against a nuclear attack. Reagan cultivated a small group of scientists and advisers to assist him. The group was sworn to secrecy and excluded the president's conventional foreign affairs advisers, for fear his dream would fall prey to bureaucratic turf battles and nay-sayers. Not long after taking office he tasked the Joint Chiefs of Staff to secretly explore the idea further.[22]

When he unveiled SDI in March 1983, President Reagan explained his motives.[23] Predecessors had sought to deter aggression "through the promise of retaliation," he noted, and this approach had worked. But the time had come "to break out of a future that relies solely on offensive retaliation for our security. . . . I've become more and more deeply convinced that the human spirit must be capable of rising above dealing with other nations and human beings by threatening their existence." A bold new approach was needed. "If the Soviet Union will join with us in our effort to achieve major arms reductions, we will have succeeded in stabilizing the nuclear balance," he explained. "Nevertheless, it will still be necessary to rely on the specter of retaliation, on mutual threat. And that's a sad commentary on the human condition."

> Wouldn't it be better to save lives than to avenge them? . . . What if free people could live secure in the knowledge that their security did not rest upon the threat of instant US retaliation to deter a Soviet attack, that we could intercept and destroy strategic ballistic missiles before they reached our own soil or that of our allies . . .

Reagan hoped that SDI research would "begin to achieve our ultimate aim of eliminating the threat posed by nuclear strategic missiles. This could pave the way for arms control measures to eliminate the weapons themselves. We seek neither military superiority nor political advantage. Our only purpose—one all people share—is to search for ways to reduce the danger of nuclear war."[24]

President Reagan sought to abolish nuclear arsenals, and SDI was a crucial part of his plan. An effective defensive system against a nuclear attack could facilitate disarmament: if both the United States and the Soviet Union had defenses, then nuclear weapons would become obsolete, thus paving the way for their elimination. Reagan sought to replace mutual assured destruction with mutual assured survival.[25]

The president repeatedly offered to share SDI with Moscow, much to his advisers' dismay. Reagan understood that only one superpower with an effective defensive system could be destabilizing: the Soviets might feel threatened by an American defensive system because the United States would be able to launch an attack without worrying about a Soviet reprisal. In Moscow's eyes, there would be nothing to deter the United States from attacking. The Kremlin might then decide to attack the United States before such a defensive system was deployed or, at the very least, to build up its own arsenals so as to be able to overwhelm US defenses. Reagan reasoned that these problems could be averted if *both* sides had effective defenses. If both superpowers could thwart a nuclear attack, retaining such arsenals would be pointless. Therefore, the weapons could be abolished. Thus, from the outset the president offered to share SDI technology with the Soviets.[26] During the Geneva summit, the Reykjavik meeting, and in letters to Soviet leaders, the president repeatedly offered to share SDI technology so as to pave the way for the elimination of nuclear weapons.

Reagan was sincere in these offers, although his Soviet counterparts did not think so. During the 1986 Reykjavik summit the president repeatedly offered to share SDI, but Gorbachev brushed him aside. "Excuse me, Mr. President," the Soviet leader interjected at the close of one session, "but I do not take your idea of sharing SDI seriously. You don't want to share even petroleum equipment, automatic machine tools or equipment for dairies, while sharing SDI would be a second American revolution. And revolutions do not occur all that often. Let's be realistic and pragmatic. That's more reliable."[27] Aleksandr Bessmertnykh, Gorbachev's aide and eventual Soviet foreign minister, later recalled, "the part about sharing technology, visiting each other's labs and so forth. We didn't trust it. We didn't trust it at all. And all our specialists said that that was absolutely impossible, that the Americans would really let us see those things developing in their laboratories. So there was no trust at all about it. It was considered a ploy."[28]

Internal Resistance to Nuclear Abolition and SDI

Reagan's advisers thought the president's views were fanciful. They opposed the abolition of nuclear weapons and tried to convince him to change his mind. "My dream [was] a world free of nuclear weapons," Reagan explained in his memoirs. "Some of my advisers, including a number at the Pentagon, did not share this dream. They couldn't conceive of it. . . . But for the eight years I was president I never let my dream of a nuclear-free world fade from my mind."[29]

"The conventional wisdom on nuclear weapons was very clear during the late 1970s," Martin Anderson recalls.

Virtually no one at the time thought seriously that there was a chance of any reduction in nuclear missiles. In fact, during the late 1970s and early 1980s, the most radical proposal put forth was a freeze on existing nuclear stockpiles. . . . And when Reagan began to talk privately of a dream he had when someday we might live in a world free of all nuclear missiles, well, we just smiled.[30]

The foreign policy experts in the administration insisted that MAD had kept the peace during the Cold War. If the threat of nuclear annihilation were removed, there would be nothing to prevent Soviet expansionism, they believed. Secretary of State George Shultz shared the president's dissatisfaction with MAD but advised that it was the best possible policy given that nuclear weapons could not be uninvented. In late 1983 Shultz prepared a paper for Reagan outlining the reasons to stick with the doctrine. "But I made little real impact on the president," he conceded. "He stuck with his own deeply held view of where we should be heading."[31]

National Security Adviser Frank Carlucci also failed to win Reagan over to the virtues of MAD. "[The president] would say to me that nuclear weapons were inherently evil," Carlucci recalled. "I'd respond with the traditional case for nuclear deterrence, saying that nuclear weapons had kept the peace for forty years."[32] But the president was never convinced.

Secretary of State Alexander Haig had wrestled with the president over the issue as well. As Haig tells it, during an early visit to Camp David Reagan had drafted a personal letter to Soviet General Secretary Leonid Brezhnev that expressed his hope for "meaningful dialogue" and ultimately the abolition of nuclear weapons. "[When I read it] I found myself astonished at his attitude when I measured it against the backdrop of what he was saying publicly and what was attributed to him as a classic cold warrior," Haig told Reagan biographer Lou Cannon. The letter "talked about a world without nuclear weapons, it talked about disarmament. . . . It reflected a demeanor that if only those two men could sit down as rational human beings, the problems of the world would be behind us." Haig considered the letter "naïve" and potentially confusing to the Soviets, so he strongly advised against sending it. Reagan complied.[33]

The president may have lost that battle, but he did not abandon his larger war against MAD. Haig's successor, George Shultz, recalls that "the arms control community cringed and did not take seriously Reagan's views about banishing nuclear weapons."[34] Consequently the speechwriting process was often "an agony of pulling and hauling" as the president inserted remarks calling for the elimination of nuclear weapons and his advisers removed them. "Every meeting I go to the president talks about abolishing nuclear weapons," Shultz once reprimanded underlings. "I cannot get it through your heads that this man is serious. We either have to convince him he is barking up the wrong tree or reply to his interests with some specific suggestions."[35]

The president's advisers did not share his devotion to SDI, either.[36] When Shultz was informed about Reagan's plans—two days before SDI was unveiled—he was incensed. "We don't have the technology to say this," he interrupted the official briefing him on the impending announcement. "This changes the whole strategic view, and the doctrine of the United States." Richard Burt, the Assistant Secretary of State, was "flabbergasted." "Not only is a nuclear-free world a pipe dream, but a speech like this by the president will unilaterally destroy the foundation of the Western alliance," he said. Shultz agreed. "This is so sweeping [that] it could hit the allies right between the eyes," he warned William Clark, the national security adviser at the time. Later that day the secretary was unusually frank with the president. "[T]his is a bombshell," Shultz advised Reagan. Technological capabilities did not warrant the sweeping language, and the president's message had not been carefully thought through. "This initiative will not be seen as a peaceful gesture," Shultz warned. "It will be seen as destabilizing." The secretary believed the initiative would "set off alarm bells among our allies [as well as] the Soviets," especially since an early draft of the speech repeated Reagan's earlier charge that the USSR was an "evil empire."[37]

Defense Secretary Weinberger was one of the few advisers who backed SDI enthusiastically, and not only because it entailed $26 billion flooding into his department. Like Reagan, he believed that the mutual vulnerability enshrined in MAD was nonsensical and defenses against Soviet nuclear missiles were imperative. It delighted him that his views offended the arms control establishment, along with most of the State Department.[38] "To those who traipse from resort to resort reading each other's papers on security and strategy, the idea that any country might try to defend itself against the nuclear missiles of another country was not only revolutionary, it was sacrilegious," he sneered.[39] Weinberger rejected this perceived elitism. "[O]bviously, if we are able to destroy incoming missiles, I don't think it would be destabilizing," he told the press in October 1981, "I think it would be extremely comforting."[40]

While Reagan was governor of California, he had discussed his desire for a defensive system with Weinberger. However, the president opted not to include him in the small group tasked to work on the project. Nonetheless, Weinberger was privy to what was going on. Although sworn to secrecy, both Bill Clark and Ed Meese surreptitiously briefed him on the project. By the time President Reagan unveiled his proposal the defense secretary "was ready to move vigorously and publicly."[41] For the remainder of his term as defense secretary, Weinberger championed the cause.

Despite serious misgivings, Reagan's other advisers came to grudgingly support SDI.[42] For one thing, Reagan was so wedded to the idea they had no choice but to go along. For another, it offered a solution to a strategic dilemma: the Soviets had far more land-based intercontinental ballistic missiles (ICBMs) than did the United States, yet Congress would not support an American buildup to match the Soviet arsenal. Nor would Moscow agree to reductions anytime soon, officials believed. Therefore, SDI provided a way to address this dilemma. An effective defensive system could neutralize this Soviet advantage.[43] Admiral James Watkins, the chief of naval operations on the Joint Chiefs of Staff and a key supporter of the program, was of this view. Watkins believed previous American attempts to match the Soviet arsenal of ICBMs had been wrongheaded. "It was a race we couldn't win, so what are we in it for?" Watkins asked. McFarlane explained, "[The United States had sought] a rough military balance, but we were always going to lose that numbers game. [The USSR] did not have a Congress to contend with and faced no limitations on quantity. But we did. So it was foolish to engage in a numerical effort to balance."[44] The United States should play to its strengths, officials reasoned. "Why don't we get in our own race, we'll play by our rules—which is high-tech, new systems, defense, doing things they probably could not do as fast as we could," Watkins reasoned.[45]

In addition, Gorbachev's unrelenting objections to SDI led Reagan officials to value the program more highly. At every summit meeting and in nearly every letter, the Soviet leader insisted that Washington must abandon its effort to build "space strike weapons," as he called SDI.[46] American officials surmised that Gorbachev was fixated on SDI because the Soviets were deeply afraid of the program, perhaps because they could not master the technology or because they could not handle the financial burden of building a system of their own. The more Gorbachev demanded restrictions on SDI, the more convinced some Americans became that it gave Washington added leverage.[47]

US officials came to believe that SDI could be a powerful bargaining chip. A comprehensive defensive system might be beyond reach, they reasoned, but SDI research might lead to technological breakthroughs. The Kremlin would be spooked by such prospects and might therefore agree to reduce its arsenal in exchange for a US commitment to restrict or abandon the project. SDI could be traded away for Soviet concessions on arms reductions, Reagan's advisers believed.[48]

This was the angle McFarlane emphasized when he was pitching the costly program to profoundly skeptical members of Congress. Persuading Congress to support SDI was no small task, given the strong support for MAD. Few thought a comprehensive defensive shield was feasible, and even fewer thought it was wise. In addition, the president's decision not to consult congressional leaders before unveiling the program had created intense ill will. Discussions and hearings about the research program were consequently "protracted and highly confrontational."[49] "It is difficult to convey the strength and the irrationality and the fury of the opposition to SDI in our Congress," Defense Secretary Weinberger recalled. "The very mention of the program seem[ed] to bring out exceptionally violent reactions."[50]

In an effort to cultivate congressional support for SDI, McFarlane focused on its potential to persuade the Soviets to reduce their nuclear arsenals. "In dozens and dozens of private one-on-one sessions [with members of Congress] I made the case for what I believed would be the Soviet reaction [to the SDI research program]," McFarlane recounted in 1998.

> I said that it seemed to me that if the Soviet Union sees the US investing in high technology, which is what we do best, that, whether or not you believe the systems would be built, you could certainly conclude that we would discover . . . sufficient new technologies that would in some fashion, some day produce, if not an effective defense, at least so many other discoveries so as to leave the Soviet Union behind. Therefore the Soviet leadership would say, "What do we need to do to stop this investment in technology?" Our answer would be "reduce nuclear weapons." In short, the argument to our Congress was that this investment would affect Soviet decision-making and force changes in their arms control positions. It would help to get them to agree to reductions.[51]

Members of Congress were suspicious of McFarlane's claims. Sam Nunn, Al Gore, and others pointed out that McFarlane was asserting that SDI would never have to be built, yet the president was telling the American people he was unwavering in his commitment to deploy the system. "Give me two years," McFarlane recalled telling these skeptics. "And if it doesn't work, you can defeat the system: don't vote for it, pull the money out." Then "they all held their breath and said, 'All right, you've got two years.'"[52]

Thus, McFarlane and others came to believe that SDI's primary value could be as a bargaining chip. If the mere prospect of American technological breakthroughs was not sufficient to induce the Kremlin to agree to arms reductions, then perhaps SDI could be traded away in exchange for such an agreement. Given its cost, congressional opposition, and technological challenges, SDI might never come to fruition anyway, officials knew. But it could be traded away in exchange for deep cuts in the Soviet arsenal.

There were certain risks to discussing this option, however. The Reagan administration had been plagued by leaks and public backstabbing, and if the Kremlin got wind that some American officials sought to use SDI as a bargaining chip, it would undermine the US position. Ideally, the administration sought to retain SDI yet force the Soviets to agree to arms reductions. "If we can keep [the Soviets] convinced that we will hold on to SDI, we will get them to agree to offensive force reductions," Weinberger told his colleagues during an NSC meeting in February 1987. If the Soviets suspected the Americans were willing to trade SDI away, the White House would lose its leverage. "SDI may be the only thing that keeps the Soviets at the negotiating table," the defense secretary argued. "The Soviets may not sign any agreement if we don't press forward. We should press forward. It will provide much better leverage."[53] Weinberger, however, opposed using SDI as a bargaining chip. "We don't have to make such a trade!" he insisted to his colleagues. "We should show them that it is in their interest, too, to seek offensive force reductions. . . . Once we signal that our approach involves such a trade, we have a real problem."[54]

The president never viewed SDI as a bargaining chip and rejected all suggestions that he engage in such horse trading. For Reagan, SDI was about protecting civilians, pure and simple. "[I] met with George Shultz about the [upcoming Geneva] summit," Reagan noted in his diary on September 11, 1985. "I sense he and Bud [McFarlane] feel that Defense is going to be uncooperative and not want to settle anything with the Soviets. I can't quite agree on that. One thing I do know is I won't trade our SDI off for some offer of weapons reductions."[55] A year later the president was still encountering resistance regarding his decision that SDI would not be bargained away. During discussions with his foreign policy advisers in July 1986 Reagan recalled that some of our arms control and State Department experts wanted me to hint to the Soviets that we might be willing to trade SDI for greater Soviet concessions on offensive weapons. Cap Weinberger, the chief evangelist, after me, of the Strategic Defense Initiative, said that if the Soviets heard about this split in the administration and decided I was wavering on SDI, it would send the wrong signals to Moscow and weaken our bargaining position. I think he was also worried that I might be persuaded by those advocating possible concessions on the SDI, but he needn't have worried. I was committed to the search for an alternative to the MAD policy and said it as emphatically and as often as I could, privately and publicly: *The SDI is not a bargaining chip.*[56]

"A certain amount of mythology grew up around the Strategic Defense Initiative," Reagan reflected in his memoirs. "[O]ne of them was that I had proposed the idea to produce a bargaining chip for use in getting the Soviets to reduce their weaponry. I've had to tell the Soviet leaders a hundred times that the SDI was not a bargaining chip. I've told them I'd share it with others willing to give up their nuclear missiles."[57]

Reagan's advisers considered the president's offers to share SDI with the Soviets to be untenable, if not a complete flight of fancy. As Weinberger advised Reagan in February 1987, the idea of sharing SDI "scared the pants off" some of his officials, including the defense secretary himself.[58] "President Reagan was not only a true believer in SDI, he was definitely a true believer in sharing," Jack Matlock explained in 1993. "[T]his was something that most of the bureaucracy, virtually the entire bureaucracy . . . said we can't do." Matlock recalled an incident in July 1986 in which he was drafting a letter to send to the Kremlin and the president wanted to insert a section proposing to share SDI technology with the Soviets. The original draft did not contain such a commitment. As Matlock recalls:

> I sent the draft in, and [Reagan] changed it. He changed the section and made a very strong commitment to sharing . . . the research. I checked this out and all the experts said, "We can't do that." So I changed it back and sent it to him. It went back to him four times.

And finally, he called me in, and he said, "Jack, is this my letter?" And I said, "Yes, sir, Mr. President." He said, "This is what I want to say." And I said, "Look, Mr. President, everybody tells me we can't do that." And he said, "Damn it, it is my letter, that's what I am going to do." And well, that's the letter he sent.[59]

Reagan continued to push the idea of sharing SDI, and his advisers continued to resist. During a September 1987 NSC meeting, Reagan again locked horns with his officials. "Why can't we agree now that if we get to a point where we want to deploy [SDI] we will simply make all the information available [to the Soviets] . . . so that we can both have defenses," Reagan pleaded.[60] "I don't believe we can ever do that," Weinberger shot back. General Robert T. Herres, the vice chairman of the Joint Chiefs of Staff, interjected, "Mr. President, there is a great risk in exchanging technical data. Much of our technology is easily convertible to other purposes and into an offensive area." Kenneth Adelman, the director of the Arms Control and Disarmament Agency, added, "Mr. President, that would be the most massive technical transfer the western world has ever known." The conversation turned to other matters, but Reagan grew frustrated. "There has to be an answer to all these questions because some day people are going to ask why we didn't do something now about getting rid of nuclear weapons. You know, I've been reading my Bible and the description of the Armageddon talks about destruction, I believe, of many cities and we absolutely need to avoid that. We need to do something *now*." "We certainly need to avoid Armageddon," Frank Carlucci said, in an attempt to soothe the president. "The answer is SDI," Weinberger added.[61]

Carlucci, who served as both Reagan's national security adviser and secretary of defense, recalled, "[The president] did, as best I could tell, sincerely believe that he could give [SDI] to the Russians and everything would be fine. And I and others tried to explain to him that technically that just was not feasible. And the only thing that finally convinced him, I remember [was] one day I said to him, 'Mr. President, you have just got to stop saying that because Gorbachev, among others, doesn't believe you.' And he said, 'Well, I guess you are right. He really doesn't believe me.' . . . But it took a number of years to get him to that realization."[62]

By 1987 Reagan was beginning to grudgingly accept that his offers to share the benefits of SDI were not being taken seriously in Moscow. He reluctantly acknowledged that the Soviets would not trust the Americans to honor such a bargain. So he came up with another plan: placing SDI under international control. Such an approach would have many benefits, the president reasoned. It would make defenses available to all nations, thus enhancing global security. It would get around the problem of mistrust. It would make it more difficult for members of Congress to oppose the project or withhold funding. And it addressed the problem posed by the Kremlin's insistence that arms reductions could not proceed until Reagan made concessions on SDI. If SDI were transferred to an international body, the president believed, the path would be cleared for an arms reduction treaty. "[T]he Soviets want an [arms reduction] agreement but are determined to force us to give up SDI," Reagan reminded his advisers during a February 1987 NSC meeting. "How about looking at going forward with deployment, but of an international SDI and an international defense against any ballistic missile? This approach would take SDI out of the bargain. This done, I can see no reason why we could not move forward with reductions."[63]

Reagan's idea derived from a similar proposal by the Truman administration in 1946, called the Baruch Plan. This plan proposed to place research on atomic energy under the auspices of an international agency, which would insure that the information would be used for peaceful and humanitarian ends. Truman's efforts fell victim to the rising Cold War, however, and his quest failed. Reagan deeply regretted this lost opportunity and frequently recalled this plan with pride. The United States "had a nuclear monopoly at the time," Reagan reminded Gorbachev during the Geneva summit meeting, "and we could have commanded the world to do our bidding."[64] Instead, the United States had opted for peace.

Administration officials were adamantly opposed to Reagan's idea of sharing SDI and only slightly more enthusiastic about his proposal to place it under international control. Weinberger thought such an approach would put Washington "in a high moral position," but would anger European allies. Arms control adviser Paul Nitze predicted the Soviets would try to gain control of any international group overseeing SDI. Lieutenant General Edward L. Rowny, Reagan's arms control adviser, cautioned that the idea might seem "too far afield from current negotiations" and therefore a "diversion." Admiral William J. Crowe, the Chairman of the Joint Chiefs of Staff, concurred.[65] Despite Reagan's enthusiasm for the proposal, his officials were able to bury it by assigning a committee to look into the matter.[66]

Driving the Soviets to Their Knees?

SDI was not introduced for the purpose of forcing the Soviet Union to surrender or collapse. "I was present at many, if not most, of the discussions on [SDI]," Rowny explained in 1998. "As the archives are opened, I would be greatly surprised if you find any serious talk about [spending the Soviets into the ground] at all. I think it did come up once or twice in passing, but by and large, throughout the period, President Reagan's idea was 'Let's defend the people of the United States.'"[67] McFarlane never thought SDI "would bring down the Soviet Union," he recalled. Rather, "all I thought that would happen is that they would want us to stop the investment."[68] Watkins concurs. The aim, he said, was to counter a perceived Soviet advantage. Officials "did not intend that the United States would 'bring the Russians to their knees' by leading a defensive arms race."[69]

At the time, Soviet experts in the CIA thought SDI would have a negligible effect on the Soviet Union. Noting that the president's vision was rather ambiguous, analysts predicted that Moscow would most likely respond through "a concerted political and diplomatic effort first to force the United States to drop its plans, or, failing that, to negotiate them away." The Soviets might take "certain limited military steps" so as to improve its bargaining position and to prepare themselves "for initial US deployment should it occur," but the CIA did not anticipate major Soviet expenditures. "We believe it highly unlikely that the Soviets will undertake a 'crash' program in reaction to US Ballistic Missile Deployment developments, but rather will seek to counter them by steadily paced efforts over the decades the United States will need to develop and deploy its overall defense. They will look for solutions that are least disruptive to their way of doing business and involve the least possible change to their planned programs."[70] It was doubtful that SDI would provoke the Kremlin into massive military outlays, the analysts concluded.

Reconceptualizing Security

President Reagan loathed Mutual Assured Destruction and sought to eliminate nuclear weapons. His aversion to nuclear weapons "was not remotely appreciated or given much attention at the time," George Shultz has observed, but his "instinctive rejection of Mutual Assured Destruction was powerful."[71] SDI was an integral part of the president's quest to abolish nuclear weapons. He did not embark on SDI for the purpose of causing the Soviet

Union to collapse. As the president repeatedly stated, his intent was to protect civilians from nuclear annihilation and to render nuclear weapons obsolete. This is why he steadfastly refused to abandon or even restrict the project to the laboratory, as Gorbachev often demanded. Other members of the administration valued SDI as a means to persuade Moscow to reduce its nuclear arsenal. For them, SDI was not a means to bankrupt the USSR, but rather a vehicle for extracting a Soviet agreement to reduce its nuclear arms. If officials had intended to use SDI to force the collapse of the Soviet Union, they would not have considered trading it away.

Moreover, if Reagan had been seeking to bankrupt the Soviet Union, he would not have repeatedly offered to share this research with the Kremlin. Sharing this technology would have removed any incentive for Moscow to invest in it itself.

Given Reagan's antipathy for MAD, it is fair to say that even if SDI had been cheap—even if it had held no prospect of placing financial pressure on the USSR—he still would have pursued it. Even if the program had had no prospect of engaging the USSR in a costly arms race the president would have embraced the idea of building a defensive system. For him, SDI was about protecting civilians and ending the scourge of MAD, plain and simple.

President Reagan's views about nuclear weapons and security were revolutionary for the time. Although often disparaged as a foreign policy dilettante, the president managed to reconceptualize the meaning of security and to revolutionize established military doctrine. When the president entered office, American experts conceived of security in a zero-sum manner: the more weapons the USSR acquired, the more vulnerable the United States became. The president initially adopted this perspective and launched the largest peacetime military buildup so as to match the perceived strength of the USSR and to force it to agree to arms reductions.

But President Reagan reconceptualized the meaning of security. He intuitively understood that the weapons themselves had become the enemy. The more nuclear weapons there were, the higher the probability of a calamitous accident and the greater the prospect of nuclear annihilation. Moreover, this was a global threat, not simply an American one. Civilians everywhere were threatened by these stockpiles. Mutual Assured Destruction insured global vulnerability. President Reagan aspired to global security. SDI was the first step on the path away from mutual assured destruction and toward mutual assured survival.[72]

4

Soviet New Thinking and the Withdrawal from Afghanistan

> How long will our military-industrial complex keep devouring our econ-
> omy, our agriculture, and our consumer goods? How long are we going to
> take this ogre? How long are we going to throw into its mouth the food of
> our children?
>
> Yegor Ligachev, Central Committee Secretary and
> Member of the Politburo

> So, for us to end the arms race was an internal domestic problem. What-
> ever Reagan might do or not do, that did not change this fact.
>
> Anatoly Chernyaev, foreign policy adviser to Mikhail Gorbachev

Did President Reagan force the Soviet Union to change its foreign policy,
reform its system, disarm, and withdraw from its war in Afghanistan? Triumphalists point out that the Soviet Union ultimately adopted many of the policy
changes the president had been calling for: Moscow became more cooperative
with the West, ended its war in Afghanistan, and embraced what it called
"universal human values," which entailed both democratic reforms at home
and free elections in Eastern Europe. Mikhail Gorbachev also embarked on a
program of "perestroika," or restructuring the Soviet economy along capitalist
lines so as to promote innovation and growth. Moscow also agreed to remove
its nuclear missiles from Europe and reduce its conventional arsenals.

Triumphalists assume that the president's military buildup and resolve
forced the Soviet Union to make these changes. The Kremlin did not *want* to
do these things; it was compelled to do so. Confronted with renewed American strength, it had no option other than to acquiesce to American demands.
Its reforms were acts of desperation. "The Soviets were terrified that they

wouldn't be able to keep up with American technology," journalist Rich Lowry has written. "Once they realized they couldn't kill SDI in the crib, greater political and economic reform was their only alternative."[1] Likewise, historian Andrew Busch asserts that "the Soviets were prodded by SDI into seeking greater modernization of their own society—which could only be achieved by liberalization. . . . [P]erestroika was a military initiative."[2] In the triumphalist view, the Reagan administration's hard-line policy had forced Moscow to reform, disarm, and withdraw from Afghanistan. In the face of overwhelming strength and determination, Moscow had no option other than to surrender the Cold War.

In order to assess the impact of Reagan's policies on the Soviet Union it is necessary to examine Soviet policy making, something triumphalists consistently fail to do. Thus, Chapters 4 and 5 consider the ending of the Cold War from Moscow's perspective. Drawing upon Soviet sources, Chapter 4 seeks to understand why the Kremlin changed its foreign policy and withdrew from Afghanistan. Chapter 5 focuses more specifically on Moscow's decision to reduce its arsenal and withdraw from the arms race.

Soviet "New Thinking"

Soviet foreign policy did indeed change dramatically in the mid-1980s. Shortly after Mikhail Gorbachev became general secretary in March 1985 the Soviet Union adopted a policy of "New Thinking," which rejected Marxist-Leninist notions about a never-ending conflict between socialism and democracy. Traditionally, Soviet foreign policy had been based on a zero-sum notion of global politics, in which a gain for Washington necessarily entailed a loss for Moscow. New Thinking rejected this Manichean view and instead emphasized global interdependence and common security. The primary threats to global security, Gorbachev argued, were the nuclear arms race, environmental degradation, and global disparities in wealth. New Thinking envisioned East and West as allies jointly facing these common dangers. It also rejected the use of force in international relations. Nuclear weapons themselves were the enemy, rather than the United States. In addition, New Thinking stressed universal human values, such as the right to free elections, freedom of speech (*glasnost*), and free trade.[3]

Within weeks of assuming office Gorbachev took steps to end the arms race.[4] In April 1985 he announced a unilateral moratorium on the deployment of new intermediate-range nuclear weapons and invited Washington to join the USSR in a moratorium on nuclear testing. When Washington opted not to join Moscow—claiming that the moratorium was unverifiable—the Soviet Union went ahead anyway, ultimately extending it until February 26, 1987, despite ongoing American tests.[5] In January 1986 the Soviet leader proposed the elimination of all nuclear weapons worldwide by 2000. By 1987 the Soviet Union had accepted the Reagan administration's Zero Option proposal to eliminate all intermediate-range forces in Europe and had agreed in principle to a 50 percent reduction in strategic arms.[6]

Another major shift in Soviet foreign policy was Moscow's decision to withdraw from Afghanistan, which it had invaded in December 1979. During the November 1985 Geneva summit meeting Gorbachev quietly informed President Reagan of his intent to pull Soviet forces out, later describing the situation publicly as a "bleeding wound."[7] Gorbachev publicly announced the withdrawal in February 1988, and one year later the last Soviet troops departed.

Gorbachev's revolutionary approach to foreign policy climaxed in his December 1988 speech to the United Nations.[8] During the address, the Soviet leader stunned his audience by effectively withdrawing from the Cold War. "The history of the past centuries and millennia has been a history of almost ubiquitous wars," he observed.

> [E]ven now many still claim that this past—which has not been overcome—is an immutable pattern. However, parallel with the process of wars, hostility, and alienation of peoples and countries, another process . . . was in motion and gaining force: The process of the emergence of a mutually connected and integral world. Further world progress is now possible only through the search for a consensus of all mankind, in movement toward a new world order.

Strikingly, the Soviet leader renounced the use of force in international relations. He announced plans to unilaterally slash the Soviet military by 500,000 troops and to significantly reduce its military presence in Eastern Europe. Six tank divisions would be withdrawn from the region, and by 1991 they would be disbanded entirely. Additional offensive arms and units in Eastern Europe would also be reduced, and remaining Soviet troops would be reorganized into "unambiguously defensive" units.

In addition, Gorbachev declared that all people had the right to freely choose their political system. He called for the rule of law and respect for human rights, both at home and abroad. "Freedom of choice is a universal principle to which there should be no exceptions," the leader of the communist world proclaimed. "[O]ur credo is as follows: Political problems should be solved only by political means and human problems only in a humane way."

After four decades of competing alliance systems, the USSR was withdrawing from the Cold War, ideologically, militarily, and politically.

In the triumphalist view the Reagan administration's hard-line policies had compelled Moscow to reform, disarm, and withdraw from Afghanistan. The Kremlin's only option was to concede to American demands. A difficulty with this argument is that President Reagan took office in January 1981, yet Soviet reforms did not begin until mid-1985. There were more than four years between the introduction of Reagan's hawkish policies and the beginning of Soviet reforms. Moreover, during these four years the Kremlin was anything but acquiescent. Leonid Brezhnev, Yuri Andropov, and Konstantin Chernenko all reviled Reagan's approach to superpower relations and adopted hard-line policies in response. By the fall of 1983 the Soviets had declared they could not do business with the Reagan administration and had stormed out of the arms talks in Geneva. None of these Soviet leaders felt compelled to adopt a more conciliatory posture toward Washington. None of them sought to appease the Reagan administration, much less concede the Cold War. The effect of Reagan's policies had been quite the opposite. As the CIA reported, by September 1983 superpower relations were as "pervasively bleak" as at any time since Stalin's death thirty years earlier.[9]

Superpower relations remained acrimonious even after the Reagan administration shifted to a more conciliatory posture in January 1984. By this time the Soviet Union was coping with infirm leaders who were incapable of major policy reform; nonetheless, there was no movement toward rapprochement. In short, President Reagan's policies—both hard-line and more conciliatory—were initially met with Soviet hostility, not compliance.

So why did Gorbachev choose to break with his predecessors and adopt a more conciliatory policy toward the West? What were the origins of New Thinking?

A Reform Movement Grows

Mikhail Gorbachev's New Thinking was not a bolt from the blue. Soviet academics and policy specialists had cautiously begun discussing ways to reform the Soviet system and foreign policy in the 1950s, when General Secretary Nikita Khrushchev ushered in an intellectual thaw. During this period pressure to conform to Stalinist policies and ideology was relaxed somewhat, thus producing a cohort of early reformers.[10] When Brezhnev became general secretary in 1964, this period of intellectual creativity initially survived. Brezhnev's policy of détente, which entailed a relaxing of tensions with the West, allowed reformers to discuss a wider range of foreign policy options for the USSR. In addition, détente brought with it an expanded range of contacts with the West. Soviet scientists and academics enjoyed new freedom to attend professional conferences abroad, and these contacts made the West appear less threatening.[11] As Soviet intellectuals gained more firsthand knowledge about the West, they began to question Marxist-Leninist principles, which depicted a world forever divided between socialist and democratic camps. Reformers began to question a class-based worldview, gravitating instead toward the notion of universal human values. In addition, they were attracted to the notion of increased trade based on market principles. Although reformers still couched their debates in classic Marxist-Leninist terminology, they began to embrace notions of interdependence, human rights, and market-based economics.

Andrei Sakharov's 1968 manifesto, *Progress, Peaceful Coexistence, and Intellectual Freedom* was a milestone in the reform movement. A physicist who had worked on the Soviet atomic bomb project, Sakharov had become disturbed about the moral and political implications of his work and sought to end the nuclear arms race. Moreover, his contact with colleagues from the West convinced him that the Soviet Union needed to adopt western notions of human rights. Drawing upon his scientific expertise and discussions with colleagues from the West, Sakharov's essay made a compelling case against the nuclear arms race and ballistic missile defense. It also included an impassioned plea for new respect for human rights and protecting the environment. Although circulated through underground channels (Sakharov's request to publish the piece under official means had been denied), the essay proved to be pathbreaking, and it influenced a generation of new thinkers.

The 1970s was a decade of contradiction for the reformers, however. "In part it was a time of great hopes, of maturation and activization of reformist thought in foreign and domestic affairs, boosted by an extensive new thaw in East-West relations," historian Robert D. English has observed. "But it was also the 'era of stagnation,' a time when the country's mounting problems were largely ignored."[12] In public, an ideocracy reigned; strict conformity to Stalinist dogma was required. In private, however, academics, scientists, and intellectuals were able to explore reformist ideas about universal human values, the Soviet Union's relationship with foreign countries, and different approaches to economic reform. While ideological conformity was enforced in the mainstream press, specialized academic journals, which had a smaller, restricted circulation, were allowed a greater degree of latitude. It was in these "closed" publications that intellectuals were able to test new ideas. The result was two separate conversations: officially sanctioned discussions in the mainstream press, which adhered to Marxist-Leninist principles; and cautiously reformist debates in more circumscribed publications.

As the 1970s wore on, Brezhnev and his allies became both more frail and more conservative. Consequently, reformers came under increasing restrictions. Some were removed from their posts, while others, such as Sakharov, were sent into exile. Alexander Yakovlev, who would go on to become a close Gorbachev confidant and was dubbed the "intellectual father of glasnost," was among the latter group.[13] In 1958 Yakovlev had been an exchange student at Columbia University before going on to head the Communist Party of the Soviet Union's Department of Ideology and Propaganda from 1969 to 1973. In 1973, however, he wrote an article in a prestigious Soviet journal criticizing conservative Russian nationalist thought. Yakovlev was promptly sacked and sent off to exile as the ambassador to Canada, where he remained for a decade.[14]

By 1975 Brezhnev was gravely ill, causing a vacuum of leadership. Three hawkish members of the Politburo—Foreign Minister Andrei Gromyko, Defense Minister Dimitri Ustinov, and then-director of the KGB, Yuri Andropov—effectively ran the government. Gromyko and Ustinov were particularly wedded to orthodoxy. Both "were in the habit of governing their subordinates with well-known severity and neither was inclined to encourage more open discussions," Andrei Grachev has recalled. This troika "drove the USSR to a position of confrontation" with most of the world. "Furthermore, this policy, which was used as an instrument to prop up the decaying political regime and justify new programs of military spending, not only placed an additional burden on the exhausted national economy but also had a crippling effect on the internal structure of Soviet society, subordinating it to the purposes of military production," Grachev believes. "The whole country was thus sentenced to become a giant war machine, and a militarized camp."[15] The succeeding decade was, "[a]bove all, a time of drift and inertia, bereft of ideological, economic and social vitality," historian Vladislav Zubok has observed. "By the 1980s the Soviet model had exhausted its innovative potential. . . . Above all, the model began to lose its appeal within Soviet society, even among the bureaucrats, educated elites, and skilled professionals who since the 1950s had formed the growing Soviet 'middle class.'"[16] Mikhail Gorbachev recalls being embarrassed and saddened by the state of the Soviet leadership during these years. "It may seem that Brezhnev's general state of physical and mental health would have brought up the issue of his retirement," Gorbachev observed in his memoirs. "Such a step would make sense from a human point of view, as well as being in the interests of the state. But neither Brezhnev himself nor his close entourage would dream of giving up their power. They convinced themselves, and tried to convince others, that Brezhnev's departure would upset the balance and undermine stability. In short, he was 'irreplaceable,' although more dead than alive."[17]

During the 1970s there was also widespread—and growing—recognition that the Soviet system was in need of reform. Stifling bureaucracy, fictitious economic "plans," empty store shelves, and apathetic workers were pervasive. A substantial underground economy had arisen so as to meet consumer's needs, yet the standard of living in the Soviet Union had fallen behind the West.

There were myriad reasons for this economic decline. "[B]y the end of the 1970s . . . the Soviet economic system was no longer functioning," recalled Oleg Grinevsky, Gorbachev's ambassador-at-large for arms control issues.

> The economy was in a pitiful state. What were the main causes? . . . First of all, the system of planned economics turned out not to be efficient and the economy was slowly deteriorating. Secondly, the military-industrial complex exerted an enormous burden upon the Soviet economy. There are different evaluations, but about 80 percent of industry, directly or indirectly, was tied into or working for the military-industrial complex. These non-productive expenses were a heavy rock that was truly depressing the economy. And the third factor was corruption. Terrible corruption was having a caustic effect upon our society year after year, and increasingly so.[18]

Georgy Shakhnazarov, an early reformer who went on to become one of Gorbachev's chief foreign policy advisers, adds two more factors to this list.

> [T]he main cause of what transpired was not economic, but the falling behind of the Soviet Union technologically. . . . It was lagging in the area of computers and high technology. . . . [B]ut [there is] one more very important factor: management. Any economic system exists more or less successfully when it has resources, when it is provided with innovation, and when it has good management. We had gerontology, we had an old folks home.[19]

"[I]t was impossible for [Brezhnev and other members of the Politburo] to react to anything," Soviet arms control expert Oleg Grinevsky explained in 1998. "They didn't know what was going on. They were sick and old people."[20] As Vladimir Slipchenko recalled, "it was a conveyor belt of funerals."[21]

Thus, by the early 1980s there was a widespread belief that the status quo in the USSR was unsustainable. However, there was disagreement over what types of reforms were needed. On the one hand, conservatives favored measures to make the current system work better. They preferred authoritarian attempts to dictate improvements in the centralized economy. On the other hand, liberal reformers believed the system itself needed to change. No amount of tinkering around the edges would create the incentives for innovation and growth that reformers saw in western democracies. In their view the USSR needed fundamental market reform as well as social and political restructuring.

Despite the absence of innovation at the top of the Soviet political hierarchy, by 1980 a well-educated cohort of reformers had matured, and they sought stronger ties with the West. "Their vision of the Soviet future was generally that of a socially-democratic type welfare state and full participant in [global affairs]," English explains. "The salience of 'capitalist-socialist' differences faded and Western 'threats' were simply no longer an issue. Informed by neoclassical precepts of mutual gains from trade, the USSR's overriding interest in fully joining the global economy was simply a given."[22] Reformers were actively calling for deeper integration with the West.

The ongoing struggle between reformers and conservatives continued throughout the early 1980s, although it was kept firmly behind closed doors. Yuri Andropov succeeded Brezhnev in November 1982 and, although in poor health himself, ushered in a period of modest change. A foreign policy hawk, he nonetheless believed there was a pressing need to revitalize the Soviet economy. "The main thing is strength," Andropov counselled Oleg Grinevsky, the Soviet ambassador for arms control negotiations, on December 16, 1983. "But strength is dependent on economic development." Andropov saw that "the economy was falling apart, all was falling apart, and that the economy should be our number one priority," Grinevsky recalled.[23] Andropov had cultivated a cadre of young reformers to study and manage a revitalization of the Soviet economy, and Mikhail Gorbachev was chief among this group. The general secretary's plans were modest, however. "Andropov knew that there was a need for changes, but his policy was to make the Soviet economy work more effectively without changing anything inside it; to simply accelerate the economy," Grinevsky observed. "[O]ne of his central policies was to make people work better."[24]

The reformers hoped Andropov would usher in foreign policy reforms as well. Soon after Brezhnev's death in November 1982 Anatoly Chernyaev, then a deputy in the International Department at the Central Committee, drafted a list of foreign policy priorities for the incoming leader. This list included the following:

— Withdrawal from Afghanistan
— A policy of noninterference in the internal affairs of Warsaw Pact countries
— Removal of Soviet SS-20 missiles from the European part of the USSR
— Curb the Military-Industrial Commission
— Reduce the Soviet army four-fold
— Allow dissidents such as Andrei Sakharov to emigrate[25]

Andropov's poor health prevented him from acting on these issues, however, and Chernyaev's agenda was consigned to a drawer. "A mood of 'waiting for Gorbachev's coming' set in . . . from the moment it became clear that Andropov wouldn't last," Chernyaev recalled.[26]

While on his deathbed in February 1984 Andropov signalled that Gorbachev should succeed him. However, in a moment of intrigue, conservatives were able to conceal Andropov's wish and install Brezhnev's protégé, Konstantin Chernenko, instead. It was not until March 1985, when Chernenko died and Gorbachev became general secretary, that reformers had a sympathetic leader capable of bringing about change.

Gorbachev's Views

By the time Gorbachev came to power there was a critical mass of reform-oriented intellectuals, scientists, economists, and political leaders in the USSR, and the new Soviet leader had established ties with many of them. As Andropov's protégé, Gorbachev had arrived in Moscow in 1979 from his home region of Stavropol as the Central Committee secretary for agriculture and a candidate for the all-powerful Politburo.[27] Believing the USSR needed revitalization, Gorbachev had set to work cultivating ties with leading reformist thinkers on everything from economics to foreign affairs to military doctrine. This was no mere politicking; by nature Gorbachev was inquisitive, and he truly sought to find solutions to the stagnation that had begun to cripple his country. Thus, he cultivated friendships with "the boldest foreign policy reformers," as historian Robert English noted, including Georgy Arbatov, Yevgeny Velikhov, and Anatoly Chernyaev, who quickly became his unofficial advisers.[28]

In 1983 Gorbachev had also successfully lobbied Andropov to bring Alexander Yakovlev back from Canada. Gorbachev and Yakovlev had developed a close bond in May of that year while Gorbachev was touring Canada as agricultural minister. Owing to a scheduling mishap, the two men found themselves with several free hours and fell into an unusually candid conversation about the Soviet Union and its challenges. The two found that they were "kindred spirits" in their assessment that economic and political liberalization were necessary in order to revitalize the USSR. Yakovlev later recalled, "We spoke completely frankly about everything. . . . The main idea was that society must change, it must be built on different principles. . . . It's clear that these thoughts didn't just appear spontaneously, accidentally in March 1985."[29] Once back in Moscow, Yakovlev became the director of the Institute of World Economy and International Relations (IMEMO), an influential think tank, where he cultivated a cadre of reform-minded thinkers.[30]

During the early 1980s Gorbachev had also had the opportunity to visit France, the United Kingdom, Belgium, and Eastern Europe. He drew several conclusions from these visits abroad. The first was that the West had clearly developed greater technological and economic expertise than the Soviet Union, and as a result its citizens enjoyed a better standard of living. Gorbachev also learned that the West was not an antagonistic monolith, as Marxist-Leninist ideology proclaimed, but rather a complex grouping of different societies. Most important, it became clear to Gorbachev that the West had no intention of invading the Soviet Union.[31]

"One should not imagine that [New Thinking] was a 'sudden revelation,'" Gorbachev cautioned in his memoirs. "[A] number of factors had convinced me of the need for a serious re-examination of our foreign policy even before my election as general secretary. I won't claim that I entered my new office with a detailed action plan in my briefcase, but I had a pretty clear idea of the first steps to be taken."[32]

By the time Gorbachev became leader of the USSR he had concluded that far too many resources had been devoted to the "military-industrial complex," as it was called. Information regarding military spending and defense systems was a closely guarded secret in the USSR, and even members of the Politburo were not privy to such data. But Gorbachev's experience as agricultural minister led him to suspect that bloated military expenditures were siphoning off an unsustainable amount of resources. When he became general secretary he was shocked to discover that by the late 1970s total defense-related expenses, including indirect costs, consumed approximately 40 percent of the Soviet budget. This was higher than Soviet defense expenditures at the outset of World War II.[33]

Within Moscow it was widely understood that defense expenditures needed to be reduced in order for economic revitalization to proceed. "[A]mong the military, we were aware that the burden of military expenses that the Soviet Union was carrying had become intolerable for it," Soviet military scientist Vladimir Slipchenko observed in 1998. "A Gorbachev had to appear in the Soviet Union. If it was not Gorbachev, it could have been any other person, but a change in our country had to happen."[34] Shakhnazarov concurs. "[I]f there had been no Gorbachev another leader would have appeared," he asserts. "He was not the only person like this. . . . [W]e had already as far back as the 1950s or 1960s, not only among dissidents, but also among our leadership, a sizeable group of people who were aware of the need for change and improvement. And they were all doing what they could, in their own way."[35]

"It was not just Gorbachev who said that we were not going to spend as much as we used to," Chernyaev recalled.

Look at his colleague, Ligachev, he was a conservative, right? A reactionary even, and yet he, at the most fierce zealous moment, would stand up, right in front of Gorbachev, and he would scream, "How long will our military-industrial complex keep devouring our economy, our agriculture, and our consumer goods? How long are we going to take this ogre, how long are we going to throw into its mouth the food of our children?" Even [Nikolai] Ryzhkov, all who were located on the conservative side, everybody was against the arms race. They were against the fact that the military-industrial complex was depressing not only the whole economy, but also the psychology. We did not want to feel like a fortress under siege.[36]

Gorbachev wanted to end the arms race so that he could reduce defense expenditures.[37] But he opposed nuclear weapons for other reasons as well. Unlike Andropov, Gorbachev doubted that Washington intended to attack the USSR, and therefore he believed Soviet arsenals were unnecessarily large. This was not only costly, it was also dangerous. He believed that the more nuclear weapons there were, the greater the probability of a cataclysmic mishap. "When I saw the monster that we and the United States had created as a result of the arms race, with all its mistakes and accidents with nuclear weapons and nuclear power, when I saw the terrible amount of force that had been amassed, I finally understood what the consequences, including global winter, would be," he has reflected.[38] "I was quite sure . . . that the people in the White House were not idiots [and would not intentionally launch a nuclear attack on the Soviet Union]," he explained. "More likely, I thought, was that nuclear weapons might be used without the political leadership actually wanting this, or deciding on it, owing to some failure in the command and control systems. They say that if there is a gun, some day it will shoot. That fear motivated me to seek an end to the arms race."[39]

Gorbachev was also repulsed by the prospect of having to order a nuclear strike, and indicated he would never do so. Recalling a Soviet military exercise that simulated a nuclear exchange with the United States, he said, "From the central control panel came the signal: missiles are flying towards our country, make a decision. Minute after minute passes, information pours in. I have to give the command for a strike of retaliation. . . . I said: 'I will not press the button even for training purposes.'"[40]

In order to end the arms race, the Soviet Union needed to improve relations with the West, and particularly with the United States. As Chernyaev explained in 1998:

> Gorbachev came to power with a very serious intent to reform the country, and reform it in a fairly brief time, because based on experience—on our history—he knew that if you take too long in reforming, then the reforms can rot before they develop. But in order to start economic and social reform, and then later political reforms, he had to deal with the arms race first. He had to stop the arms race. That was his priority. . . . And Gorbachev could only end the arms race if he was successful in changing relations with the United States.[41]

The Soviet leader reasoned that the United States would not agree to end the arms race as long as it viewed the USSR as an actively threatening adversary. Thus, it was imperative to change the image of the Soviet Union in the eyes of the West and to build a modicum of trust.[42] Such an improvement in superpower relations would have the additional benefit of bolstering domestic support for perestroika, Gorbachev believed. If superpower relations were on the mend, he would encounter less resistance to cuts in defense spending.

"[T]he fundamental reform of both our economic and political systems would have been impossible without . . . corresponding changes in Soviet foreign policy and the creation of propitious international conditions," Gorbachev explained in his memoirs. "As a first step, we had at least to clear up the 'snow drifts' left over from the Cold War times and to alleviate pressure that had borne down on us due to our involvement in conflicts all over the world and in the debilitating arms race. We had to understand that 'we couldn't go on living like this,' both inside our country and in world politics. This understanding was the starting-point for everything."[43]

Within hours of becoming general secretary, Gorbachev jotted down his foreign policy priorities on a piece of paper: "stop the arms race, withdraw troops from Afghanistan, change the spirit of the relationship with the USA, [and] restore cooperation with China."[44] In later years Gorbachev noted that ending the arms race was the linchpin upon which all other reforms rested. "[W]ithout that," he noted, "any plans for *perestroika* would have had to remain in the realm of fiction."[45]

Over time Gorbachev fleshed out his vision for change. In his book *Perestroika: New Thinking for Our Country and the World* (1987) he explained his plans to a western audience. "[T]he new world order had to be based [on the following principles]," the Soviet leader wrote: "interdependence of countries and nations, the balance of interests, freedom of choice, common responsibility and the finding of universally accepted solutions for today's global problems."[46] Gorbachev rejected his country's long tradition of self-imposed isolation from the West. "[I]n today's world of mutual interdependence, progress is unthinkable for any society which is fenced off from the world by impenetrable state frontiers and ideological barriers. A country can develop its full potential only by interacting with other societies, yet without giving up its own identity," he wrote. Moscow "could not insure our country's security without reckoning with the interests of other countries. . . . [I]n the nuclear age, [we can] not build a safe security system based solely on military means."[47]

Reformers in Power

Initially Gorbachev enjoyed broad support for his reforms. "Why was there no resistance on the part of conservatives?" Shakhnazarov asked in 1998. "At first, everybody wanted change, and everybody thought that it would be the strengthening of socialism, improvement, democratization, but in principle, the Soviet Union would continue to be a great power. Therefore, the Politburo, science, public opinion, the military, directors of enterprises—everybody supported Gorbachev, unanimously. Everybody thought that he would do what was necessary."[48] Tradition also played a role. "[I]n the beginning everyone was afraid: the general secretary occupied a position like that of a Russian emperor," Shakhnazarov observed. "The emperor is a person who is given to the country by God. Therefore, everybody must listen to him, no questions permitted."[49]

Nonetheless, Gorbachev grew frustrated with the entrenched bureaucracy and officials who were incapable of moving beyond old ways of thinking. "Changes were far too slow," he recalled. The Politburo had "adopted a number of decisions [and] we had worked out a plan of progress toward a nuclear-free world and replaced a number of cadres, but the diplomatic wagon train was moving slowly along the same old beaten track. Our diplomatic style was 'toughness for toughness sake.' The main thing was to demonstrate an unyielding spirit and an attitude of arrogant pride which was justified neither by political nor practical considerations."[50]

Gorbachev had appointed Yakovlev to lead the Propaganda Department of the Central Committee in 1985, but this had not been sufficient to bring about change. Thus, he began to replace old-style thinkers with reformers. One of the first to go—and most pivotal—was Foreign Minister Andrei Gromyko, one of the troika who had been de facto leaders during Brezhnev's final years. Gromyko had been foreign minister since 1957 and was the embodiment of traditional, hard-line Soviet foreign policy. His Western counterparts had dubbed him "Mr. Nyet" owing to his legendary inflexibility—an assessment that was shared in Moscow. Owing to his long tenure, Gromyko had an ironclad grip on Soviet foreign policy. Reform could not proceed until he was removed. In a strange turn of events, however, Gromyko had been key in ensuring that Gorbachev had become general secretary. Thus, removing him from office was especially delicate, yet essential. "It was not simply a question of being indebted to Gromyko," Gorbachev's adviser and spokesperson Andrei Grachev observed. "Rather, the problem lay in the fact that Gromyko personally was implicated in precisely those crucial decisions of the Soviet leadership (deployment of SS-20 missiles to Europe and the invasion of Afghanistan), that Gorbachev was inclined to reconsider. . . . [A]s long as Gromyko continued to occupy the post of Foreign Minister there was no way Gorbachev could challenge him openly in the area that had become his exclusive territory."[51]

In July 1985 Gorbachev "promoted" Andrei Gromyko and replaced him with Eduard Shevardnadze. Shevardnadze, a reform-minded Georgian with no foreign policy experience, proved to be an ideal proponent of New Thinking. As a Kremlin outsider he was not beholden to the old-school network of bureaucrats and foreign policy experts in Moscow. He was also affable and naturally excelled at diplomacy. In the West he was considered a striking—and most welcome—contrast to Gromyko. After years of being stonewalled by Gromyko, western diplomats greeted Shevardnadze's appointment with both relief and hope.

On February 1, 1986, Gorbachev also appointed longtime reformer Anatoly Chernyaev as his foreign policy adviser. Finally free of Brezhnevites, the Soviet leader now had a strong team of foreign policy reformers anxious to implement New Thinking.

However, Gorbachev encountered increasing resistance from conservative military leaders. There was need for reform, these officials believed, but Gorbachev was going too far and too fast. Steep cuts in defense spending were not in their self-interest, but military leaders did not dwell on this point. Instead, they insisted that deep cuts would render the USSR vulnerable, especially during a time in which the American president was hurling insults and threatening Soviet security with a massive military buildup.

Gorbachev and his fellow reformers did not have close ties to the conservatives in the military-industrial complex, so they had to tread carefully at first. Although the general secretary had supreme authority, he could not afford to alienate such a powerful group.[52] He needed their support to implement his reforms.

Over time Gorbachev was able to co-opt, marginalize, or dismiss many of these hawks. In one instance in the spring of 1987, he used an embarrassing security breach as an excuse to sack military hard-liners. On May 28—Border Guard's Day in the USSR—a nineteen-year-old German citizen, Mathias Rust, managed to fly his rented Cessna over the general secretary's office and land just outside Red Square in the heart of Moscow. An inexperienced pilot, Rust had nevertheless managed to stymie the supposedly impregnable Soviet air defense. Soviet forces had tracked and then lost the plane repeatedly. Owing to bureaucratic confusion—and clouded judgment brought on by celebratory shots of vodka—border officials twice recognized the Cessna as a friendly aircraft. Ultimately, it was identified as a domestic training plane, a low priority in terms of surveillance. After landing not far from the Kremlin, Rust signed autographs for two hours before officials managed to arrest him.[53]

The affair was a profound embarrassment for the Soviet military. Normally a symbol of unquestioned authority, defense officials became the object of ridicule. "Did you hear that the Politburo is renaming Red Square?" went one joke that spread through Moscow at the time. "It will be called Sheremetyevo-3." (Sheremetyevo-1 and Sheremetyevo-2 were the two main airports in the region.)

Gorbachev used the incident as an excuse to purge conservatives from the military. He fired Defense Minister Sergey Sokolov, as well as the chief of air defense, Alexander Koldunov. In addition, he placed more than 150 top military officers on trial, leading to their dismissal. By 1988 Gorbachev had managed to replace most of the top echelon of military officers. This was the biggest purge since Stalin's time.[54]

Chernobyl and the Evolution of New Thinking

On April 26, 1986, the Soviet Union suffered a devastating accident: its nuclear reactor at Chernobyl exploded, spewing huge amounts of radioactive material into the atmosphere across the USSR and Europe, especially Scandinavia. The explosions themselves were a disaster, ruining the environment, causing mass relocation of the local population, and sickening thousands. The Soviet response to the explosions was a second disaster. First responders were woefully unprepared, and medical facilities were overwhelmed and ill equipped. Civilian and military leaders alike were unfortunately slow to understand the gravity of the situation. Moreover, military officials responsible for the reactor tried to cover up the truth, lying to Gorbachev and other Politburo members about what had occurred. Gorbachev and Shevardnadze, in turn, misinformed foreign governments about events surrounding the accident.

The response to the Chernobyl accident unmasked many of the problems with the Soviet system. It "further exposed the backwardness and corruption of the Stalinist system, particularly the failures of central planning with its haste, sloppiness, and disregard for [what the Soviets called] 'the human element,'" historian Robert English observed.[55] Shevardnadze nearly resigned over the manner in which military leaders had lied about the incident. It was "outright sabotage of the New Thinking [and of] the trust we had worked so hard to build," he charged. He and Gorbachev had been "betrayed" by the hard-liners within their own government.[56]

Gorbachev was both devastated and furious. The accident reflected poorly on his leadership, made a mockery of his campaign for "openness," caused foreigners to question his integrity, and humiliated the USSR. It also underscored the ineptitude of the Soviet military, despite its preponderant power. "For thirty years you've been telling us that everything is safe!" he fumed at military leaders during a July 3 Politburo meeting. "And you expected us to take it as the word of God! This is the root of our problems. Ministries and research centers got out of control, which led to disaster. And so far, I do not see any signs that you've learned your lesson from this. . . . The system is plagued by servility, boot-licking, and clannish management. We're now putting an end to all this."[57]

The Chernobyl disaster also drove home the potentially devastating effects of a nuclear war and inspired Gorbachev to pursue an end to the arms race with even greater vigor. "The accident at Chernobyl showed again what an abyss will open if nuclear war befalls mankind," Gorbachev told his fellow citizens during a televised address on the accident on May 14, 1986. "For inherent in the stockpiled nuclear arsenals are thousands upon thousands of disasters far more horrible than the Chernobyl one."[58] During the address Gorbachev extended the Soviet moratorium on nuclear testing and beseeched the United States to join him in ending the arms race. "We again urge the United States to consider most responsibly the measure of danger looming over humanity, and to heed the opinion of the world community. . . . The nuclear age forcefully demands a new approach."[59]

The Chernobyl accident was "an event that cast its shadow on everything from that moment forward: on the economy, on the moral and psychological state of society, on trust in the new leadership, and on people's hopes for change," Anatoly Chernyaev has written.[60] The disaster had a profound effect on the general secretary. "One can say that [Chernobyl] marked the border between two Gorbachevs: one before, the other after 26 April," Andrei Grachev has observed.

> In a way Chernobyl became for him the equivalent of his personal Cuban missile crisis. Before 26 April his intention to propose a curb on the arms race along with a radical reduction of nuclear weapons was mostly based on economic and security concerns, while after Chernobyl his attitude towards nuclear weapons transformed into a psychological aversion, a moral rejection bringing him in this respect closer to Reagan. The fight for a non-nuclear world . . . became a personal challenge.[61]

Reformer Yevgeny Velikhov recalled that the Chernobyl accident induced Gorbachev to make "a great, instinctive leap to break the old cycle of secrecy, stubbornness, and deadlocked negotiations [with the United States]."[62] "We need negotiations," Gorbachev informed the Politburo on May 8, 1986. "Even with this gang [in Washington], we need to negotiate. If not, what remains? Look at the Chernobyl catastrophe. Just a puff and we can all feel what nuclear war would be like."[63]

While Gorbachev's desire to end the arms race began as part of a quest for economic reform, by the spring of 1986 it had become a moral crusade. Having seen the horrors of a nuclear accident, the general secretary became determined to end the threat of nuclear annihilation. In this, he had widespread domestic support. Chernobyl spurred an antinuclear movement both in the USSR and abroad. "After Chernobyl the nuclear threat stopped being an abstract notion for our people," Marshal Sergei Akhromeyev has recalled. "It became tangible and concrete. The people began to see all the problems linked with nuclear weapons much differently."[64] Chernobyl "tore the blindfold from our eyes and persuaded us that politics and morals could not diverge," Eduard Shevardnadze noted.[65]

The Soviet Withdrawal from the War in Afghanistan

In the late 1970s the Soviet leadership had quietly warned Marxist factions in Afghanistan against using violence so as to seize power. However, these warnings were ignored, and in April 1978 leftist officers staged a coup in Kabul without first consulting Moscow.[66] This had created both a problem and an opportunity for the Politburo. On the one hand, a motley bunch of Afghan rebels had flagrantly disregarded the Kremlin's directives and seized power. Owing to Marxist-Leninist ideology—which posited competing socialist and democratic camps—Moscow became obligated to provide "fraternal assistance" to its ideological ally. This obligation was all the more acute because Afghanistan was right on the Soviet Union's doorstep. It was a classic case of the tail wagging the dog: a small group of rebels was forcing the Soviet Union to take action. On the other hand, the Kremlin was presented with an unexpected opportunity to expand Soviet influence southward. Politburo members ultimately found this prospect too tempting to ignore, and Soviet-Afghan contacts in trade, construction, education, and politics blossomed.

When a rebellion broke out in western Afghanistan in March 1979, however, the Politburo had to determine the degree of its commitment to Afghanistan. Soviet leaders were initially ambivalent, finding Afghan president Noor Mohammad Taraki's politics and outlook distasteful. Politburo members Alexey Kosygin and Andrei Kirilenko argued that the Afghan communists themselves were to blame for the rebellion. "We gave very, very good support to Afghanistan. We gave it everything," Kirilenko fumed to his comrades. "And what has come of it? Nothing of any value. After all, it was they who executed innocent people for no reason and told us that we also executed people in Lenin's time. You see what kind of Marxists we have found."[67] Kirilenko was especially concerned that Soviet forces would be drawn into a civil war, fighting against civilians rather than an army. In March both Andropov and Gromyko opposed Soviet military intervention in Afghanistan. "I completely support Comrade Andropov's proposal to rule out . . . the deployment of our troops into Afghanistan," Gromyko informed his comrades on March 18. "The army there is unreliable. Thus, our army, when it arrives in Afghanistan, will be the aggressor. Against whom will it fight? Against the Afghan people first of all, and it will have to shoot them."[68] Gromyko argued that a deployment would carry many costs yet yield few benefits.

> [A]ll that we have done in recent years with such effort in terms of détente, arms reductions and much more—all that would be thrown back. China, of course, would be given a nice present. All the non-aligned countries will be against us. . . . There will no longer be any question of a meeting [between Brezhnev] and Carter . . . or Giscard d'Estang. . . . And one must ask, what would we gain? Afghanistan with its present government, with a backward economy, with inconsequential weight in international affairs. . . . [F]rom a legal point of view, too, we would not be justified in sending troops. . . . This is [Afghanistan's] internal affair, a revolutionary internal conflict, a battle of one group of the population against the other. . . . [It is] a situation where the leadership of the country, as a result of the serious mistakes it has allowed to occur, has ended up not on the high ground, not in command of the support from the people.[69]

The Politburo concluded that "in no case will we go forward with a deployment of troops to Afghanistan."[70]

Andropov changed his mind, however, as the situation in Afghanistan deteriorated in the fall, and Taraki was assassinated by his lieutenant, Hafizullah Amin.[71] Together with Ustinov, he began urging a reluctant Brezhnev to deploy Soviet troops to Afghanistan. The USSR needed to "defend the achievements of the April revolution, resurrect the Leninist principles of state and party building in the Afghan leadership, and strengthen our positions in that country," Andropov wrote to Brezhnev in early December 1979. More ominously, Andropov warned that if Moscow did not step in, Washington might, leading to American forces along Soviet borders. "We are receiving information about Amin's behind-the-scenes activities which might mean his political reorientation toward the West," Andropov related. "In closed meetings, he attacks Soviet policy and the actions of our specialists." If Amin became a US ally, he warned, there would be the spectre "of American short-range missiles being deployed in Afghanistan and aimed at strategic objectives in Kazakhstan, Siberia, and other places [in the Soviet Union]."[72]

Although the professional military officers of the Soviet general staff had serious reservations about a deployment to Afghanistan, Ustinov and Andropov were able to prevail. The Politburo decided on December 12, 1979, to send military forces into Afghanistan. The intent was to conduct a "lightning operation" with a limited contingent of forces to remove Amin, and then to withdraw rapidly.[73] On Christmas Day, Soviet troops invaded.

Soviet leaders were surprised by the intensely hostile international reaction to the invasion. Superpower détente—which had already been on its last legs—collapsed.[74] The USSR became more isolated, both politically and economically. The invasion was also unpopular at home. The decision to intervene had been made by a small circle of leaders; and, as news spread within Moscow, shock and widespread criticism followed. Anatoly Chernyaev, a member of the Central Committee's International Department, learned of the invasion from the radio, as did most other foreign policy experts.[75] Soviet reformers were repulsed. They viewed the invasion as an act of naked imperialism that flew in the face of both socialist *and* democratic values. The "whole [Soviet] system began to lose its remaining ideological justification in the eyes of the idealistically motivated portion of the intellectual elite," Andrei Grachev recalled.[76]

It quickly became clear that a lightning strike followed by a rapid withdrawal was not tenable. In January 1980 Andropov visited Kabul, where he learned that Afghan resistance fighters were both more tenacious and better armed than the Politburo had initially believed. Soviet troops would have to stay in Afghanistan indefinitely, Andropov reported to his comrades.[77]

Faced with the prospect of a long, unpopular war, the Politburo immediately began backpedaling. Within a month after launching the invasion, it was searching for a face-saving way to withdraw. However, it had boxed itself into a corner: the Politburo had justified the invasion to the Soviet public by stating that the USSR was responding to a request for assistance from a fellow socialist regime. The Soviet Union was providing fraternal assistance to an ideological ally. How could leaders explain to the Soviet people that Moscow was now abandoning this so-called ally? Brezhnev was simply not up to the task. Ideological, intellectual, and physical constraints limited his ability to develop an innovative solution to the Soviet predicament. By June 1980 domestic opposition to the war in Afghanistan had grown to the point that Georgy Arbatov and other reform-minded foreign policy specialists were comfortable pressing Brezhnev and Andropov to withdraw.[78] Yet Soviet leaders remained imprisoned in the ideological jail they had created for themselves.

When Andropov took over in November 1982 little changed. He, too, sought to end the debacle, and even welcomed UN mediation in the matter. The question was not *whether* to withdraw from Afghanistan, but *how*. Soviet military leaders did not want to leave without a clear-cut victory, or a face-saving way out. Nonetheless, the USSR was drawn deeper into the conflict. Afghan leaders begged for additional troops and resources, further entrapping Moscow. In 1984 the Reagan administration dramatically increased its military assistance to the Afghan resistance, complicating matters further. While the American aim had previously been to increase the costs of the Soviet deployment, President Reagan changed the objective: the United States now sought to force the Soviet Union out of Afghanistan.[79] This was tragically ironic: Washington was trying to force the Soviets out of Afghanistan, and the Soviets *wanted* to leave Afghanistan. Yet they could not find a way to exit gracefully. They were entrapped by both Marxist-Leninist ideology and, increasingly, Cold War geopolitics: a Soviet withdrawal in the face of Afghan resistance and US support to the mujahedin would smack of defeat. The Socialist East would be conceding to the Imperialist West. American assistance to the mujahedin inhibited Moscow's ability to withdraw. "[B]ack in Andropov's time there was a clear understanding that we needed to leave Afghanistan," Soviet arms control negotiator Oleg Grinevsky recalled in 1998. "[T]he understanding in Moscow [was] that the Americans would not let us leave Afghanistan, that this was a calculated US policy to keep the Soviet Union in Afghanistan and draw blood and weaken the Soviet Union."[80]

The absence of easily discernible policy options, in combination with the poor health of first Andropov and then Chernenko, precluded a resolution to the conflict. "[T]he problem was how to justify the losses and the expenses of the entire Afghanistan campaign [to our people]," Sergei Tarasenko, the former principal Policy Assistant to Foreign Minister Eduard Shevardnadze, explained in 1998.

> People perished, there were many tragedies, and a lot of money was spent. How are we going to explain why we went there? . . . We went

in to make a certain regime stronger and the regime did not want to get stronger, it kept getting shakier and shakier. If we could get some kind of a ghost of a justification and then leave, we would have loved that, but at the time the real situation kept drawing us in deeper and deeper. More money, more people, more technology, more help, more aid, how could we tell it to our people? We needed something to save face.[81]

Gorbachev came to power intending to end the war in Afghanistan quickly. Unlike his predecessors, he had had no role in the original decision to intervene, nor was he tethered to Marxist-Leninist ideology. Gorbachev rejected both the ideological and the geopolitical constraints that were compelling the USSR to remain in Afghanistan. The invasion had been an "unjustified political folly" with mounting and unforgivable costs, he believed.[82] As casualties had risen, the war had become increasingly unpopular at home, the financial burden was growing, and the diplomatic isolation that had resulted undermined his plans to improve relations with the West. The USSR had paid a heavy price for its mistake, Gorbachev argued. It was time to end the debacle. The Politburo agreed unanimously.

In October 1985 Gorbachev held a secret meeting with Afghan leader Babrak Karmal, informing him that the Soviets would be withdrawing and that he should seek to strengthen his position at home beforehand. Gorbachev told Karmal:

[B]y the summer of 1986 you'll have to have figured out how to defend your cause on your own. We'll help you, but with arms only, not troops. And if you want to survive you will have to broaden the base of the regime, forget socialism, make a deal with the truly influential forces, including the Mujahideen commanders and leaders of now-hostile organizations. You'll have to revive Islam, respect traditions, and try to show the people some tangible benefits from the revolution. . . . Support private trade, you won't be able to create a different economy any time soon.[83]

"Karmal was dumbfounded," Anatoly Chernyaev recalls Gorbachev reporting to the Politburo. "[H]e's been counting on us to stay there for a long time—if not forever." Not only did Gorbachev advise Karmal that the USSR was leaving, remarkably, he also counseled the Afghan communist to "forget socialism" and adopt democratic reforms.[84]

Gorbachev adopted a "dual approach" to ending the war. On the one hand, he pursued a diplomatic solution through multilateral talks in Geneva, and on the other he stepped up military pressure on the Afghan resistance. Soviet military leaders insisted they could win the war, and pressured Gorbachev for one final chance to do so. The new Soviet leader needed the military's support for perestroika and did not have many close ties with hawkish military leaders. Thus, he conceded. Consequently, 1985 and 1986 were the most destructive years of the war as Soviet military leaders made one final attempt to end the conflict in victory. In November 1985 Gorbachev told President Reagan during the Geneva Summit that he intended to withdraw Soviet forces and asked for his support in the matter.[85] Given the increased violence in Afghanistan, however, the Reagan administration questioned Gorbachev's sincerity and did little to help. In 1986 Washington began sending Stinger missiles to the mujahedin, effectively weakening Soviet air power and thus undermining Moscow's efforts to force a conclusion to the conflict. Gorbachev grew increasingly frustrated, both with his military leaders and with the Americans. The Soviet Union intends to leave Afghanistan, Gorbachev complained to US Secretary of State George Shultz in 1987, but the United States keeps "putting sticks in our spokes."[86] By 1988 it was clear that there would be no military resolution to the war. On February 8, 1988, Gorbachev announced to the Soviet people that the USSR would begin withdrawing its forces in the spring. On February 15, 1989, the final Soviet forces departed Afghanistan.

Triumphalists argue that President Reagan's hard-line policies compelled the Soviet Union to reform, disarm, and withdraw from Afghanistan. Absent the US president's military buildup and resolve, the USSR would not have adopted any of these policies. Examining Soviet decision making enables us to understand the reasons for Soviet behavior, and thus the impact that Reagan's policies had on Moscow. As this chapter demonstrates, triumphalist claims are unsubstantiated. A reform movement had been growing in the USSR since the 1950s. When reformers finally came to power in 1985 they embarked on a program to revitalize the Soviet system, which included reducing defense expenditures, ending the arms race, and concluding the Cold War. Ending the Cold War was a critical part of Gorbachev's plan to reform and modernize the Soviet Union.

Nor did Washington compel Moscow to withdraw from Afghanistan against its will. Soviet leaders immediately regretted the 1979 invasion and within a month had begun seeking a way out. The Soviet Union withdrew from Afghanistan because Soviet leaders believed the incursion had been a costly mistake. Moscow had become mired in a decade-long war with an unacceptable number of casualties, unsustainable economic costs, and steep political penalties. Tragically, it took the Kremlin a decade to find its way out of the ill-conceived operation.

In short, the Reagan administration did not compel Moscow to adopt policies it did not want to adopt. Nor did it force the Kremlin to adopt policies that were counter to Soviet interests. "[T]he roots [of New Thinking] were in our country . . . not elsewhere," Georgy Shakhnazarov has explained. "We came to these reforms through our suffering, ourselves. There was a growing understanding in our society that we could not live like this any longer, that it was abnormal."[87] He added that the Soviets recognized the need for reform as early as the 1950s. "If the West had given a better response to Khrushchev's proposals, then the process probably could have begun then. . . . Alexey Kosygin was nurturing the idea of reforms, even Brezhnev was ready for them. Brezhnev proposed a Plenum on economic reform, but then changed his mind because he did not want complications [with conservatives]. Therefore, Gorbachev grew on this wave of reforms, of reform ideas, which had been maturing for a long time in our society."[88]

"I do not believe that the anti-Communist, anti-Soviet rhetoric, and the increase in the armaments and military power of the United States played a serious role in our decision making," Anatoly Chernyaev reflected in 1998. "I think perhaps they played no role whatsoever. The United States is a colossal power, a military superpower, it was clear to us, but it was a constant. What was important was that we came to the realization that we needed to stop the arms race. . . . So, for us to end the arms race was an internal domestic problem. Whatever Reagan might do or not do, that did not change this fact."[89] Soviet reformers sought to restore the health of the Soviet system. New Thinking was the medicine.

Examining Soviet decision making makes clear that President Reagan's hard-line policies actually impeded Soviet efforts to disarm and reform. Reagan's buildup, combined with his threats and name-calling, had the unintended effect of strengthening the position of Soviet conservatives, who favored a more traditional, antagonistic posture toward Washington. The more belligerent the president acted, the more Soviet conservatives became convinced that Gorbachev was on the wrong course and so resisted his reforms. "Reagan's tough policy . . . made the life for [Soviet] reformers, for all who yearned for democratic changes in their life, much more difficult," Georgy Arbatov, the director of the Soviet Institute for the Study of the United States and Canada, has explained. "In such tense international situations the conservatives and reactionaries were given predominant influence [in the USSR]. That is why . . . Reagan made it practically impossible to start reforms after Brezhnev's death, (Andropov had such plans) and made things more difficult for Gorbachev to cut military expenditures."[90]

Thus, President Reagan's initially hawkish posture undermined US interests. Reagan made it more difficult for Gorbachev to reduce Soviet arsenals, adopt New Thinking, and implement democratic reforms. The Reagan administration's hard-line policies hampered the conclusion of the Cold War.

5

Moscow Calls Off the Arms Race

> It is crystal clear that in the world we live in, the world of nuclear weapons, any attempt to use them to solve Soviet-American problems would spell suicide. Even if one country engages in a steady arms buildup while the other does nothing, the side that arms itself will all the same gain nothing.
>
> Mikhail Gorbachev

> Our concessions were the result of . . . logic: we were not going to fight a war, we wanted to end the Cold War, we wanted nuclear disarmament and the liquidation of nuclear arms. That was New Thinking.
>
> Anatoly Chernyaev, Gorbachev's foreign affairs adviser

Triumphalists claim that the US military buildup—and the Strategic Defense Initiative in particular—compelled the Soviet Union to concede the Cold War and ultimately to collapse. Faced with the prospect of having to match increases in American strength, Moscow realized it did not have the financial or technical resources to keep up. The buildup forced the USSR to the brink of bankruptcy, thus leading it to surrender and finally to dissolve. The Strategic Defense Initiative "threw the Soviet leadership into a state of despair," historian Andrew E. Busch explains. "SDI changed the strategic environment threatening the Soviets with the choice of an unacceptable strategic defeat or an unacceptable technological and economic burden. In the end, the pressures produced by SDI contributed as much as any single factor to the successful termination of the Cold War."[1] After leaving office, President Reagan himself suggested that the buildup and SDI were pivotal in ending the Cold War. "[I]f I had to choose the single most important reason, on the United States' side, for the historic breakthroughs that were to occur . . . in the quest for peace and a better relationship with the Soviet Union," he reflected in his memoirs, "I would say it was the Strategic Defense Initiative, along with the overall modernization of our military forces."[2]

This story, however, is a myth. The Soviets never sought to match Reagan's buildup. There was no massive increase in Soviet arsenals, nor was there a large, prolonged spike in Soviet defense expenditures in the 1980s. As the CIA belatedly discovered, the Soviet Union had not been building up its arsenal at an increasing clip during the late 1970s and 1980s. The rate at which the Kremlin procured new weapons peaked in 1975 and remained stable for the ensuing decade. This meant that the rate of growth in Soviet military spending (which had declined between 1970 and 1974) decelerated even more sharply between 1975 and 1984.[3]

Under Gorbachev there was a brief period in which the rate at which the Soviet Union procured new weapons ticked upward. For the most part, this reflected an earlier decision to modernize the ABM system around Moscow.[4] It also included increased purchases of aircraft and missiles for what was hoped to be the final push to victory in Afghanistan. In addition, the Soviet habit of hanging on to obsolete equipment meant that the overall size of Soviet arsenals grew, increasing the costs for operations and management.[5] Consequently, between 1985 and 1987 Soviet military spending grew approximately 3 percent per year, but this was considerably below the 7 percent a year increases that the Reagan administration enjoyed. These small and short-lived increases were also not sufficient to destroy the Soviet economy. Moreover, by 1988 Soviet defense spending dropped abruptly, decreasing to 1980 levels of spending. The following year the Soviet Union cut its military budget by 14 percent while reducing arms production by nearly 20 percent.[6]

Nor did the Soviets exhaust themselves seeking to build an SDI system of their own. Initial concerns about SDI dissipated by the mid-1980s as Soviet scientists concluded that the system could be countered cheaply and, in all likelihood, would never be built.

In short, the Reagan military buildup had a negligible impact on the Soviet Union. There was no devastating spike in Soviet defense spending in response to Washington's policies. While the forty years of Cold War had certainly strained the Soviet economy, the Reagan buildup did not push the USSR into financial collapse.

Reforming Military Doctrine and Abandoning the Arms Race

Reagan's military buildup did not provoke the Soviets into a buildup of their own because Soviet thinking about the arms race had shifted significantly by the early 1980s. Soviet reformers had come to believe that building and maintaining large arsenals had in fact undermined Soviet security. Their reasoning was threefold.

For one thing, the thirty-year arms race had taken a serious toll on the Soviet economy. Owing to the secrecy and complexity of the Soviet system, no one knew exactly how much money had been poured into defense over the decades, but by the late 1970s most understood that such spending had been onerous and was increasingly unsustainable.[7] The arms race had robbed the Soviet Union of the ability to innovate and grow. The Soviet economy needed to be revitalized. Moscow needed to invest more heavily in consumer products and technology, and the only way to do so would be to slash defense spending.

Second, reformers had come to believe that the traditional Soviet military doctrine—which called for large arsenals—was outmoded.[8] The traditional doctrine was based on the country's experiences during World War II, when it had suffered a devastating surprise attack from Hitler's Germany. This experience had left an entire generation with "1941 syndrome," or an overwhelming fear of another invasion. These fears sometimes bordered on paranoia.[9] Soviet military leaders had fixated on thwarting another such attack and had reasoned that the best way to do so was to build overwhelming offensive capabilities: if a war with the West seemed imminent, the Soviet Union would launch a massive strike of its own. A strong offense was the best defense, they believed. Such a policy required an arsenal focused on offensive—rather than defensive—capabilities, as well as military forces that were on hair-trigger alert.

By the early 1980s, however, reform-minded military officials were rethinking these traditions. Younger officials had little memory of World War II, and thus were less susceptible to "1941 syndrome." In their view, the fixation on thwarting an invasion was outdated.[10] More important Moscow's large arsenal of offensive weaponry was perceived as threatening in the West and had prompted the United States to increase its arsenals. Building up offensive forces had ultimately undermined Soviet security, reformers observed.

Military leaders were rethinking other aspects of the military competition with the West as well. Traditional military doctrine embraced the notion of "parity," or the need to match US military capability. If the United States built a new system, the USSR would follow suit. This tit-for-tat strategy drove the arms race.[11] By the early 1980s, however, reformers had come to believe that the drive for parity had been nonsensical. Ongoing attempts to match US forces had resulted in a glut of weapons. The USSR had more than enough weapons to deter a surprise attack or to retaliate decisively in the improbable event of an invasion. The Soviet Union had excessive military capability, and building and maintaining this excess capacity was costly.

Reformers believed the USSR should abandon parity: Moscow should no longer focus on matching US military capabilities. Instead, it should shed its excess military capacity. The Soviet Union should shift to a doctrine of "sufficient defense," in which the objective would be to reduce its arsenal to the lowest level possible. The USSR would retain only enough weapons so as to be able to defend itself in the event of an attack.

Moscow would not only reduce its forces, it would also shift to a less threatening posture. The Soviet Union would divest itself of much of its offensive arsenal and emphasize defensive capabilities instead. The focus would be on "nonprovocative defense."[12]

Sufficient defense—or "reasonable sufficiency," as it was sometimes called—made strategic sense, reformers argued. More weapons did not necessarily bring more security. In fact, at a certain point more weapons undermine security by appearing threatening to the adversary. The adversary will then respond with its own buildup. The reformers' conclusion was paradoxical: having too many weapons undermines security. According to this logic, then, security would be enhanced by reducing armaments, particularly those suited for offense rather than defense. The doctrine of sufficient defense, therefore, opened the door to slashing Soviet arsenals. As Colonel Makhmut Gareyev, head of the Military Science Administration of the Soviet General Staff, explained, genuine security "is guaranteed by the lowest possible level of strategic balance, not the highest."[13]

The new military doctrine also made economic sense. If the USSR only needed enough weapons to thwart an invasion, it could divest itself of its excess capacity. Defense expenditures could be reduced not only by foregoing the production of new offensive weapons, but also by eliminating the costs of maintaining and securing bloated arsenals. The emphasis would be on quality, not quantity, of weapons. Reformers further argued that Soviet security was not based exclusively on its military capacity; economic strength was crucial as well. Reducing defense expenditures would ultimately strengthen the Soviet Union by bolstering its economy.[14] Thus, the doctrine of sufficient defense provided the logic for slashing both arsenals and defense expenditures.

Finally, during the 1980s Soviet officials were also rethinking the purpose and capabilities of their nuclear arsenal. Nuclear weapons were costly to develop and maintain, reformers observed. They were also of questionable value: they could not be deployed owing to their horrific destructive capability, which meant their primary purpose lay in deterring an American nuclear attack. But such an attack was improbable, reformers believed. The logic underlying the Soviet nuclear arsenal was akin to the joke about the salesman selling elephant repellant in Moscow. "There are no elephants in Moscow!" a citizen tells the salesman. "See, it works!" he replies.

Soviet nuclear weapons also appeared threatening to the West. Increases in the Soviet nuclear arsenal prompted the United States to build up its nuclear capabilities, which in turn threatened the USSR. The result was a never-ending security dilemma that was both costly and futile. In short, the Soviet nuclear arsenal was worse than useless; it was counterproductive.

By 1985 there was agreement within the Politburo that "nuclear arms have to stop being used in a political role because it is impossible to achieve our goals using [them]," Anatoly Chernyaev recalled. "The members of the Politburo thought that we really had to emphasize the idea of the non-nuclear world."[15] Even Andrei Gromyko, the infamously hawkish foreign minister, changed his views about nuclear weapons. During a June 1988 Politburo meeting Gromyko accepted responsibility—albeit obliquely—for dangerously fanning the flames of the arms race:

> In Khrushchev's time we produced 600 nuclear bombs. Khrushchev himself from time to time asked the question: "When should we stop?" Later, under Brezhnev we should have taken a more reasonable position. But we remained attached to the same principle: since [the US is] running ahead, we should do the same, as if it were a sports competition. . . . It was evidently a primitive approach but our supreme military commanders were convinced that if a war started, we could win it. That was evidently an erroneous position, completely erroneous. And the political leadership was completely responsible for it.[16]

Gorbachev explained the futility of the nuclear arms race in 1987.

> It is crystal clear that in the world we live in, the world of nuclear weapons, any attempt to use them to solve Soviet-American problems would spell suicide. Even if one country engages in a steady arms buildup while the other does nothing, the side that arms itself will all the same gain nothing. . . . This is why striving for military superiority means chasing one's own tail.[17]

Aware of the overwhelming costs of defense expenditures, in 1985 the Ministry of Defense tasked a small group of scientists to secretly study the ramifications of abolishing nuclear weapons.[18] What would happen, the scientists were asked, if the USSR eliminated its nuclear arsenal? What would be the risks and benefits to the Soviet Union? The scientists were also asked to examine the implications for regional and global security. Owing to the controversial nature of the study, the officials were sequestered in a secret location, where they worked intensely.

When the study was completed the scientists were taken aback by what they had discovered. "The conclusions we [made] were very shocking for us at the time," General Vladimir Slipchenko, a leading military scientist who served on the Soviet General Staff, has recalled. "We concluded that there was not one nuclear state which could adequately protect itself through the use of its nuclear arsenal. . . . We came to the conclusion that we had to start thinking about the inevitability of peaceful coexistence."[19]

Eliminating nuclear weapons appealed to Gorbachev, as did the notion of sufficient defense, and not only because he sought to reduce defense expenditures. The Soviet leader understood that changing the threatening image of the USSR was critical to ending the arms race. The doctrine of sufficient defense called for steep reductions in offensive military capabilities and a shift to purely defensive positions. Such a shift could reduce Western perceptions of threat. If Moscow could convince the West that it had no intention of attacking, there would be less support in the United States for the Reagan administration's military buildup and more pressure on the White House to agree to arms reductions. Embracing the new military doctrine would enable Gorbachev to end the arms race and focus instead on revitalizing the Soviet system.

In February 1986 Gorbachev announced that the Soviet Union had formally adopted the doctrine of sufficient defense, or, as he called it, "reasonable sufficiency."[20] Moving forward, Soviet conventional forces would be reduced and restructured to be clearly defensive, rather than offensive. Soviet forces would be structured so as to be able to defeat an attack but not to carry out a large-scale invasion. In December 1988 the Soviet Union took a major step toward implementing this doctrine when Gorbachev announced at the United Nations that the USSR would unilaterally demobilize 500,000 troops and withdraw 10,000 tanks, 8,500 artillery pieces, and 800 combat aircraft from Europe. This was a significant reduction in the Soviet Union's offensive capability.[21]

In short, for a variety of strategic and financial reasons, Moscow had quit the arms race. The Kremlin never sought to match the Reagan administration's military buildup because it had come to believe that large arsenals undermined security.

By 1985 "a new political thinking emerged," Vladimir Sliphchenko, a leading defense scientist, has explained. "We, the military—I think of myself as being a purely military expert—started developing completely new military views having to do with rational defense sufficiency. [We concluded that] peace should not rest on preparation for war." Moreover, "the Soviet Union began to treat nuclear armaments in a completely different way. We began to understand that they had outgrown the goals for which they were created and that no strategic or political goals can be achieved by means of nuclear armaments. . . . In the nuclear age wars cannot be a continuation of politics."[22] Soviet security would not be enhanced by matching the increases in American expenditures, the Politburo had decided.

Soviet Missile Defense

Triumphalists insist that the Strategic Defense Initiative was the straw that broke the Soviet back. As Robert Gates tells it, "By 1983, already panting hard as they tried to keep pace with current and prospective military deployments, the Soviet leaders were left breathless by one US military initiative that, in its ambition and implications, truly horrified them—Reagan's determination to build a space-based ballistic missile defense."[23] Other members of the administration shared Gates's view of the pivotal nature of SDI and concluded that Soviet fears about the program were driving the changes in Soviet foreign policy. "We were gaining quite extraordinary leverage from a system that was a long way from being operational," Assistant Secretary of

Defense Richard Perle has recalled. "It was just wonderful."[24] According to Kenneth Adelman, Reagan's arms control adviser, the general secretary's insistence on restricting SDI made it plain to him that the program "was the engine driving [Moscow] to negotiate over deep reductions in categories of strategic arms."[25] He elaborated:

> None of us—not Ronald Reagan, not any of his advisors—could have imagined SDI's impact when he launched the notion in March 1983. . . . We could not conceive that it would *significantly* help end Soviet power altogether. . . . Along with the Chernobyl accident, SDI marked the beginning of the end. . . . The record does show that only after SDI came along in force did Moscow adopt the notion of deep reductions and begin serious negotiations on that basis. Having helped end the Cold War, the Soviet Union, and the acute threat of Soviet nuclear attacks that loomed for a generation, SDI has given us more protection than ever imaginable—even if it is never deployed![26]

These views are mistaken. Not only did Moscow opt not to invest heavily in an SDI system of its own; by 1985 its initial concerns about Reagan's program had largely dissipated.

The Soviet Union had been working on missile defense systems and antisatellite weapons for decades before President Reagan announced his Strategic Defense Initiative. Drawing upon their success with Sputnik in 1957, the Soviets began applying their technological and scientific expertise to military systems. In the late 1950s they had constructed a large experimental facility for missile defense in Sary Shagan, Kazakhstan, where they developed a number of ground-based lasers over the subsequent two decades. By the early 1970s the Soviets had built a ground-based missile defense system around Moscow, as well as a rudimentary antisatellite weapon that could adopt the same orbit as its target and fire at it with conventional weapons. After signing the 1972 Anti-Ballistic Missile (ABM) Treaty, the USSR continued research on defense-related technologies, as did the United States. The Soviets also investigated ways to deploy laser weapons in space, which expanded their expertise in both space shuttle design and lasers.[27]

In 1978 Soviet military scientist Vladimir Chelomei proposed a new project: the construction of small space shuttles that would carry antisatellite weapons into space. Chelomei, a star weapons designer, was responsible for several generations of Soviet cruise missiles, the SS-19 ICBM, and early antisatellite weapons. He liked to refer to himself as "the most expensive man" in the Soviet Union, owing to the size of his institute's budget for military research.[28] On paper, there were important similarities between Chelomei's proposal and the program Reagan would propose five years later. Both plans envisioned a space-based system of lasers capable of destroying incoming missiles. A key difference, however, was that the president envisioned a purely defensive system, whereas the Soviet proposal included the ability to attack enemy satellites.[29]

As was customary, the Kremlin had commissioned a committee of experts to investigate the merits of Chelomei's proposal. The committee delved into the technological, scientific, and engineering details of building such a missile defense system; and their investigation gave them a deep appreciation for the many challenges of such a task. After careful consideration, it determined that pursuing a comprehensive ballistic missile defense system was not worthwhile.[30]

By 1980 much of the Soviet research on ballistic missile defense had stalled. Soviet information technology had proven too primitive to handle the rapid-fire calculations necessary for laser weapons. At a time when *Time* magazine was conferring its "Person of the Year" award on the personal computer, such devices were virtually unheard of in the Soviet Union. It was woefully behind the West in computer technology.[31] Even with sophisticated computers, the technological challenge of hitting a speeding missile with a laser was daunting. Such weapons would require vast amounts of energy, precision targeting, and impeccably constructed materials, all of which the Soviets lacked. While they excelled in weapons design, they often ran into difficulties during construction owing to substandard materials.[32]

Initial Soviet Reactions to SDI

The Soviets were initially alarmed about SDI. "When we [at the Soviet military institutions] received the information that the United States was ready to create a multi-stage anti-missile defense system, we . . . initially were put into a state of fear and shock because we understood that this could be realistic due to the economic and financial capabilities of the United States," General Slipchenko recalled in 1998. "The Soviet Union was not ready or prepared to respond adequately."[33] Soviet Foreign Minister Aleksandr Bessmertnykh has agreed, recalling that the Soviets initially considered SDI "something very dangerous. . . . [It] made us realize we were in a very dangerous spot."[34] General Secretary Yuri Andropov responded to Reagan's SDI announcement in a typically vitriolic manner. "Should this conception be converted into reality," he warned ten days after Reagan's surprise announcement, "this would actually open the floodgates of a runaway arms race of all types of strategic arms, both offensive and defensive."[35] Victor Karpov, the Soviet representative at the ongoing arms talks in Geneva, also denounced the proposal. SDI was an unacceptable violation of the ABM Treaty, he declared to General Edward Rowny, the US arms control specialist. "It violates the spirit of the ABM Treaty, if not the letter, and this is perfidious of the United States." Karpov then walked out of the talks.[36]

In late 1983 the Kremlin commissioned a committee to evaluate President Reagan's proposed Strategic Defense Initiative. The committee was chaired by Yevgeny Velikhov, who had been on the committee that had considered the Chelomei proposal years earlier, and included the best and the brightest Soviet military scientists and professionals. Owing to the investigation of the Chelomei proposal, the committee members had unparalleled expertise in the many challenges of missile defense. After careful consideration of Reagan's vague proposal and US options, the Velikhov committee "concluded that building a global anti-missile system that could protect against a first strike by the Soviet Union was impossible—at least it would not be possible during the next 15 to 20 years."[37] SDI was not an imminent threat, Soviet experts believed.

Their previous research on missile defense systems enabled Soviet scientists "to respond to Reagan's speech rapidly and energetically," Velikhov has recalled. "The Chelomei affair was killed and this was a very good inoculation for Russia against the Star Wars proposal by Reagan, because five years before, we had already had these internal discussions, with a very detailed analysis on the technical engineering level."[38]

Velikhov, director of the Soviet Space Research Institute Roald Sagdeev, and others urged the Politburo not to bother trying to build a Soviet version of SDI. Their preferred path was arms control, and, if necessary, cheap countermeasures that would overwhelm SDI.[39] Pursuing such countermeasures would not only be far less costly than building a Soviet version of SDI, it could also be put off until the Americans had deployed their system—something that might never happen, Velikhov reasoned.

While the Velikhov committee had rejected the possibility that the United States could build a comprehensive defensive system, SDI did generate other concerns in Moscow. For one thing, the Soviets believed the SDI proposal violated the 1972 ABM Treaty, in which the superpowers had agreed to forego building new defensive systems. Moscow considered this pact to be the foundation of all subsequent arms accords; a flagrant violation called into question the entire arms control architecture. The Kremlin repeatedly called on Washington to reaffirm its commitments and to strengthen the treaty.[40]

Moreover, Soviet scientists respected American technology, and some were initially concerned that an investment of billions of dollars would lead to technological breakthroughs that could be disadvantageous to the USSR.[41] "The danger of the SDI program was that it would lead to the development of new kinds of weapons," Lieutenant General Nikolai Detinov, a former Soviet arms control expert, reflected in 1998. "New space armaments, lasers, or other things of this nature could be produced, arms that could be placed in space and could aim at the surface of the globe. They could aim at our airplanes, not just our missiles."[42]

Finally, some initially feared that SDI might be part of an American plan to launch a surprise nuclear attack against the USSR. (Yuri Andropov was among this group.) While the United States would most likely not be able to build a comprehensive defensive system to intercept thousands of missiles across a broad territory, Soviet scientists thought it might be able to develop a more limited system that could effectively absorb a smaller retaliatory strike. If so, the United States would be able to launch a surprise attack on the USSR without having to fear Soviet retaliation. Mutual Assured Destruction would be dangerously undermined. "We all shared the view that an SDI system that would protect 100 percent of the population of the country from a planned attack was quite impossible," Detinov explained. "But we thought it would be possible to create a system of anti-missile defense in order to intercept a counterattack which was not planned and on a small scale." Such a prospect "alarmed scientists and our [military] general staff and a number of the leaders of our country," he reflected.[43] As one Soviet official explained in 1993, "[T]he danger lay not in the fact that [SDI] was offensive, but in the fact that it was defensive, because by creating these strong defenses you have denied the Soviet Union the possibility for a retaliatory response if we are attacked."[44] There would be nothing to deter Washington from attacking

Moscow. From this perspective, SDI made an American nuclear strike seem more probable.[45]

Thus, SDI provided an excuse for conservatives in the Soviet military to lobby for the revival of missile defense programs. As journalist David E. Hoffman described it, these officials behaved like "a hunting dog sensing new quarry."[46] They played up the potential threat of Reagan's SDI and quickly got to work repackaging old programs to sell to the Politburo as a way to meet the new American threat. According to Andrei Grachev, Gorbachev's political adviser and spokesperson, the response "proposed by Soviet generals and weapons manufacturers envisaged 117 scientific [programs], 86 research projects and 165 experimental programs with approximate spending during the ten-year period amounting to between 40 and 50 billion rubles."[47] Many of these programs had originated years earlier.

Soviet Concerns about SDI Dissipate

The more Soviet scientists delved into SDI, however, the more their initial concerns were allayed. General Slipchenko, a leading military scientist, explained that the initial "fear and shock" over SDI soon gave way to a more composed perspective.

> [I]n figuring out our response we modeled many times the kind of SDI that the US could realistically have created. We became convinced that even the most reliable system of anti-missile defense, let's say 99 percent effective, still has holes, and out of 6400 warheads which could be launched in the direction of the United States, 60 warheads would have found their targets. . . . [T]he retaliatory strike of even one nuclear warhead would cause unacceptable damage to a country. Therefore, we decided that this American policy must be of a political nature. To be more specific, the US was trying to economically ruin the Soviet Union by involving it in an arms race.[48]

However, SDI did not require a costly response, these scientists concluded. They determined that it would be considerably less expensive to try to counter SDI than to match it. "We found over 200 alternative solutions [to SDI]," Slipchenko recalled in 1998. "We chose 20 to 30 of them to look at more closely. We evaluated our anti-SDI measures against a realistic SDI of the

United States and found out that it would cost us about 10 percent of what the Americans would have to spend on SDI. Then we were happy. Actually, we would have been quite glad if the Americans continued building SDI . . . because we realized that SDI could be fought very successfully—not by means of creating a similar system, but by way of creating means to overcome the system."[49]

Soviet officials began to suspect that SDI was a hoax of sorts—a large-scale disinformation campaign aimed either at goading the Soviets into wasting their own resources on building a similar system or a bargaining chip that Reagan would offer to trade away in exchange for reductions in the Soviet arsenal. SDI "was a fuss about nothing," Soviet scientists counseled Gorbachev. "We suspect that this SDI is nothing but a bluff."[50] After careful consideration Marshal Sergei Akhromeyev, the Chief of the General Staff, concluded that SDI was nothing more than a "chimera."[51] The KGB was tasked with searching for information to determine whether SDI was a large-scale disinformation operation calculated to extract concessions on nuclear weapons from Moscow in exchange for a US commitment to abandon the program.[52]

Gorbachev's Diplomatic Offensive against SDI

When Mikhail Gorbachev came to power in March 1985 he too opposed SDI, but for different reasons than his predecessors. He was not as paranoid about an American attack as Andropov, nor did he believe a comprehensive defensive shield was possible—by the mid-1980s few Soviets did.[53] Security concerns did not prompt his opposition. Rather, Gorbachev opposed SDI because it threatened his plans to reduce defense spending. Conservatives in the military-industrial complex were using SDI as an excuse to lobby for additional funding for Soviet missile defense projects, while others advocated building enough weapons to overwhelm SDI. Both responses required additional investments in armaments. Gorbachev sought to end the arms race, yet SDI threatened to ramp it up.

Soon after Gorbachev became general secretary he asked Yevgeny Velikhov to once again evaluate President Reagan's Strategic Defense Initiative. Gorbachev had a firm grasp on economic problems, but in 1985 he was less confident about foreign policy, particularly arms control. Two years had passed since Velikhov first assessed Reagan's proposal, but SDI remained more of a dream than a substantive plan. Thus, Velikhov briefed Gorbachev by reiterating his earlier findings: a comprehensive defense system was not feasible, and the Soviet Union would be foolish to pursue such a costly project. There were preferable alternatives, he told the Soviet leader. An arms reduction treaty would obviate the need for costly defensive systems, while inexpensive countermeasures could overwhelm an SDI system—if one were ever to be deployed.[54]

Gorbachev found Velikhov's arguments to be persuasive and promptly appointed him to become the science director of a program to develop measures for countering SDI. This was a politically savvy move. Velikhov was deeply respected within the military-industrial complex and would be able to build support for Gorbachev's plans. At the same time, the esteemed scientist would be able to control both the scope and the cost of any Soviet response to SDI.

Nonetheless, the new general secretary had to be careful not to alienate powerful conservative military leaders who were seeking funding for missile defense. In order to placate them, in 1985 he approved proposals to revive some of the existing missile defense research programs. After a decade of reduced expenditures for strategic defense, investments returned to traditional levels.[55]

Gorbachev did not intend to invest heavily in countering SDI, however. Velikhov had advised him that SDI could be countered relatively cheaply by building enough missiles to overwhelm the system when and if it were ever built. But Gorbachev preferred the most cost-effective response of all: a full-court diplomatic press intended to persuade Reagan to abandon SDI. Unlike his predecessors, the Soviet leader was a natural diplomat. He was a "genuine born missionary," one Soviet military official observed, with a talent for converting people to his views through reason and dialogue.[56] Gorbachev sought to marshal his persuasive powers so as to convince Reagan to focus on arms reduction and abandon the Strategic Defense Initiative. If he could meet with Reagan and persuade him to discontinue SDI, he reasoned, Soviet military leaders would have little reason to request or receive additional funding. Gorbachev could then proceed to his primary task, which was ending the arms race. Consequently, the general secretary launched a diplomatic offensive against SDI. During every summit meeting, every discussion about arms control, and in virtually every letter, Gorbachev sought to persuade Reagan to abandon his program. Thus, the Strategic Defense Initiative came to dominate superpower relations.

The Package: Linking SDI and Arms Reduction

Gorbachev's strategy was to link SDI to nuclear arms reduction; Moscow would agree to reduce its arsenal if Washington would agree to jettison SDI. In Soviet parlance, the two issues were a "package." The Politburo already sought to end the arms race, so trading arms reductions in exchange for American concessions on SDI would be squarely in Moscow's self-interest. Such an exchange would also be in keeping with the doctrine of sufficient defense, which meant Gorbachev could count on support from reform-minded quarters of the military-industrial complex.[57]

The general secretary knew that negotiating and concluding arms accords would be a time-consuming affair, especially given the degree of mistrust between the superpowers. Thus, he sought to jump-start the process. Less than a month after taking office Gorbachev announced a unilateral moratorium on the deployment of new intermediate-range missiles, and ten days later he announced a moratorium on nuclear testing, inviting the United States to join in.[58] The Soviet leader hoped such goodwill gestures would convey his sincerity in ending the arms race, thus building trust. In late September the newly appointed Soviet foreign minister, Eduard Shevardnadze, delivered a letter from Gorbachev to the White House. The letter's intent was to pave the way for a historic agreement in the upcoming Geneva summit meeting, and it began by discussing at length the superpowers' mutual interest in "terminating the arms race on earth and preventing it in space." "[P]reventing war and removing the threat of war is our mutual, and for that matter, primary interest," Gorbachev wrote."[59] He urged the president to join the Soviet moratorium on nuclear testing and lamented the lack of progress in the ongoing arms talks in Geneva. He then made a proposal: the Soviet Union would agree to a 50 percent reduction in the superpowers' nuclear arsenals in exchange for a complete ban on "space attack weapons," as the Soviets called SDI. Although the president had himself proposed cutting nuclear arsenals in half in 1983, he rejected Gorbachev's package owing to the stipulations about SDI.

Gorbachev persevered. "Ending the arms race is of critical importance," he told the president during the Geneva summit meeting in November 1985. "The first priority of this meeting should be to give impetus toward resolving the arms race."[60] Gorbachev agreed to Reagan's proposal to cut strategic offensive arms by 50 percent and to pursue the eventual elimination of intermediate-range missiles in Europe—in exchange for the president's agreement to abandon SDI. Reagan again refused, insisting that SDI was purely defensive. The president offered to share SDI technology, but Gorbachev dismissed the idea out of hand.

Although the Geneva meeting was ultimately hailed as a success by both sides, the heated disagreement over SDI left both leaders frustrated. "Gorbachev is adamant we must cave in our SDI," Reagan fumed to his diary. "Well this will be a case of an irresistible force meeting an immovable object."[61] Gorbachev was equally adamant. "Reagan appeared to me not simply a conservative," he complained, "but a political dinosaur."[62]

The Soviet leader found Reagan's tenacious commitment to SDI both perplexing and irritating, especially given the dim prospects for the program's success. The president's "advocacy of the Strategic Defense Initiative struck me as bizarre," Gorbachev recalled. "Was it science fiction, a trick to make the Soviet Union more forthcoming, or merely a crude attempt to lull us in order to carry out the mad enterprise—the creation of a shield which would allow a first strike without fear of retaliation?"[63]

The Soviet leader remained determined to reduce nuclear arsenals and eliminate SDI, despite what he perceived to be American intransigence. Gorbachev decided a bold move was necessary. On January 15, 1986, he unveiled a proposal to eliminate all nuclear weapons worldwide by 2000.[64] The three-stage plan was detailed and ambitious, beginning with reductions in superpower arsenals and ending with the elimination of nuclear arsenals in France, Britain, and China as well. It also called for an end to nuclear testing as well as a renunciation of "space-strike weapons." "My impression is that [Gorbachev has] really decided to end the arms race no matter what," Chernyaev observed in his diary the following day. "He is taking this 'risk' because as he understands, it's no risk at all—because nobody would attack us even if we disarmed completely. And in order to get the country out on solid ground, we have to relieve it of the burden of the arms race, which is a drain on more than just the economy."[65] Soviet reformers hoped the radical proposal would spur the Americans to cooperate.

However, Washington failed to respond to the offer as Moscow had hoped. President Reagan was captivated by the proposal to abolish nuclear weapons, but no one in his administration shared his enthusiasm. The Kremlin had foolishly unveiled the plan in public before the administration had had time to read through it carefully, thus raising suspicions it was nothing but propaganda. "Most US government agencies considered Gorbachev's proposal nothing more than smoke-and-mirrors and advised a flat rejection," Jack Matlock has recalled.[66] Ultimately, the president rejected the proposal owing to its stipulations regarding SDI. The first stage of Gorbachev's plan called for a ban on "space strike weapons," which Reagan found unacceptable.[67]

Gorbachev's frustrations with the Reagan administration grew. His radical initiative to end the arms race had failed, and the Americans had not only continued to refuse to join the nuclear test moratorium, but had also detonated a nuclear device in Nevada on March 22, 1986. Two days later Gorbachev lamented to the Politburo, "The moratorium helped us to clarify the genuine motives of the Western partners—precisely that they are not inclined to disarm. When will New Thinking reach them?" He then erupted,

> Maybe we should just stop being afraid of the SDI! Of course, we cannot be indifferent to this dangerous program. But still—can we get rid of the complex [i.e., the irrational obsession]? They are betting on precisely the fact that the USSR is afraid of the SDI—in the moral, economic, political and military sense. That is why they are putting pressure on us—to exhaust us! . . . [Y]es we are against the SDI *because we are in favor of abolishing nuclear weapons.*[68]

Gorbachev was beginning to reconsider his strategy of making arms reductions dependent upon an agreement on SDI.

At the same time, Soviet reformers came to appreciate that they had allies in Washington: domestic support for Reagan's military buildup was dissipating.[69] The US Congress was beginning to cool to Reagan's defense expenditures, and by the autumn of 1986 it had cut military funding by one-third. In addition, the US Senate was challenging the administration's reinterpretation of the ABM Treaty, and thus the legality of the SDI program.[70] It seemed increasingly unlikely that Washington would deploy a comprehensive defense system; therefore, it was increasingly unlikely that the Soviet Union would have to invest in countermeasures.

Nonetheless, Gorbachev grew more frustrated throughout 1986.[71] None of his reforms was bearing fruit. The Geneva arms talks were stymied owing to disagreements over the Strategic Defense Initiative, and this standoff had impeded plans for revitalizing the Soviet economy. On top of all this, the

Chernobyl disaster had underscored the potential horrors of a nuclear war as well as the urgent need to stop the arms race. Gorbachev could not understand American indifference to his proposals, but he vowed to press on. "If we take the position of the imperialist—toughness and toughness again, to insist on our position, we will not achieve anything," he remarked to the Politburo in May 1986. "And everything will be as it used to be. And that means that it would be worse."[72] Determined to reduce superpower arsenals, on September 16, 1986, the general secretary invited President Reagan to a meeting in Reykjavik, Iceland. Unlike traditional summit meetings, which took months to plan, Gorbachev urged Reagan to meet as soon as possible.

The Soviet leader intended to "sweep Reagan off his feet" in Iceland with "a major step toward disarmament."[73] "In order to move Reagan we should give him something," he instructed the group of advisers preparing for the November meetings. "We should do something to push him until a breakthrough occurs." Gorbachev's "supertask" was "to prevent the next round of the arms race." The "end goal" was the "abolition of nuclear weapons"; but, anticipating that the Americans would find fault with this objective, the group prepared other proposals as well.[74]

Gorbachev began the Reykjavik summit by introducing a comprehensive package of sweeping proposals, many of which echoed earlier American positions. The Soviets would accept a 50 percent reduction in strategic weapons and the complete elimination of intermediate-range missiles in Europe— proposals the Americans had made earlier. In addition, the Soviet leader proposed a comprehensive ban on testing nuclear weapons and expressed an interest in stricter verification measures to insure that the superpowers abided by their treaty commitments, something President Reagan had long wanted. Gorbachev also pulled back from earlier demands that Washington abandon SDI. Instead, he now sought to "strengthen the ABM Treaty" with a mutual commitment not to withdraw from the agreement for ten years. Such a pledge would have the practical effect of restricting SDI to the laboratory for a decade. Reagan would not have to abandon his beloved SDI, but neither could it be developed or deployed during this time period.

After the first negotiating session in Reykjavik the Americans were elated. "Everyone was surprised," Secretary of State George Shultz later recalled. "Gorbachev's proposals were heading dramatically in our direction. He was laying gifts at our feet—or more accurately, on the table—concession after concession."[75]

President Reagan was unprepared for such sweeping proposals, however, and responded in a flat-footed manner. He dutifully worked through the details of Gorbachev's plan, focusing on its difficulties. The Soviet leader grew irritated, fearing the talks would get bogged down in minutia the way they did in Geneva. "Let's not slurp the soup that [our arms negotiators] have been cooking all these years," he urged Reagan.[76] Gorbachev pressed on, seeking areas of agreement. Eventually, the president launched into an impassioned defense of SDI, explaining once again his desire to protect the American people from nuclear Armageddon. Gorbachev's temper flared, but the two sides agreed to work through the night to hammer out an agreement.

On the second day the two leaders parried back and forth, fleshing out proposals and counterproposals, going over and over the same ground, anger ebbing and flowing. In the midst of an exasperating discussion over the difference between "strategic" and "ballistic" missiles the president said, "It would be fine with me if we eliminated all nuclear weapons." Gorbachev leapt on the idea. "We can do that. Let's eliminate them. We can eliminate them."[77] It was a historic moment: the abolition of nuclear weapons would revolutionize world politics and pave the way for significant reforms in the USSR. Such an agreement could profoundly alter the course of history.

But the moment passed. While reiterating his approval for eliminating nuclear weapons, Gorbachev insisted that SDI must be confined to the laboratory. The president refused, and a landmark agreement slipped away.

Reykjavik was not a failed summit, however. Although the two leaders were unable to forge an agreement to abolish nuclear arms, they gained a far better understanding of each other's antipathy to nuclear weapons and desire for peace. According to Chernyaev, after this meeting "it became perfectly clear to Gorbachev that there was not going to be a war and that neither side was going to attack the other."[78] Therefore, the argument that SDI would allow the United States to launch a nuclear first strike with impunity was no longer credible. Armed with this knowledge, Gorbachev was better able to resist his military leaders when they played up the American threat in an effort to secure additional funding. After Reykjavik "Gorbachev always bristled [at requests for military spending]," Chernyaev recalled. He would ask military leaders, "'Are you going to war? I'm not going to war. So all of your suggestions are unacceptable.' All of the Politburo supported him."[79]

For Gorbachev, the Reykjavik meeting was pivotal in ending the Cold War. "I believe it was then, at that very moment, that [Gorbachev] became convinced it would 'work out' between him and Reagan," Chernyaev has written. "A spark of understanding was born between them, as if they had winked to each other about the future."[80]

After leaving office Gorbachev confided to George Shultz that his discussions with Reagan in Reykjavik had been profoundly important. Gorbachev had come to greatly admire the secretary of state and went to visit him in California after both had retired. "We sat in the backyard," Shultz has recalled, "and I said to him 'When you entered office and when I entered, the Cold War was about as cold as it got, and when we left office it was over. So what do you think was the turning point?' And he didn't hesitate one second. He said, 'Reykjavik.'"[81]

Untying the Package

By 1987 many of Gorbachev's advisers had become exasperated with their leader's fixation on SDI and were urging him to drop the matter so as to focus on the more important goal of arms reduction. The general secretary's tirades over the US program smacked of old-style Soviet foreign policy, they advised, something Gorbachev claimed to want to abandon. As early as May 1985 Anatoly Chernyaev had confided to his diary that Gorbachev's position made the USSR look weak. "The reason is that Gorbachev is still following Gromyko's well-worn path (and thus losing his grip on foreign policy). . . . We've shortsightedly become fixated on the US's military space research programs, making their termination a condition for success in Geneva. . . . Gorbachev has now committed himself personally to these demands. . . . The Western press is beginning to sense that the Gromyko era in foreign policy still hasn't ended."[82]

Gorbachev's fixation only strengthened the American commitment to SDI, others pointed out. The Soviet leader had even joked about this during the Reykjavik summit. "I think that I am helping the president with SDI," Gorbachev told Reagan. "After all, your people say that if Gorbachev attacks SDI and space weapons so much it means the idea deserves more respect. They even say that were it not for me no one would listen to the idea at all."[83]

Others argued that SDI was a distraction. It was of dubious military value and might even be an elaborate propaganda campaign. "In 1986–87 we in the Foreign Ministry at working levels were writing all kinds of papers about how we should deemphasize SDI in our positions, in our

policies, that it is counterproductive to emphasize SDI," recalled Pavel Palazhchenko in 1993.

> And then, once we felt it was beginning perhaps to be [accepted] by
> the leadership . . . there would be something like a spy scandal or
> Secretary [of Defense Caspar] Weinberger's idea of early deployment
> . . . or something else that would undermine [the position that Mos-
> cow should downplay SDI]. . . . [Soviet Foreign Minister Eduard]
> Shevardnadze . . . was convinced in 1986 that we should deempha-
> size SDI, that it would be good for us and for the US and for the
> process of arms control. And then always something would happen
> that would create the atmosphere in which the military industrial
> complex . . . could continue to push their line that SDI is something
> that we should emphasize. So it was very difficult.[84]

Chernyaev and other reformers thought that linking SDI with arms reduction in one "package" had proven counterproductive. Reagan's stubborn position on SDI had rendered it impossible to achieve an arms accord. The strategy
of tying the two issues together had backfired. In February 1987 Gorbachev's
confidant and adviser, Alexander Yakovlev, wrote a long memo to the Soviet
leader urging him to "untie the package" and deal with SDI and nuclear arms
reductions separately.[85] "In politics, maximum freedom of maneuver is always
valuable," the reformer told Gorbachev. "The 'package' in its present form
only ties our hands." Initially, the strategy had been a good one, Yakovlev
reflected. "We needed a powerful initiative . . . [to] capture public opinion"
and to reveal President Reagan's intransigence. Opposition to SDI has been
growing, he pointed out, both in the United States and in Europe. But the
president's inflexibility had turned the package into a "dead end." Arms
reduction talks had stagnated. "We should not let this American trick go
unanswered," he opined. "For us the 'package' is not a goal, but a means. The
Soviet side should not allow Washington to sow doubts about our intentions,
shifting the responsibility for the absence of progress in the negotiations to
the USSR." A separate agreement on reducing intermediate-range nuclear
weapons would be in Soviet interests, he advised. "For us it would be tanta-
mount to the removal of a very serious threat. It would raise our reputation in
Europe. In the end, it would make our relations with China easier." Yakovlev
continued, "In any case, it is unlikely that we would have to penetrate

SDI—if it is ever built—with intermediate range missiles. Untying the 'package' makes this agreement obtainable; preserving the 'package' blocks it."

Yakovlev cautioned, however, that Washington might remain intractable even if SDI and INF were "untied." "Will the US go for such decisions?" the reformer asked. "It is already clear, not under Reagan!" He continued, "We don't have . . . grounds to expect that everything will work out on its own; that Reagan will have an epiphany—in Reykjavik he missed his best chance to go down in history not as a clown, but as a statesman. For that, Reagan is not intelligent enough, and too limited in his freedom of choice." But the USSR should pursue separate agreements regardless of Reagan. Yakovlev concluded, "In general, partial agreements—both on the issue of SDI and on all other issues—are in our interests."

Influential voices outside the Kremlin also urged Gorbachev to abandon his fixation on SDI. For example, in December 1986 Soviet dissident Andrei Sakharov urged Gorbachev to de-link SDI and arms reduction and to focus exclusively on the latter. A nuclear physicist, Sakharov had been on the scientific team that had developed the Soviet atomic bomb and had played a key role in the development of the hydrogen bomb. During the 1960s, however, Sakharov became an increasingly outspoken critic of the arms race and was especially opposed to the idea of ballistic missile defense. As a result of these and other activities, in 1980 Sakharov was sentenced to internal exile in Gorky, a closed city, where he remained for six years. In December 1986, Gorbachev released Sakharov as part of his new glasnost policy, allowing him to return to Moscow. Sakharov used the media attention surrounding his release to press the Soviet leader to focus on arms reduction rather than SDI.

Sakharov was only one (albeit famous) voice in a large and increasingly influential transnational group of scientists seeking to pressure the superpowers to reduce nuclear weapons. Velikhov and Sagdeev were part of this network, as were Frank von Hippel and Jeremy Stone of the American Federation of Scientists, and Christopher Paine, an arms expert on US Senator Edward Kennedy's staff. In mid-February 1987 Sakharov, von Hippel, and Stone spoke at an international disarmament conference in Moscow that Gorbachev attended. All three emphasized the folly of tying SDI to arms reduction talks. "A significant cut in ICBMs and medium-range and battlefield missiles and other agreements on disarmament should be negotiated as soon as possible, independently of SDI," Sakharov declared to a rapt audience. "I believe that a compromise on SDI can be reached later."[86] Von

Hippel and Stone had the honor of sitting with the general secretary during the concluding dinner, providing all three the opportunity to discuss "untying the package" in greater detail. Gorbachev's desire for nuclear disarmament should not be held captive to President Reagan's obstinacy regarding SDI, Von Hippel and Stone asserted.[87]

Gorbachev later explained that his discussions with the scientists at the forum "made a big impression" on him.[88] He discussed the conference with the Politburo shortly after it concluded. Borrowing the phrase that Yakovlev had used in his long memo, Gorbachev told his comrades that the Geneva arms talks had become a "dead end." "We have to rise to a new level of conversation," he urged them. "We start from the assumption that as difficult as it is to do business with the United States, we are doomed to do it. We have no choice. Our main problem is to remove confrontation." Gorbachev then explained, "The biggest measure that would make an impact on the outside world, on public opinion, will be if we untie the package." Yegor Ligachev, the Politburo member who headed the Department of Organizational Party Work, jumped on the idea. "If we agree to cut the number of missiles at once, we will win at once. And our defense capability will not suffer. We will also gain a lot in terms of public opinion." Gorbachev noted his approval and then attempted to one-up his comrade, saying, "I am in favor of [this] proposal, plus a reduction of a thousand more. Without it Western Europe will not agree to remove the [Pershing missiles.] And we will pressure the United States through public opinion, arguing that we are in favor of mutual trust."[89] The Soviet Defense Minister, Marshal Sergey Sokolov, then attempted to throw cold water on the idea, noting that the British and the French had nuclear missiles as well. "You are losing the political elements here, Marshal Sokolov," Gorbachev scolded. "There will be no war with Britain or France. It is impossible. And our medium-range missiles, if we remove them, it does not change anything here."[90]

On February 28, 1987, Gorbachev untied the package, leading to a major breakthrough in superpower relations. Gorbachev announced that the Soviet Union would be willing to discuss the reduction of nuclear missiles separately from the Strategic Defense Initiative. "The Soviet Union suggests that the problem of medium-range missiles in Europe be singled out from the package of issues, and that a separate agreement be concluded on it, and without delay," the general secretary declared.[91] This decision was pivotal in ending the Cold War. Alleviated of the need to find common ground on SDI, the two sides quickly reached an agreement to eliminate intermediate-range nuclear forces (INF) in Europe. In December 1987 the superpowers signed the historic INF Treaty. Based on the Reagan administration's earlier Zero Option proposal, the treaty was the first agreement to eliminate an entire class of nuclear weapons.

After the spring of 1987 the Politburo rarely discussed SDI.[92] The matter had been, as they say, "overtaken by events."

SDI: An Impediment to Ending the Cold War

Reflecting upon the Reykjavik summit as he flew back to Moscow in October 1986, Gorbachev fumed over the manner in which Reagan's obstinacy on SDI had precluded an agreement on the elimination of nuclear weapons. "By this negotiating package we wanted to show the entire world—and the Europeans first of all—that the SDI is the main obstacle to nuclear disarmament," he grumbled to Chernyaev.[93] SDI was the main impediment to reducing nuclear arsenals and improving superpower relations, the general secretary insisted.

Gorbachev was correct, but both leaders bear the blame for this roadblock. President Reagan's initially harsh rhetoric and military buildup combined to give the impression that the Strategic Defense Initiative had offensive purposes. It appeared to the Soviets that the president was launching a new arms race in space. In addition, SDI made President Reagan's repeated calls for the abolition of nuclear weapons seem insincere. In the Kremlin's eyes, launching a new weapons system while calling for the elimination of nuclear arms seemed contradictory. The president's stubborn refusal to restrict SDI to the laboratory was also ill considered: it was implausible that SDI could have been deployed within a decade. As Shultz later remarked, agreeing to such a restriction would have been like "giving [Gorbachev] the sleeves from our vest."[94]

Reagan's inflexible position on SDI impeded progress on arms reduction. But this was only because Moscow had linked the two issues. If Gorbachev had not made arms reduction dependent upon restrictions on SDI, disarmament could have proceeded more quickly. The Soviet decision to "package" the two issues together prevented earlier progress on reducing intermediate-range nuclear missiles.

Moreover, Gorbachev's fixation on SDI had the paradoxical effect of strengthening American support for the program. Most of Reagan's advisers were initially tepid about the plan, as were many leading members of Congress. But the more Gorbachev demanded restrictions, the more American officials prized SDI. They came to see it as a valuable bargaining chip. If the Soviet leader had opted to focus primarily on nuclear arms reduction—as many of his advisers recommended—there might well have been less support for SDI at home.

Gorbachev also erred by dismissing Reagan's repeated offers to share SDI technology. The Soviet leader had little to lose by accepting such a gesture, but plenty to gain. If Gorbachev had accepted Reagan's offer, US officials would have had to either renege on the offer or find ways to follow through. The White House would have faced the prospect of US technology being transferred to Moscow, which would have caused a maelstrom within Washington. The US Congress might well have slashed funding for the program, thus completing Gorbachev's task for him.

The Strategic Defense Initiative also made it more difficult for Gorbachev to reduce defense spending and seek an end to the arms race. Conservatives in the Soviet military-industrial complex claimed SDI was evidence of the looming American threat and used the program as an excuse to lobby for increased funding. SDI strengthened the position of those conservatives who favored an antagonistic approach to the United States. Thus, it prevented Moscow from disarming earlier. "Star Wars was exploited by [Soviet] hardliners to complicate Gorbachev's attempt to end the Cold War," Alexander Yakovlev has explained.[95]

SDI did not force the Soviet Union into bankruptcy, nor did it compel Moscow to accept policies that were antithetical to its interests. In fact, it had a negligible impact on Soviet attitudes toward nuclear weapons, military doctrine, and ending the Cold War. Absent SDI, Gorbachev would still have pursued an end to the arms race and the elimination of nuclear weapons. Moscow sought to end the Cold War because this was squarely in the Soviet Union's self-interest.

In September 1983 the CIA released a study that speculated on the Soviet Union's possible responses to SDI. The president had unveiled the research program five months earlier, and senior officials wanted to understand what impact it might have on the Kremlin. The report considered a wide variety of potential political and military responses, but argued that the Politburo would be "reluctant to divert scarce assets to expensive technological efforts."

Given economic constraints, it was unlikely that Moscow would invest in a "crash program" to mimic SDI. The Soviets might take "certain limited military steps" so as to improve its bargaining position and to prepare themselves "for initial US deployment should it occur," but the Agency did not anticipate major increases in Soviet expenditures. Rather, the CIA thought it most likely that the Soviets would "look for solutions that are least disruptive to their way of doing business and involve the least possible change to their planned programs." Moscow would probably respond with "a concerted political and diplomatic effort to force the US to drop its . . . plans, or failing that, to negotiate them away."[96] The Agency also warned that US efforts to build SDI could have the unintended effect of bolstering support for similar projects already underway in the USSR.

These predictions were astonishingly accurate. Contrary to what triumphalists believe, the Soviet Union did not attempt to replicate SDI, nor did it invest heavily in countering the program. Instead, Gorbachev launched a diplomatic offensive, hoping to persuade Reagan to abandon the project. By 1987, however, it was clear both that the diplomatic effort had failed and that SDI posed little real threat. Gorbachev then shifted his attention to his primary objective, which was reducing nuclear arsenals.

The military buildup and SDI did not force the Soviet Union into bankruptcy. Nor did it compel Moscow to "concede" the Cold War. The US buildup was initially followed by a period of increasing superpower hostility, culminating in the war scare in the fall of 1983. Moreover, supposed Soviet concessions on nuclear arms came in late 1986, just as public and congressional support for Reagan's defense policies was dissipating.

Changes in Soviet policy were a response to domestic needs and objectives, not American pressure. The Kremlin sought to end the arms race in order to be able to reduce defense spending and revitalize the Soviet economy. The Politburo adopted the doctrine of "sufficient defense" as part of its plan to diminish western perceptions of the Soviet threat, reduce superpower arsenals, and decrease defense expenditures. These positions were adopted regardless of the US military buildup, not because of it.

Moscow did not "knuckle under" American pressure. Rather, Gorbachev and his fellow reformers viewed arms reduction as a way to promote not only the Soviet national interest, but also global security. "We [were] looking for points of mutual interest," Chernyaev has reflected. "When [Gorbachev] made concessions, they were justified from the moral and political standpoint. . . .

Our concessions were the result of . . . logic: we were not going to fight a war, we wanted to end the Cold War, we wanted nuclear disarmament and the liquidation of nuclear arms. That was New Thinking."[97] As historian Raymond Garthoff has explained, "Gorbachev understood that the Soviet Union could not afford to match or overmatch the US militarily, but more important, he understood that it did not need to. He understood that both countries, and the world, would be better off without a Cold War military confrontation and a permanent arms race. He did not lose the arms race, he called it off."[98]

6

The Triumph of Diplomacy and Leadership

> Our challenge is peaceful. We do not threaten the Soviet Union. We have never fought each other. There is no reason we ever should.
>
> President Ronald Reagan, January 16, 1984

Triumphalism has become the conventional wisdom in the United States and has been promoted by political leaders, media personalities, and scholars. It is commonplace to believe that President Reagan "won" the Cold War by compelling the Soviet Union to surrender and then collapse. But this triumphalist description of the ending of the Cold War is built upon a series of fallacies.

For one thing, triumphalists misstate the impact that President Reagan's policies had on the Soviet Union. Reagan's initial hard-line posture did not compel Moscow to withdraw from Afghanistan or to agree to arms reductions and democratic reforms. Soviet leaders did not acquiesce to American demands; rather, they dug in their heels, hurled accusations of their own, and walked out of arms control talks. In fact, Reagan's name-calling and saber rattling brought the superpowers to the precipice of war in 1983. Moreover, these US policies provided an excuse for Soviet hard-liners to play up the American threat, lobby for increases in defense spending, and resist Gorbachev's plans for ending the arms race. The more belligerent they perceived Reagan to be, the more these conservatives resisted reform. President Reagan's initially hawkish posture undermined US interests and caused superpower relations to deteriorate dangerously.

And when Soviet reforms did come—five years into the Reagan presidency—they were not concessions to American pressure, but rather were a response to domestic needs. New Thinking in foreign policy and perestroika were rooted in decades-long discussions within the USSR about the need to reform the Soviet system. Soviet reformers sought to end the arms race and conclude the Cold War so that they could focus resources on revitalizing the Soviet Union. "Perestroika was the result of internal demands [and] analysis of the internal situation in the Soviet Union, not pressure from Ronald Reagan or SDI," Anatoly Chernyaev has stated.[1]

Nor did the US military buildup compel Moscow to disarm and collapse. By the mid-1980s the Politburo had concluded that large arsenals were counterproductive. They were costly to build and maintain and incited fear in the West, prompting the United States to increase its arsenal. The Soviet Union would be more secure, the Politburo reasoned, if both nuclear and conventional arsenals were greatly reduced. Thus, Moscow chose not to match the US buildup. There was no devastating spike in Soviet defense expenditures that caused the economy to collapse. Rather, the USSR imploded owing to structural flaws in the Soviet system, combined with Gorbachev's misbegotten attempts at reform.[2]

Triumphalists also misstate the impact that the Strategic Defense Initiative had on the Soviet Union. While some Soviets were initially alarmed about SDI, these concerns dissipated by the mid-1980s as military scientists concluded the system could be countered cheaply and in all likelihood would never be built. Moscow therefore did not launch an SDI program of its own in response to the US initiative. By 1986 Gorbachev's advisers pressed him to ignore SDI and to focus instead on getting the Americans to agree to reduce nuclear arms. This shift was pivotal, and it cleared the way for the conclusion of the 1987 INF Treaty, which was the first agreement to eliminate an entire class of nuclear weapons.

But SDI certainly impeded progress in ending the arms race. The program was the main stumbling block in superpower relations between 1983 and 1986, and disputes over SDI dominated both the Geneva and the Reykjavik summit meetings. Both sides bear the blame for this roadblock. President Reagan proved unable (or unwilling) to recognize the manner in which SDI could appear to be threatening to Moscow. And, owing to his hope that SDI would protect civilians from nuclear annihilation, he was unwilling to accept restrictions on the project. But Gorbachev made the tactical mistake of demanding that progress in other arms reductions talks be dependent upon an agreement to restrict SDI. No progress could be made, therefore, until the president conceded on his pet project. Thus, the entire arms reduction process—and improvements in superpower relations more generally—were held hostage to discussions on SDI.

Triumphalists not only misstate the impact that Reagan's policies had on the Soviet Union, they also mischaracterize the president's intentions and policies. They suggest that President Reagan's greatest legacy is the collapse of the Soviet Union. This is curious because Reagan had left the White House long before the Soviet Union collapsed. Moscow lowered the Soviet flag for the last time on December 31, 1991—almost three years after Reagan had retired.

But, more important, the president was not seeking to destroy the USSR. Rather, he sought to improve superpower relations so that the two sides could reduce, and hopefully eliminate, their nuclear arsenals. Reagan sought dialogue and disarmament, as he and his key foreign policy advisers repeatedly stated.

Triumphalism overlooks Reagan's deep antipathy to nuclear weapons and his quest to eliminate them.[3] "No *one* could win a nuclear war," he insisted. "Yet as long as nuclear weapons were in existence, there would always be risks they would be used, and once the first nuclear weapon was unleashed, who knew where it would end? My dream, then, became a world free of nuclear weapons. . . . [F]or the eight years I was president I never let my dream of a nuclear-free world fade from my mind."[4]

President Reagan's military buildup was intended to bring about arms reductions, not the collapse of the USSR. Reagan officials assumed—wrongly, as it turned out—that the Politburo would not agree to such reductions until confronted by an adversary of equal strength and resolve. Erroneously believing that the United States was behind in the arms race, they launched a buildup so as to catch up.[5] Officials reasoned that once the United States had regained its strength it would be better able to persuade the Kremlin to agree to arms reduction talks. The administration sought "peace through strength," as Reagan officials were fond of saying.

The Strategic Defense Initiative was part and parcel of the president's plan to eliminate nuclear weapons. Reagan hoped SDI would protect civilians from both an intentional and an accidental nuclear attack. SDI was a means for reducing the risk of nuclear Armageddon. Moreover, an effective defensive system would render nuclear weapons useless, thus paving the way for their elimination. This is why the president refused to abandon the project. It is also why he repeatedly offered to share it with Moscow, much to his advisers' chagrin. As Reagan explained in March 1988:

The fact is that many Americans are unaware that . . . the United States has absolutely no defenses against a ballistic missile attack. If even one missile were to be accidentally fired at the United States, the president would have no way of preventing the wholesale destruction of American lives. All he could do is retaliate—wipe out millions of lives on the other side. This is the position we find morally untenable. . . . People who put their trust in MAD must trust it to work 100 percent—forever, no slip-ups, no madmen, no unmanageable crises, no mistakes—forever. . . . Isn't it time we invented a cure for the madness? Isn't it time to begin curing the world of this nuclear threat? . . . We can create a better, more secure, more moral world, where peace goes hand in hand with freedom from fear—forever.[6]

Triumphalists also overlook the role that diplomacy played in ending the Cold War. They suggest that the president refused to engage with the Soviet Union until it agreed to reduce its arsenal and adopt reforms, but Reagan corresponded regularly with Soviet leaders. The president reached out to Moscow when superpower relations were dangerously strained, and he invited Gorbachev to a summit meeting on the day the Soviet leader took office—years before the introduction of New Thinking and perestroika. President Reagan wound up meeting with Gorbachev five times in three years—more frequently than any of his predecessors had met with their Soviet counterparts.

In fact, Reagan believed discussions with adversaries were crucial. Military strength was necessary—but insufficient—for peace. Military threats might deter an adversary from attacking, but they are unable to resolve underlying disputes. Conflicts can only be resolved through dialogue. "Strength and dialogue go hand in hand," he explained in 1984. "[W]e want more than deterrence; we seek genuine cooperation; we seek progress for peace."[7] The aim of this dialogue was to reduce uncertainty, build trust, and seek areas of common interest, such as nuclear disarmament.

President Reagan did not wait for his adversary to reform before seeking cooperation and disarmament. Rather, he sought dialogue in the hopes of bringing about reform and disarmament. Reagan did not waver in his anti-communism; he rose above it.

Another myth about President Reagan—albeit one that is not exclusive to triumphalism—is that he was "the Great Communicator."[8] Reagan was a gifted orator who had the ability to write and deliver stirring speeches. In these addresses he was able to discuss complicated matters, such as arms control treaties and fiscal policy, in a simple, homespun manner.[9] In addition, his sincere optimism had broad appeal. But when it came to more private exchanges, the president had difficulty. Reagan was often unable to communicate his intentions and decisions clearly and effectively to his subordinates. He hated conflict, and when his advisers disagreed Reagan would try to avoid picking sides, preferring instead to tell humorous anecdotes so as to dispel tension. During meetings the president would often listen politely, interject sparingly, and the meeting would adjourn.[10] Advisers were left to divine the president's wishes. It is easy to understand why the administration was plagued by "school boy scuffles," as Alexander Haig called them, with different factions claiming to represent the "true Reagan."[11] These contradictory understandings of the president's aims continue to this day.

Reagan's inability to communicate decisively to his advisers had a pernicious effect on the administration's ability to form a coherent policy toward Moscow. This, in turn, undermined superpower relations. A classic example of this difficulty came in April 1981 when President Reagan was convalescing at the White House after being shot. Sitting in the sun-drenched solarium, he was introspective, wondering whether he had been spared for a reason. "Perhaps having come so close to death made me feel I should do whatever I could in the years God had given me to reduce the threat of nuclear war," Reagan recalled. "I didn't have much faith in Communists or put much stock in their word. Still, it was dangerous to continue the East-West nuclear stand-off forever, and I decided that if the Russians wouldn't take the first step, I would." Reagan decided to write a letter to General Secretary Brezhnev so as to "convince him that, contrary to Soviet propaganda, America wasn't an 'imperialist' nation and we had no designs on any part of the world. . . . [I] wanted to send a signal to him that we were interested in reducing the threat of nuclear annihilation."[12] Writing in longhand on a pad of yellow legal paper, the president drafted a missive to Brezhnev that emphasized the superpowers' common interests and underscored America's peaceful intentions. Noting that the United States had not taken advantage of its monopoly on nuclear weapons after World War II, Reagan stressed his desire for "meaningful and constructive dialogue which will assist us in fulfilling our joint obligation to find lasting peace."

Secretary of State Haig was not enthralled with this letter, to put it mildly. As Reagan recalled, Haig "was opposed to conciliatory gestures toward the

Russians until they gave us evidence that they were willing to behave."[13] The administration needed to stand firm and reiterate its demand that the Soviets must change their behavior before relations can improve, the secretary insisted. If the president wanted to write to the Kremlin, Haig scolded, the State Department should compose the letter. Reagan initially complied. "Well, I guess you fellows know best," he conceded. "You're the experts." The State Department duly drafted a stiff, formal letter that conveyed none of the hopes for peace and disarmament that Reagan had expressed in his personal note. It was "typical bureaucratese," Reagan's adviser, Michael Deaver, recalled. Deaver urged the president to stand up to Haig. "If you think [your] letter ought to be sent to Brezhnev, don't let anybody change it. Why don't you just send it?" he counseled.[14]

But it was not Reagan's style to confront an adviser, especially in his weakened state. A compromise was broached: Reagan would send his hand-written note emphasizing the superpowers' common interests, and the State Department would send its formal letter chastising Moscow for its aggressive conduct. The only thing the two letters had in common was the date and Reagan's signature at the bottom.

Understandably, the Soviets found the two letters frustratingly perplexing. Reagan was subsequently disappointed with Brezhnev's "icy" reply.[15]

The Soviets found the president and his administration to be confusing, to say the least. Anatoly Dobrynin, the longtime Soviet ambassador to the United States, recalled, "There seemed to be no strict discipline or clear guidance within the administration in dealing with the Soviet Union, and its members seemed to delight in staging petty conflicts, to Moscow's irritation."[16] Reagan called for dialogue and cooperation, yet he initially avoided summit meetings, armed the mujahedeen in Afghanistan, and insisted that the United States would confront communism around the globe. Reagan claimed he wanted to eliminate nuclear arms, yet he engaged in a military buildup and introduced SDI.

Ambassador Dobrynin has explained the Soviet view:

What seemed most difficult for us to fathom were Reagan's vehement public attacks on the Soviet Union while he was secretly sending—orally or through his private letters—quite different signals seeking more normal relations. On March 8 [1983], less than a month after our first White House conversation when he seemed to

be trying to open up a working relationship with the Soviet leadership, he publicly described the Soviet Union . . . as the "evil empire."
. . . The entire episode demonstrated a certain paradox about Ronald
Reagan: a contradiction between words and deeds that greatly
angered Moscow, the more so because Reagan himself never seemed
to see it. In his mind such incompatibilities could coexist in perfect
harmony, but Moscow regarded such behavior at that time as a sign
of deliberate duplicity and hostility.[17]

Owing to the mixed signals emanating from the White House, it took a
long time for Soviet leaders to appreciate President Reagan's desire to improve
relations and eliminate nuclear weapons. Gorbachev believed *he* was leading
the way toward ending the arms race and the larger Cold War, coaxing an
unwilling adversary. The Soviet leader "was painfully struggling, on the highest level, to start a real disarmament process on equal footing with the West,"
Anatoly Chernyaev recalled. "But if not for Gorbachev's persistence, his
dogged determination to prove to all that nuclear weapons were an absolute
evil and unacceptable as a foundation for world politics, the process would not
have started and we would not have had the subsequent historic reversal in the
arms race."[18] From Moscow's perspective, the Soviets made overture after
overture—a moratorium on nuclear testing, a moratorium on the deployment
of new intermediate-range forces, a call for the global elimination of nuclear
weapons, the withdrawal of Soviet forces from Europe—hoping to coax
Washington into joining them to end the arms race. As Gorbachev confided
to UN Secretary General Javier Perez de Cuellar in June 1987, "Our tactic is
to tow our partners behind us. Somebody has to take the initiative of taking
the first step—if our partners are not ready to do it, we must do it ourselves."[19]
Gorbachev was repeatedly frustrated that his initiatives to disarm were not
only not reciprocated but dismissed by the Reagan administration as propaganda. The Soviet leader had naïvely believed that these initiatives, in combination with his personal charm, would improve superpower relations quickly.
For example, after the 1985 Geneva summit meeting Gorbachev grew frustrated over the lack of progress on disarmament. President Reagan was continuing to throw "fuel" on an ideological fire, the Soviet leader lamented.

Again, it was Reagan who led anti-Communist hysteria, reiterating
his attack on "the evil empire." No effort was spared to discredit our

initiatives and to dismiss our genuine invitation to disarm as a utopian scheme. The tragedy of Chernobyl was exploited as an alleged proof that we had no intention of really "opening up," that we remained treacherous and not to be trusted. The Americans continued to proclaim in public their readiness for serious arms control negotiations, but in reality they were again undermining the talks and adopting new weapons programs which sent the arms race spiralling ever upward. Try as I would, I simply could not understand this behaviour.[20]

While Gorbachev was gratified that Reagan had nearly agreed to abolish nuclear weapons during the 1986 Reykjavik summit, he was frustrated at the plodding progress of disarmament talks. During a Politburo meeting on October 22 he complained that Reagan officials "don't have any constructive program and are doing everything to inflame the atmosphere. In addition to this they are acting very rudely and are behaving like bandits."[21] The general secretary remained committed to finding a way forward, however. "We need to continue to put pressure on the American administration, explaining our positions to the population and showing that the American side is responsible for the breakdown in the agreement over the questions of reduction and liquidation of nuclear weapons."[22]

In April 1988 Gorbachev complained about the president to Secretary of State George Shultz:

> We've met three times and should have reached an understanding by now. We signed a document of utmost importance—the first agreement on nuclear weapons reductions. And now it turns out that you are impossible to please. You're still operating under the assumption that there's a real threat of communist aggression. In refusing to change your stance you disregard the fact that there won't be any aggression and objectively can't be.[23]

"What was our interpretation of the United States and Reagan in the mid-1980s?" Anatoly Chernyaev asked in 1998. "Reagan was the leader of imperialism, of an aggressive superpower and that was absolutely beyond doubt, that was absolutely clear for the leadership of our country. But Gorbachev also based his thinking on the fact that there were some reasonably-thinking people in Washington, that they could see where the arms race was leading humankind, that it was already verging on a catastrophe, and doing major damage to the US economy too, and that common sense could be a foundation for [a] common process [to improve relations]."[24] In order to end the Cold War the Kremlin would need to work around the Reagan administration. "[T]he steps we took to carry out our new policy were met by a wall of prejudice and refusal in the political centres of the West," Gorbachev has recalled. "But in the end Western politicians yielded to pressure from the general public, who understood that the world was on the brink of a catastrophe, and that we could not allow this to continue."[25]

In short, the Soviets saw themselves as advancing the cause of peace and disarmament and the Americans as the spoilers. "These differences [in view] illustrate the problems we and the Soviet leaders faced in communicating our real intentions and in establishing the measure of trust required to solve major problems," Jack Matlock has reflected.[26] The miscommunication between the capitols was profound.

Reagan sought to resolve what he called the "dangerous misunderstandings" between the superpowers, but he bears significant blame for creating such confusion.[27] The president sent mixed signals to the Kremlin, his vitriolic language drowned out most everything else he was saying, and his inability to end the battles within his administration further muddled his message.

On occasion, the president's communications fell victim to Kremlin intrigue. As administration officials toiled over the president's pivotal address of January 16, 1984, they decided they would take extraordinary measures to call attention to it. Senior officials held off-the-record backgrounders with members of the press to underscore the importance of the upcoming speech and Reagan's call for dialogue and disarmament, while the State Department contacted key allies. In addition, it delivered copies in advance to the Soviet ambassador to the United States as well as to the Soviet Foreign Ministry in Moscow. This speech will be a watershed, US officials told their Soviet counterparts; the president hopes it will be a turning point in superpower relations.[28]

But the speech did not have the impact on Moscow that US officials had hoped. In fact, it barely caused a ripple. As it turns out, few Soviet officials learned of the address. General Secretary Yuri Andropov was on his deathbed at the time, and the Kremlin was on the cusp of another transition. Moscow's future direction was uncertain. Hawkish Foreign Minister Andrei Gromyko decided not to circulate the text widely, so as to insure he would retain influence over Moscow's response. Soviet officials did not have access to Western press at the time, so they depended upon the Foreign Ministry and the official news agency, TASS. Gromyko effectively prevented Reagan's message from reaching the political leadership.[29] Gorbachev's advisor on international affairs, Anatoly Chernyaev, first read Reagan's address in the late 1990s, when Jack Matlock showed it to him. "I was shocked," he recounted, "because I, an international adviser to the general-secretary[,] didn't know about [the speech or similar subsequent statements]. I wasn't aware of the existence of these documents. . . . What they stressed wasn't the arms race, rather . . . [Washington] moved to the foreground the desire to have talks, to have human contact,. . . . We didn't know about this."[30]

Resolving the Cold War through Reassurance and Engagement

The peaceful resolution of the Cold War was astonishing. At the time, most viewed the conflict to be an enduring feature of the international system. For forty years leaders had simply tried to manage the conflict and prevent it from becoming unacceptably violent, rather than to resolve its fundamental disputes. Triumphalism not only claims to explain the surprising end of the Cold War, it stipulates how to cope with current and future conflicts. In this view, Reagan's threats and military buildup compelled the Soviet Union to acquiesce to American demands and ultimately to collapse. Post–Cold War leaders should therefore follow Reagan's lead. They should employ tough rhetoric, increase defense spending, avoid negotiations, and pursue regime change abroad. Conflicts will be resolved when adversaries are compelled into submission.

However, in this case, compellence failed miserably. Reagan's initially hawkish policies not only did not end the Cold War, they also undermined US interests. They strengthened the position of Soviet hard-liners who opposed disarmament, made it more difficult for Gorbachev to pursue arms reductions and reform, and brought the superpowers to the brink of war.

The Cold War was resolved through diplomacy, not threats. By 1983 the Reagan administration had largely embraced a strategy of engagement and reassurance, which was pivotal to bringing about the peaceful resolution of the Cold War. This strategy had three components.

First, beginning in 1984 the Reagan administration repeatedly reassured Moscow that its security was not threatened. These messages were delivered both in public and in private. "Our challenge is peaceful," Reagan declared in January 1984. "We do not threaten the Soviet Union. Our countries have never fought one another. There is no reason we ever should."[31] These assurances were crucial, and they implicitly recognized the trauma the Soviets had endured when they were invaded by Germany during World War II. They also provided Gorbachev with the leverage he needed to counter domestic opposition to his reforms. The less threatening Reagan appeared to be, the more Gorbachev was able to resist Soviet hard-liners who favored higher defense expenditures and an antagonistic approach to Washington. Soviet reformers thus had more latitude to pursue arms reductions, improved superpower relations, and domestic reforms. Ambassador Dobrynin observed in his memoirs, "It may sound like an historical paradox . . . but if the President had not abandoned his hostile stance toward the Soviet Union for a more constructive one . . . Gorbachev would not have been able to launch his reforms and his new thinking. Quite to the contrary, Gorbachev would have been forced to continue the conservative foreign and defense policies of his predecessors."[32]

The Reagan administration's assurances also helped to clarify US intentions. Once Gorbachev came to understand Reagan's sincere desire to abolish nuclear arms and improve superpower relations, the less important disputes over SDI became. A war between the superpowers seemed increasingly improbable, thus freeing Gorbachev to pursue reforms and arms reductions with greater vigor.

The second element of this strategy was to focus on common interests. Reagan's decision to focus on the superpowers' mutual interest in abolishing nuclear arms was pivotal. "[T]he people of our two countries share with all mankind the dream of eliminating the risks of nuclear war," the president noted in 1984.[33] Gorbachev shared this dream. The two leaders had many differences of opinion, but on this one issue they had a sense of shared purpose. Just as important, neither leader could accomplish this task on his own. Each was dependent upon the other. Cooperation was essential. As Gorbachev told the Politburo on April 3, 1986, "Despite all the contradictions in our relations [with the United States], the reality is such that we cannot do anything without them, and they cannot do anything without us. We live on the same planet. We will not be able to preserve peace without America."[34] It was this mutual desire to end the threat of nuclear annihilation—and their inherent inability to accomplish this goal alone—that was the basis upon which Reagan and Gorbachev built a more cooperative relationship.

The third element was trust-building. Both Reagan and Gorbachev understood that nuclear arms could not be abolished until there was a modicum of trust between the superpowers. The Cold War was built upon a foundation of mistrust. If mutual suspicions could be resolved, other policy disputes would dissipate as well. This was especially true regarding arms control. "We don't mistrust each other because we're armed," Reagan was fond of saying. "We are armed because we mistrust each other." If the superpowers could eradicate the mistrust, the arms race would take care of itself. Soviet reformers agreed. "The problem of the Cold War was a problem of trust, and of differences in how we understood each other's efforts in the areas of security and defense," Anatoly Chernyaev observed in 1998. "It was this absence of understanding, or incorrect understanding, or lack of desire to understand that was the root of the problem."[35]

Gorbachev and his fellow reformers sought to build trust through a series of unilateral arms reductions and moratoria intended to prove that the Soviet Union sincerely sought to end the Cold War and the arms race. These gestures, it was hoped, would reassure Washington of Moscow's benign intentions.

The Reagan administration sought to build trust by engaging in dialogue and expanding the range of topics under discussion so as to foster mutual understanding. "By broadening the agenda to include not just arms control, but other issues we hoped to relieve some of [the Soviet] leaders' fears that we would attack," National Security Adviser Robert McFarlane has explained.[36] Toward this end, Jack Matlock prepared over forty papers for the president on various aspects of Soviet history and Russian culture. Reagan devoured them and urged his advisers to study them as well. "[T]hey were the most important papers of the past 20 years," McFarlane has recalled.

> We'd give them to President Reagan once a week and they were on these fundamental issues of Russian character, Russian history, Russian structure. And Reagan, from a time in 1981 and 1982 when he used to be bored to death over all these arcane issues of numbers, throwweights, cruise missiles, and so on, came alive. We'd go into his meeting on a morning and he'd give me back one of Jack's papers and it would be scribbled all over and he would look at Don Regan and he would say, "Read this. This is good; this is really worth knowing." And when the president tells you that you really ought to read something you usually do.[37]

McFarlane credits these papers with a transformation within the administration. "[I]t was a result of the knowledge and scholarship provided by Jack Matlock which helped educate the bureaucracy in the fall of 1983 and then throughout 1984 and 1985 that this broader, more balanced agenda became the American approach," he believes.[38] This process culminated with the Geneva summit meeting in 1985. "A year earlier President Reagan would not have had the grasp of the Russian character and as heartfelt an appreciation for Russian history as he did in Geneva," McFarlane has explained. "But in those sessions, early on, one-on-one, just [the leaders] and their interpreters, his focus was not on arms control, not on SDI, but on why Gorbachev mistrusted us and why Gorbachev should not [mistrust us] and on why Reagan mistrusted Gorbachev. Reagan invited him to say 'Why shouldn't we trust each other?' . . . It wasn't over issues of beancounting . . . our missiles that we finally turned a corner in our relationship."[39]

The Cold War was resolved through diplomacy. President Reagan focused on the superpowers' mutual interest in reducing nuclear arms and engaged in meaningful dialogue so as to ease security concerns and build trust. It was this policy of reassurance and engagement that led to the peaceful conclusion of the Cold War.

Vision and Leadership

The ending of the Cold War was a triumph of diplomacy. It was also a triumph of leadership. In the fourth volume of his biography of President Lyndon Johnson, Robert Caro observes that while power can be pernicious, it can also be liberating.

> [A]lthough the cliché says that power always corrupts, what is seldom said, but what is equally true, is that power always reveals. When a man is climbing, trying to persuade others to give him power, concealment is necessary: to hide traits that might make others reluctant to give him power, to hide also what he wants to do with that power; if men recognized the traits or revealed the aims, they might refuse to give him what he wants. But as a man obtains more power, camouflage is less necessary. The curtain begins to rise. The revealing begins.[40]

This is especially true of presidents during their final term in office. No longer burdened by the need to please potential supporters both inside and outside the government, a second-term president has more freedom to focus on the long-term interests of the United States. He is able to pursue what is right, not simply what is possible. Reagan's brush with death in March 1981 rendered such moral issues even more compelling and prodded him to consider his legacy at an early stage in his presidency.

At a time when most Americans believed the Cold War to be an enduring feature of the international system, President Reagan envisioned a world beyond the arms race. "Peace," he believed, must be something more than the mere absence of nuclear war. "Security" had to be more substantive than a never-ending threat of nuclear Armageddon. Consequently, Reagan introduced radical new ideas about global security.

First and foremost, Reagan rejected Mutually Assured Destruction, which was the core of US strategic doctrine. According to MAD, both superpowers were deterred from launching a nuclear attack on the other by the fact that neither side had defenses. If one were to attack, the other could retaliate and both would be obliterated. A first strike would prove suicidal; therefore, such an act would deter a would-be aggressor. Foreign policy experts insisted that this precarious vulnerability had kept the peace since the end of World War II. This was the gospel, accepted as an article of faith within the foreign policy community.

Reagan rejected this gospel. He believed MAD was both a dangerous and a morally bankrupt conception of security. "For forty years nuclear weapons had kept the world under a shadow of terror," the president asserted. "[MAD] was the craziest thing I ever heard of. . . . We were a push button away from oblivion."[41]

Second, the president rejected the traditional approach to nuclear arms control, which sought to limit the rate at which arsenals could continue to grow. Reagan sought to eliminate nuclear arsenals altogether. At the time, the most radical proposal was to "freeze" nuclear arsenals at their current levels. Reagan rejected a freeze, reasoning that such a move would allow arsenals to remain at dangerously high levels and do nothing to limit the possibility of a catastrophic accident. Moreover, the president believed that the United States was behind in the arms race, and a freeze would institutionalize this disadvantage.

The Strategic Defense Initiative was Reagan's third radical notion about security. While the idea of creating defenses against nuclear attack preceded the president, the foreign policy establishment had rejected it because it would upend MAD. The superpowers had even agreed to forego defenses in the 1972 ABM Treaty. Reagan not only embraced the idea, he sought to push science and technology to new frontiers so as to build a cutting-edge space-based laser system that would defend civilians from attack. The president was committed to finding a way to protect civilians from an accidental or intentional nuclear strike.

Finally, and perhaps most shockingly, President Reagan wanted to share SDI technology with the Soviets. His reasoning was simple: if the United States had defenses, Soviet nuclear weapons would become useless. But if both superpowers had defenses, nuclear weapons would become obsolete and so could be eliminated. SDI was a crucial part of the president's plan to eliminate nuclear weapons.

President Reagan confronted steadfast opposition to his ideas about global security. His most trusted advisers did not share his belief that MAD was both dangerous and immoral. Nor did they think the elimination of nuclear weapons was desirable, much less possible. They considered SDI to be fanciful. And they firmly rejected the president's repeated suggestions to share SDI technology with Moscow.

At first, many of Reagan's advisers did not take him seriously. The president was neither an arms control expert nor a foreign policy specialist. He articulated his views in very simple, accessible language, which at times led others to conclude that the ideas themselves were lacking in substance. In addition, his grasp of basic facts about nuclear weapons could be tenuous. At times he confused different types of weaponry, offered questionable facts, and as late as 1983 indicated that he did not know that the Soviets relied primarily upon land-based intercontinental missiles (ICBMs) for their defense.[42] In retrospect Reagan may have garbled these facts because he thought they were beside the point. His objective was to reduce and eventually eliminate nuclear weapons. Everything else was just detail.

At the time, however, Reagan's halting grasp of arms control issues combined with his fanciful talk about a nuclear-free world and space-based defenses did not inspire confidence from his advisers or allies. For many, the president was a foreign policy dilettante who needed to be educated about the virtues of MAD. While no one was enthralled with the idea of a never-ending threat of nuclear annihilation, most thought it was the least bad avenue to peace. MAD had prevented the Cold War from becoming hot, most believed.

Secretary of State George Shultz, who normally deferred to the president's directives, counseled Reagan to abandon his calls for the elimination of nuclear weapons. "I told the president that I shared his dissatisfaction with our dependence on the threat of nuclear annihilation as the means for keeping the peace. But nuclear weapons cannot be un-invented," he recalled. In 1984 Shultz advised Reagan that "the present structure of deterrence and of our alliances depends on nuclear weapons and the best approach is to work for large reductions in nuclear arsenals." Shultz lamented, however, that he "made no real impact" on the president.[43]

As best they could, foreign policy advisers removed from Reagan's letters and speeches passages that called for the elimination of nuclear weapons. For example, in the spring of 1982 Reagan read a column by Ann Landers in which a citizen expressed fears about an impending nuclear war. The president decided to write a letter to Landers himself. A nuclear war was "unthinkable," he wrote, which is why "we must have a true verifiable reduction [in nuclear arsenals] leading to the eventual elimination of all such weapons." National Security Council staff quickly struck the reference to abolishing nuclear weapons. Reagan conceded and signed a version that called only for the reduction of nuclear arsenals.[44]

Conservative Republicans, who strongly supported Reagan's strident anticommunism, were appalled by his calls to eliminate nuclear weapons. "Reagan had a totally naïve view against nuclear weapons, which I saw time and again," recounted Kenneth Adelman, who had been director of the Arms Control and Disarmament Agency (ACDA). "All of us who were conservative thought that when [President] Carter said, 'I want to eliminate nuclear weapons,' that was the stupidest thing we'd ever heard. We all made fun of it. And then we had our hero who says things really more extreme than Carter ever does, and he's unstoppable in doing it."[45] Conservative opinion makers such as George Will and Charles Krauthammer publicly lambasted the president for nearly agreeing to eliminate nuclear weapons during the 1986 Reykjavik summit, while conservative interest groups conveyed their disapproval privately.[46] Reagan's performance in Reykjavik prompted Richard Nixon and Henry Kissinger—who had been estranged from each other for more than a decade—to join forces to denounce the idea of a nonnuclear world. Eliminating nuclear weapons could provoke the "most profound crisis" in the history of the NATO alliance, they warned. "Any Western leader who indulges in the Soviets' disingenuous fantasies of a nuclear-free world courts unimaginable perils."[47]

NATO allies were equally concerned about a nonnuclear world. Super-power relations were extraordinarily tense in the early 1980s. Sitting on the Soviet Union's doorstep, the allies counted on the American nuclear arsenal to deter a Soviet attack on Western Europe. Reagan's close friend British Prime Minister Margaret Thatcher was especially wary of talk about elimi-nating nuclear weapons. "Next year we will have had peace in Europe for forty years," she told the president during a meeting in December 1984. "That is a very long period of peace. We are going to have to live with [MAD] for a considerable period of time," she insisted. Reagan replied, "I don't think there's any morality in that at all."[48]

President Reagan defied experts, counselors, longtime friends, and key allies in pursuit of his vision of a more moral, more humane approach to global security. Perhaps even more difficult, he rose above ideological differ-ences and reached out to his adversary to accomplish his goals. And he did so at a time when the Soviet Union had not even begun to reform. The president began calling for the elimination of nuclear weapons years before Gorbachev came to power, at a time when Soviet leaders were clinging to traditional Cold War hostility. Reagan sought to reconceptualize security during the height of the Cold War. He understood that nuclear weapons themselves had become the enemy. The overwhelming stockpiles, the destructive capacity, the hair-trigger alert, and the never-ending threat of nuclear annihilation all constituted a fundamental threat to global security. Ronald Reagan hated communism, but he hated Mutually Assured Destruction even more. Com-munism was a dumb idea, but MAD was a potentially catastrophic one.

Rosalynn Carter once observed that "a leader takes people where they want to go, while a great leader takes people not necessarily where they want to go, but where they ought to be."[49] By these standards Ronald Reagan and Mikhail Gorbachev were great leaders. They sought to reconceptualize secu-rity and to move beyond the Cold War, despite opposition. "Our people look to us for leadership, and nobody can provide it if we don't," the president wrote to Gorbachev in November 1985. "But we won't be very effective lead-ers unless we can rise above the specific but secondary concerns that preoc-cupy our respective bureaucracies and give our governments a strong push in the right direction."[50] Reagan's initial calls for the elimination of nuclear weapons were met with resistance and derision, both at home and abroad. Gorbachev's New Thinking and his desire to end the arms race also provoked conservative opposition within the USSR. But thirty years later, the idea of eliminating nuclear weapons has become mainstream. Political leaders, military officials, and security experts across the world support the idea of abolishing nuclear weapons—including former Reagan officials and officials from the former USSR.[51] Ronald Reagan and Mikhail Gorbachev were pivotal in moving the idea of a nonnuclear world from the realm of the preposterous to the realm of the possible.

President Reagan's policy was peace through strength, but it was his initiatives for peace, rather than his efforts to build strength, that resolved the Cold War. Would the Cold War have ended absent the US military buildup? Most likely. It was not the buildup that brought the two sides together, but rather Reagan and Gorbachev's mutual desire to eliminate the threat of nuclear annihilation. "[Gorbachev and Reagan] were very idealistic . . . ," Soviet Foreign Minister Aleksandr Bessmertnykh reflected in 1993. "[T]his is what they immediately sensed in each other and this is why they made great partners. . . . And if it were not for Reagan, I don't think we would have been able to reach the agreements in arms control that we later reached: because of Reagan, because of his idealism, because he really thought that we should do away with nuclear weapons. Gorbachev believed in that. Reagan believed in that. The experts didn't believe, but they did."[52]

President Reagan and General Secretary Gorbachev were partners in ending the Cold War, and their shared desire to eliminate nuclear weapons was the foundation upon which the conflict was resolved. It took years for the two leaders to appreciate the depth of each other's commitment to nuclear disarmament. Decades of mistrust inhibited progress toward eliminating nuclear weapons. But it was this shared dream that enabled them to overcome their differences and place the superpowers on the path toward peace.

The ending of the Cold War was indeed a triumph for President Reagan, although not in the manner that triumphalists suggest. It was the growing spirit of superpower collaboration and the reduction of nuclear arsenals—not the collapse of the USSR—that was Reagan's greatest victory. It was Reagan's far-sighted leadership—his revolutionary antinuclearism—that led to the peaceful conclusion of the Cold War. This is President Reagan's most enduring legacy.

Acknowledgments

This book was a long time in the making. Several jobs, several moves, and several children all insured that progress was sporadic. On my more upbeat days I joked that I was "savoring the process." More frequently, I referred to the book as "The Beast."

I am enormously grateful to the Norwegian Nobel Institute for its early and frequent support of this project. My fellowship there enabled me to lay the foundation for this book, and the camaraderie of Geir Lundestad, Olav Njolstad, and other Nobel Fellows encouraged me to persevere. Ongoing discussions over the years with Frederic Bozo, Archie Brown, Mick Cox, Ben B. Fischer, Mel Leffler, Leopoldo Nuti, Marie-Pierre Rey, Jeremy Suri, Odd Arne Westad, and Vlad Zubok improved the final product immeasurably.

Over the years I have also benefited from discussions with Svetlana Savranskaya, whose detailed and thoughtful work has enriched my understanding of Soviet decision making. Likewise, I owe thanks to Tom Blanton, Philipp Gassert, Ron Granieri, and Bernd Greiner.

I have had the opportunity to collaborate with others on projects about President Reagan that have enabled me to think more deeply about the president's legacy. For example, I owe thanks to W. Elliot Brownlee, Jeff Chidester, Brad Coleman, and Paul Kengor. Peter M. Robinson was generous with his time while I was conducting research at the Hoover Institution, and Dale Reed's archival support was most helpful.

I have the good fortune to work at the University of Toronto's Woodsworth College, a supportive community that seeks to enhance the success of students and faculty alike. It has been a pleasure working there for the past five years. My discussions with Carol Chin were pivotal in reimagining the central argument of this book, and her advice on the publishing process was much appreciated. I owe similar thanks to Bob Bothwell.

Jean Edward Smith read early drafts of this book, and his feedback greatly improved the readability of the text. Likewise, thank you to Dave O'Reilly and Nick McLean.

It has been a pleasure working with the University Press of Kentucky, most notably Andrew Johns, Melissa Hammer, Ila McEntire, and Natalie O'Neal. I appreciate their efforts in championing this book and shepherding it to completion. Donna Bouvier's superb editing skills significantly improved my writing.

Lynn Fischer took good care of my children while we were in Oslo, during the crucial early stages of my research. Without her support I would not have been able to get this project off the ground.

And finally, to my family: Gerard, Kate, Andrew, and Jack. To be honest, they really didn't do anything to expedite this book. But they sure make life fun.

Notes

Introduction

1. Bruce W. Jentleson, *American Foreign Policy: The Dynamics of Choice in the 21st Century,* 3rd ed. (New York: W. W. Norton and Co., 2007), 170.

2. Lawrence Eagleburger, Under Secretary of State for Political Affairs, "Review of US Relations with the Soviet Union," February 1, 1983, *American Foreign Policy: Current Documents, 1983* (Washington, DC: Department of State, 1985), 499–504.

3. For other perspectives on Reagan's role in ending the Cold War, see Beth A. Fischer, "The United States and the Transformation of the Cold War," in Olav Njolstad, ed., *The Last Decade of the Cold War* (New York: Frank Cass, 2004), 226–240; and Beth A. Fischer, "Reagan and the Soviets: Winning the Cold War?" in W. Elliot Brownlee and Hugh Davis Graham, eds., *The Reagan Presidency: Pragmatic Conservativism and Its Legacies* (Lawrence: University Press of Kansas, 2003), 113–132.

4. William D. Jackson, "Soviet Reassessment of Ronald Reagan, 1985–1988," *Political Science Quarterly* 114, no. 4 (Winter 1998–1999): 623–624. See also Robert G. Kaiser, *Why Gorbachev Happened: His Triumph, His Failure, and His Fall* (New York: Simon & Schuster, 1992), 11–13.

5. In earlier works I referred to this perspective as "the Reagan Victory School," which is somewhat clunky. Throughout this book I use "triumphalism" instead. I intend the two terms to be synonymous.

6. Caspar Weinberger, *Fighting for Peace: Seven Critical Years inside the Pentagon* (New York: Warner, 1990). See also Robert M. Gates, *From the Shadows: The Ultimate Insider's Story of Five Presidents and How They Won the Cold War* (New York: Simon & Schuster, 1996); and Richard Pipes, *Vixi: Memoirs of a Non-Belonger* (New Haven: Yale University Press, 2003).

7. Peter Schweizer, *Victory: The Reagan Administration's Secret Strategy That Hastened the Collapse of the Soviet Union* (New York: Atlantic Monthly Press, 1994). Schweizer and Weinberger collaborated on several books during the 1990s. See Andrew Preston, "George Shultz versus Caspar Weinberger," in Andrew L. Johns, ed., *A Companion to Ronald Reagan* (New York: Wiley Blackwell, 2015), 549.

8. For examples of triumphalism see Jay Winik, *On the Brink: The Dramatic, Behind-the-Scenes Saga of the Reagan Era and the Men and Women Who Won the Cold War* (New York: Simon & Schuster, 1996); Paul Lettow, *Ronald Reagan and His Quest to Abolish Nuclear Weapons* (New York: Random House, 2005); Francis Fukuyama, *The End of History and the Last Man* (New York: Free Press, 1992); Ann Coulter, *Treason: Liberal Treachery from the Cold War to the War on Terrorism* (New York: Crown Forum, 2003); Francis H. Marlo, *Planning Reagan's War: Conservative Strategists and America's Cold War Victory* (Washington, DC: Potomac Books, 2012), and Douglas E. Streusand, Norman A. Bailey, and Francis H. Marlo, *The Grand Strategy That Won the Cold War: Architecture of Triumph* (Lanham, MD: Lexington Books, 2016). For a discussion of triumphalism, see Ellen Schrecker, *Cold War Triumphalism* (New York: Free Press, 2004), 1–9.

9. Terri Lukach, "Hope was Ronald Reagan's Secret Weapon," June 11, 2004, Armed Forces Press Service, available at http://osd.dtic.mil/news/Jun2004 /n06112004_200406111.html.

10. The CNN poll is available at www.cnn.com/POLLSERVER/results/11313 .exclude.html, accessed June 5, 2004.

11. Joshua Muravchik, "Losing the Peace," *Commentary,* July 1, 1992, available at www.commentarymagazine.com/articles/losing-the-peace/.

12. Fukuyama, *The End of History,* 75.

13. John McCain, "Reagan Stood Tall, So Must We," Address to the California Republican Party Convention, September 8, 2007. For similar remarks see McCain's June 23, 2006, address at the Reagan Presidential Library, available at "McCain Address to Reagan Presidential Library," June 23, 2006, mccain.senate.gov/press _office/view_article.cfm?id=13&fontsize=big.

14. On the lack of US intelligence sources in the Kremlin during the 1980s and the uncertainty this created in terms of understanding Soviet behavior, see the President's Foreign Intelligence Advisory Board Report, February 15, 1990, in Nate Jones, *Able Archer 83* (New York: New Press, 2016), 29, 80, 83, 110.

15. On Reagan administration officials' beliefs about nuclear arms, see Paul Lettow, *Ronald Reagan and His Quest to Abolish Nuclear Weapons* (New York: Random House, 2006).

16. Among the most enlightening memoirs from Soviet officials are Mikhail Gorbachev, *Memoirs* (New York: Doubleday, 1995); Anatoly Chernyaev, *My Six Years with Gorbachev* (University Park: University of Pennsylvania Press, 2000); Anatoly Dobrynin, *In Confidence: Moscow's Ambassador to America's Six Cold War Presidents* (New York: Random House, 1995); Andrei Grachev, *Gorbachev's Gamble: Soviet Foreign Policy and the End of the Cold War* (Malden, MA: Polity, 2008); Roald Z. Sagdeev, *The Making of a Soviet Scientist: My Adventures in Nuclear Fusion and Space from Stalin to Star Wars* (New York: John Wiley & Sons, 1994); and Mikhail Gorbachev and Zdenek Mlynar, *Conversations with Gorbachev: On Perestroika, the Prague Spring, and the Crossroads of Socialism* (New York: Columbia University

Press, 2002). Among the most easily accessible oral history collections are the Gorbachev Foundation Oral History Archives, available at the Hoover Institution, Stanford University; and the Presidential Oral History Series at the Miller Center for Public Affairs, University of Virginia. The National Security Archive at George Washington University is also an invaluable resource.

17. For example, see Stephen Kotkin, *Armageddon Averted: The Soviet Collapse, 1970–2000* (New York: Oxford University Press, 2001); Vladislav M. Zubok, *A Failed Empire: The Soviet Union in the Cold War from Stalin to Gorbachev* (Chapel Hill: University of North Carolina Press, 2007); Archie Brown, *Seven Years That Changed the World: Perestroika in Perspective* (New York: Oxford University Press, 2007); Robert D. English, *Russia and the Idea of the West: Gorbachev, Intellectual, and the End of the Cold War* (New York: Columbia University Press, 2000); and Svetlana Savranskaya, Thomas Blanton, and Vladislav Zubok, eds., *Masterpieces of History: The Peaceful End of the Cold War in Europe, 1989* (New York: Central European University Press, 2010).

18. There were skeptics, of course. As late as 1990 Caspar Weinberger described Gorbachev's reforms as a superficial public relations ploy, adding, "My feeling has always been that no general secretary of the Communist Party of the Soviet Union will be allowed to alter in any fundamental way the basically aggressive nature of Soviet behavior." See Caspar Weinberger, *Fighting for Peace*, 347–348.

19. Jack F. Matlock, *Autopsy on an Empire: The American Ambassador's Account of the Collapse of the Soviet Union* (New York: Random House, 1995), 148–149 (advance copy).

20. Don Oberdorfer, *The Turn: From Cold War to a New Era, the United States and the Soviet Union, 1983–1990* (New York: Poseidon Press, 1991), 299.

21. John Mueller, "When Did the Cold War End?" Paper presented to the annual meeting of the Society for the Historians of American Foreign Relations (SHAFR), Princeton University, June 24–26, 1999, p. 7, and Figure 2, p. 18.

22. Ibid.

23. Quoted in Michael R. Beschloss and Strobe Talbott, *At the Highest Levels: The Inside Story of the End of the Cold War* (Boston: Little, Brown, 1993), 165.

1. Engaging the Enemy

1. In a final humiliation to President Carter, the hostages were released minutes after Reagan was inaugurated.

2. Prime rate interest history available at http://www.fedprimerate.com/wall _street_journal_prime_rate_history.htm. Interest rates would climb to 21 percent during 1980–1981.

3. Ronald Reagan, *An American Life* (New York: Pocket Books, 1990), 279. Reagan's plan became law in August 1981.

4. Ibid., 314–315.

5. On January 17, 1983, the Reagan administration issued National Security Decision Directive (hereafter NSDD) 75, entitled "US Relations with the USSR." On this document, see Jack F. Matlock, *Reagan and Gorbachev: How the Cold War Ended* (New York: Random House, 2004), 52–55; and George P. Shultz, *Turmoil and Triumph: My Years as Secretary of State* (New York: Charles Scribner's Sons, 1993), 275–276. In May 1982 President Reagan signed NSDD 32, which dealt with national security more broadly. Substantial portions of this document focused on the Soviet threat. Nonetheless, Reagan insisted the bureaucracy develop a more coherent framework for policy specifically toward the USSR. On NSDD 32, see Melvyn P. Leffler, *For the Soul of Mankind: The United States, the Soviet Union, and the Cold War* (New York: Hill and Wang, 2007), 350–351; and Paul Lettow, *Ronald Reagan and His Quest to Abolish Nuclear Weapons* (New York: Random House, 2005), 64–69.

6. Donald Regan, *For the Record: From Wall Street to Washington* (New York: St. Martin's, 1988), 159–161.

7. Alexander M. Haig Jr., *Caveat: Realism, Reagan, and Foreign Policy* (New York: Macmillan Publishing Co., 1984), 355–356. See also Kenneth Adelman, interview for the Miller Center of Public Affairs Presidential Oral History Project, 2003, available at http://millercenter.org/president/reagan/oralhistory/kenneth-adelman.

8. Matlock, *Reagan and Gorbachev,* 62.

9. "US Repudiates a Hard Line Aide," *New York Times,* March 19, 1981, A8.

10. George P. Shultz, *Turmoil and Triumph: My Years as Secretary of State* (New York: Charles Scribner's Sons, 1993), 159.

11. Vice President George H. W. Bush was out of town at the time, and Haig believed that the secretary of state was next in line to the office of the president. While the US Constitution had stipulated that the secretary of state was second in line to the presidency, the Presidential Succession Act of 1947 had changed this order. The secretary of state is now fourth in line, after the vice president, the speaker of the House of Representatives, and the president pro tempore of the Senate.

12. Leaks became an ongoing problem, and in the fall of 1983 the administration considered requiring all top officials to undergo a polygraph test so as to determine their source. See Ronald Reagan, *The Reagan Diaries,* ed. Douglas Brinkley (New York: HarperCollins, 2007), 61–62; and Lou Cannon, *President Reagan: The Role of a Lifetime* (New York: Simon & Schuster, 1991), 423–427.

13. Richard Pipes, *Vixi: Memoirs of a Non-Belonger* (New Haven: Yale University Press, 2003), 153.

14. Caspar Weinberger, *Fighting for Peace: Seven Critical Years in the Pentagon* (New York: Time Warner Books, 1983), 29.

15. Reagan, *Reagan Diaries,* 88.

16. See Shultz, *Turmoil and Triumph,* Part 3.

17. Bernard Gwertzman, "The Shultz Method: How the New Secretary of State Is Trying to Stabilize Foreign Policy," *New York Times Magazine,* January 2, 1983,

15, 28; Anatoly Dobrynin, *In Confidence: Moscow's Ambassador to America's Six Cold War Presidents* (New York: Times Books, 1995), 512–516.

18. Shultz, *Turmoil and Triumph*, 12.

19. James Kelly, Douglas Brew, and Bruce W. Nelan, "More a Ladle than a Knife," *Time,* December 20, 1982, available at http://www.time.com/time/magazine/article /0,9171,923169,00.html.

20. See Shultz, *Turmoil and Triumph*, especially 110, 141–142, 144; and Weinberger, *Fighting for Peace.* Budget Director David Stockman describes Weinberger's refusal to collaborate so as to correct Stockman's error in calculating the defense budget in Stockman, *The Triumph of Politics: Why the Reagan Revolution Failed* (New York: Harper and Row, 1986). On the Shultz-Weinberger relationship, see Andrew Preston, "A Foreign Policy Divided against Itself: George Shultz versus Caspar Weinberger," in Andrew L. Johns, ed., *A Companion to Ronald Reagan* (New York: Wiley Blackwell, 2015), 546–564.

21. See the memoirs of the members of the Reagan administration, especially Haig, *Caveat;* Weinberger, *Fighting for Peace;* Shultz, *Turmoil and Triumph;* Robert C. McFarlane with Zofia Smardz, *Special Trust* (New York: Caddell and Davies, 1994); Regan, *For the Record;* and Matlock, *Reagan and Gorbachev,* among others.

22. Haig, *Caveat,* 57.

23. The first national security adviser was Richard Allen. In January 1982 he was replaced by William Clark. McFarlane took over in October 1983. In December 1985 John Poindexter replaced McFarlane. Frank Carlucci was appointed national security adviser in January 1987, and Colin Powell succeeded him in November of that year.

24. Matlock, *Reagan and Gorbachev,* 30–31. Moscow extended conditional offers for a summit meeting; however, they appeared to be designed to be unacceptable. Brezhnev passed away November 10, 1982, and was succeeded by Yuri Andropov. Andropov suffered a debilitating kidney failure in February 1983 and passed away February 9, 1984. Andropov's successor, Konstantin Chernenko, died on March 10, 1985.

25. Alexander Haig, "A New Direction in US Foreign Policy," April 24, 1981, *Department of State Bulletin,* June 1981, 6.

26. Alexander Haig, "A Strategic Approach to American Foreign Policy," August 11, 1981, *Department of State Bulletin,* September 1981, 11.

27. Ronald Reagan, Remarks at Rancho del Cielo, August 13, 1981, *Weekly Compilation of Presidential Documents, 1981,* vol. 17, p. 874. See also "Excerpt from Weinberger Statement on Military Budget Outlay," *New York Times,* March 5, 1981.

28. Others in the administration, such as Secretary Haig, were more cautious, asserting that current *trends* suggested that the United States could find itself in a position of vulnerability. These claims about Soviet military superiority remained in dispute long after the Cold War ended. See Raymond L. Garthoff, *The Great Transition* (Washington, DC: Brookings Institution, 1994), especially 505–509. See also

remarks by Nikolai Detinov and response by Ed Rowny in Nina Tannenwald, ed., "Understanding the End of the Cold War, 1980–1987," an oral history conference sponsored by the Watson Institute, Brown University, Providence, Rhode Island, May 7–10, 1998 (hereafter "Brown Conference"), transcript, pp. 34–35.

29. Ronald Reagan, "Speech on Strategic Arms Limitation Talks," November 18, 1981, available at: millercenter.org/the-presidency/presidential-speeches/november -18-1981-speech-strategic-arms-reduction-talks.

30. The Carter administration had initiated this military buildup during its final year in office. Secretary Weinberger and David Stockman, the budget director, initially agreed to an increase of 7 percent per year. However, owing to a mathematical error by Stockman the actual increase was more than 10 percent. See David A. Stockman, *The Triumph of Politics: Why the Reagan Revolution Failed* (New York: Harper and Row, 1986), 107–108, 273–278; and Nicholas Lemann, "Caspar Weinberger in Reagan's Pentagon: The Peacetime War," *Atlantic Monthly,* October 1984, 71–71; and "Calculator Error—or Calculated Error?" *Washington Post,* July 10, 1986, A23.

31. Richard Halloran, "Reagan to Request $38B Increase in Military Outlays," *New York Times,* March 5, 1981; and William Kaufmann, *A Reasonable Defense* (Washington, DC: Brookings Institution, 1986), 25.

32. Alexander Haig, appearance on ABC-TV's *Issues and Answers,* July 19, 1981, *Department of State Bulletin,* September 1981, 24.

33. Alexander Haig, interview with Ken Sparks, March 16, 1981, *Department of State Bulletin,* June 1981, 24–25.

34. The Soviet Union had approximately 1,000 warheads on SS-4, SS-5, and SS-20 missiles based in the region, while the deployment of 572 warheads on US Pershing II and ground-launched cruise missiles (GLCMs) was scheduled to begin in November 1983.

35. A nuclear freeze involved "freezing" superpower arsenals at their current levels.

36. Hedrick Smith, "Reagan's Arms Plan: a Shift in Tone," *New York Times,* November 19, 1981, A16.

37. Haig, *Caveat,* 229. Haig maintains that the Zero Option idea originated with the West German government of Helmut Schmidt.

38. "Reagan's Arms Cut Proposal Assailed," November 20, 1981, *Current Digest of the Soviet Press* 33, no. 47: 7. See also Shultz, *Turmoil and Triumph,* 123.

39. However, it did ultimately agree to abide by the terms of the SALT II treaty.

40. The plan proposed a cap of 2,500 land-based missiles. The Soviets had about 5,500 such weapons, while the United States had 2,152. Reagan proposed the idea of START in November 1981, during the same speech in which he unveiled the Zero Option. However, he did not unveil specific American proposals for START until May 1982. See Reagan, "Arms Reduction and Nuclear Weapons," November 18, 1981, *Weekly Compilation of Presidential Documents, 1981,* vol. 17, p. 1273; and Reagan, commencement address at Eureka College, May 9, 1982, *Weekly Compilation of Presidential Documents, 1982,* vol. 18, p. 603.

41. For example, see NSDD 75 (January 1983) and NSDD 100 (July 1983), available at www.fas.org/irp/offdocs/nsdd/.

42. Ronald Reagan, remarks to the National Association of Evangelicals, March 8, 1983, *Public Papers of the Presidents: The Presidency of Ronald Reagan, 1983,* 364.

43. Ronald Reagan, Address to the Nation, March 23, 1983, *Weekly Compilation of Presidential Documents, 1983,* vol. 19, pp. 442–448.

44. SDI will be discussed at length in Chapter 3.

45. Benjamin B. Fischer, *A Cold War Conundrum: The 1983 Soviet War Scare,* Intelligence Monograph CSI 97-10002, Central Intelligence Agency (Center for the Study of Intelligence, September 1997), available at https://www.cia.gov/library /center-for-the-study-of-intelligence/csi-publications/books-and-monographs/a-cold -war-conundrum/source.htm.

46. See Seymour M. Hersh, *The Target Is Destroyed* (New York: Random House, 1986); Alexander Dallin, *Black Box* (Los Angeles: University of California Press, 1985); and R. W. Johnson, *Shootdown: The Verdict on KAL 007* (London: Chatto and Windus, 1986). On the final 1993 report on the investigation of the tragedy by the International Civil Aviation Organization (ICAO) of the United Nations, see Richard Witkin, "Downing of KAL 007 Laid to Russian Error," *New York Times,* June 16, 1993, A7.

47. "Soviet Attack on Korean Civilian Airliner," September 1, 1983, *Weekly Compilation of Presidential Documents, 1983,* vol. 19, p. 1191. See also George Shultz, Remarks on the Downing of KAL 007, September 1, 1983, *Department of State Bulletin,* November 1983, 66; and Ronald Reagan, "US Measures in Response to the Soviets' Korean Airline Massacre," September 5, 1983, *American Foreign Policy: Current Documents, 1983* (Washington, DC: Department of State, 1985), 545–546.

48. Andropov statement of September 28, 1983, as translated in *Current Digest of the Soviet Press* 35 (October 26, 1983): 39.

49. Don Oberdorfer, *The Turn: From Cold War to a New Era, the United States and the Soviet Union, 1983–1990* (New York: Poseidon Press, 1991), 68.

50. Able Archer was the final phase of a larger series of NATO maneuvers that began in August called "Autumn Forge 83." Autumn Forge simulated a conventional war with the Soviet bloc, while Able Archer rehearsed the transition from conventional to nuclear war. The most comprehensive account of the 1983 war scare can be found in Nate Jones, *Able Archer 83* (New York: New Press, 2016). See also Nate Jones, "The 1983 War Scare: 'The Last Paroxysm' of the Cold War," Parts 1–3, at http://nsarchive.gwu.edu/NSAEBB/NSAEBB426/; B. B. Fischer, *Cold War Conundrum*; Christopher Andrew and Oleg Gordievsky, *KGB: The Inside Story of Its Foreign Operations from Lenin to Gorbachev* (New York: HarperCollins, 1992); Beth A. Fischer, *The Reagan Reversal: Foreign Policy and the End of the Cold War* (Columbia: University of Missouri Press, 1997), 122–137; Robert M. Gates, *From the Shadows: The Ultimate Insider's Story of Five Presidents and How They Won the Cold War* (New York: Simon & Schuster, 1996); and Fritz W. Ermarth, "Observations on

the 'War Scare' of 1983 from an Intelligence Perch," Parallel History Project on NATO and the Warsaw Pact, November 11, 2003, available at http://web.archive .org/web/20060724160027/http://www.isn.ethz.ch/php/documents/collection_17 /texts/ermarth.pdf.

51. Nicholas Thompson, "Nuclear War and Nuclear Fear in the 1970s and 1980s," *Journal of Contemporary History* 46, no. 1 (January 2011): 141–142; and Jones, *Able Archer 83,* 11–13.

52. See Jones, "The 1983 War Scare"; Christopher Andrew and Oleg Gordievsky, *KGB: The Inside Story* (London: Hodder and Stoughton, 1990), 488–489; Gordon Brook-Shepherd, *The Storm Birds: The Dramatic Stories of the Top Soviet Spies Who Have Defected since World War II* (New York: Weidenfeld & Nicolson, 1989), 267, 329–330; and the transcript from *Ideas* (radio program on Operation RYAN), Canadian Broadcasting Corporation (CBC), November 4–5, 1992, 1, 6. The East German spy agency (HVA) and the East German military intelligence unit (VA) also played important roles in Operation RYAN. See B. B. Fischer, *Cold War Conundrum.*

53. B. B. Fischer, *Cold War Conundrum,* n. 45.

54. Andrew and Gordievsky, *KGB,* 492–493; *Ideas* (CBC), 2.

55. "Romanov Keynotes Nov. 7 Celebration," *Current Digest of the Soviet Press* 35: 45, 5–6. The two leading newspapers in the USSR, *Izvestia* and *Pravda,* carried the "white hot" comment on their front pages, indicating the seriousness of the statement. At the time, there was much concern among the general public about an American invasion. See B. B. Fischer, *Cold War Conundrum.*

56. Richard Rhodes, *Arsenals of Folly: The Making of the Nuclear Arms Race* (New York: Vintage, 2007), 165. See also Gates, *From the Shadows,* 271–272.

57. Information about Soviet decision making during the 1980s was scarce. Initially, American intelligence characterized the Soviet actions as saber rattling, believing that Moscow was trying to sow panic and discord within the Western alliance. The US intelligence community dismissed the notion that the Soviets truly feared an American nuclear attack. However, a 1990 investigation by the President's Foreign Intelligence Advisory Board (PFIAB) concluded that the Soviets were sincerely alarmed. The American military buildup, combined with threatening rhetoric, had made the Soviets "hyperdefensive" and had "inadvertently placed our relations with the Soviet Union on a hair trigger." Nate Jones's book *Able Archer 83* (2016) is the most comprehensive account of this crisis and includes the PFIAB report on pp. 67–178. See also Jones, "The 1983 War Scare"; Gates, *From the Shadows,* 270–273; B. B. Fischer, *Cold War Conundrum;* and Ermarth, "Observations on the 'War Scare' of 1983."

58. George L. Church, "Time's Men of the Year," *Time,* January 2, 1984, 8.

59. Hedrick Smith, "Andropov Is Spotted Being Driven to Work," *New York Times,* December 8, 1983, A8.

60. Henry Kamm, "Vatican Seeks to Mediate US and Soviet Rift," *New York Times,* December 5, 1983, A3. The Vatican Secretary of State, Cardinal Casaroli, met with Reagan on November 22, 1983. See Reagan, *Reagan Diaries,* 200.

61. Church, "Time's Men of the Year."

62. For the text of the speech, see Ronald Reagan, "The US-Soviet Relationship," January 16, 1984, *Department of State Bulletin* February 1984, 1–4, available at www.reaganlibrary.gov/research/speeches/11684a. For more detail about this address and its consequences, see B. A. Fischer, *Reagan Reversal;* "A Retrospective on the End of the Cold War," Oral History Conference sponsored by the Woodrow Wilson School of Public and International Affairs, Princeton University, February 26–27, 1993 (hereafter "Princeton Conference"), pp. 44–46; and Robert McFarlane and Jack Matlock remarks, Brown Conference, transcript.

63. See Jack Matlock's remarks, Brown Conference, transcript, p. 92. The US ambassador to Moscow, Arthur Hartman, also hand-delivered a copy to the Soviet Foreign Ministry and spoke with officials there about it.

64. McFarlane, *Special Trust,* 295; Michael Getler, "Positive Tone May Be Change of Tune," *Washington Post,* January 17, 1984. See also Matlock, *Reagan and Gorbachev,* 80–85; Shultz, *Turmoil and Triumph,* 463–467; and B. A. Fischer, *Reagan Reversal,* 32–40.

65. Matlock, Brown Conference, transcript, p. 85. Matlock went on to become the US ambassador to the USSR between 1987 and 1991.

66. Ibid., 89.

67. McFarlane briefing, January 1984, WHORM subject file SP 833 (Soviet/US Relations, WH 1/16/84) 168687–194999, available from the Reagan Presidential Library, White House Office of Record Management, www.reaganlibrary.gov /document-collection/whormsub.

68. Matlock, *Reagan and Gorbachev,* 78–79.

69. For a more detailed discussion of the events of fall of 1983 and their impact on subsequent policy toward the Soviet Union see B. A. Fischer, *Reagan Reversal,* 102–143.

70. Author interview with Robert McFarlane, July 7, 1995.

71. Reagan, *Reagan Diaries,* 199. This was the entry for November 18, 1983.

72. Douglas MacEachin in Brown Conference, transcript, pp. 243–244.

73. Jack Matlock in ibid., p. 243.

74. Douglas MacEachin in ibid., pp. 181–182, 242–245. See also Fritz W. Ermarth, "Observations on the 'War Scare' of 1983 from an Intelligence Perch," November 11, 2003, Parallel History Project on NATO and the Warsaw Pact, available at http:// web.archive.org/web/20060724160027/http://www.isn.ethz.ch/php/documents /collection_17/texts/ermarth.pdf.

75. Reagan, *Reagan Diaries,* 210.

76. Reagan, *An American Life,* 588–589.

77. Author interview with Robert McFarlane, July 7, 1995.

78. "Peace through strength" will be discussed in more detail in Chapter 3.

79. Ronald Reagan, Address to the Nation on Arms Reduction and Deterrence, November 22, 1982, *Weekly Compilation of Presidential Documents, 1982,* vol. 18, p. 1519.

80. Reagan, *An American Life,* 549. For a more detailed account of the president's antipathy to nuclear weapons, see Chapter 4.

81. Matlock, *Reagan and Gorbachev,* 78–79.

82. Reagan, *An American Life,* 269, 272–273.

83. Just as there is disagreement over whether the Reagan administration initially exaggerated the Soviet military threat, there is disagreement over whether the increase in US defense expenditures significantly increased US military capabilities. For instance, Raymond Garthoff, a longtime CIA Soviet military analyst, argues that, while the administration cultivated a perception of added strength in the mid-1980s, "[t]he real military relationship remained stable. The United States was not so weak in 1980 as pictured, nor so much stronger by 1984 or 1988; what changed was the official rhetoric and the public impression." Garthoff, *Great Transition,* 505.

84. Officials were also aware that Congress would not support unlimited increases in military spending. Increases in defense expenditures peaked in 1984, but by 1985 the rate of increase began to slow. The Reagan administration spent more than $2 trillion over eight years. See Garthoff, *Great Transition,* 505; and Lettow, *Ronald Reagan and His Quest,* 136–137.

85. George P. Shultz, memorandum to the president, "US-Soviet Relations in 1983," January 19, 1983, in Brown Conference, archival document no. 2.

86. Shultz, *Turmoil and Triumph,* 162–167.

87. Ibid., 270–271.

88. Matlock comments in Eric J. Schmertz, Natalie Datlof, and Alexej Ugrinsky, eds., *President Reagan and the World* (Westport, CT: Greenwood Press, 1997), 123. See also Matlock remarks, Princeton Conference, p. 44.

89. For example, see Reagan's handwritten note to Yuri Andropov dated July 11, 1983, in which he assured the Soviet leader that the United States was dedicated to "the course of peace and the elimination of the nuclear threat." "You and I share an enormous responsibility for the preservation of stability in the world," he added. "I believe we can fulfill that responsibility but to do so will require a more active level of exchange than we have heretofore been able to establish." Ronald Reagan to Yuri Andropov, letter dated July 11, 1983, Executive Secretariat, National Security Council (NSC), Head of State, Box 38, Ronald Reagan Presidential Library, Simi Valley, California.

90. Matlock, *Reagan and Gorbachev,* 77.

91. Ibid., 81.

92. Author interview with Robert McFarlane, July 7, 1995.

93. Author interview with Caspar Weinberger, July 31, 1995.

94. Author interview with Robert McFarlane, July 7, 1995.

95. Matlock, *Reagan and Gorbachev,* 75.

96. Author interview with Jack Matlock, September 19, 1995.

97. Shultz, *Turmoil and Triumph,* 531–532.

98. Reagan, *An American Life,* 12.

99. Reagan remarks during Afternoon Plenary, November 19, 1985. Reagan-Gorbachev Meeting in Geneva, Transcript of Afternoon Plenary, November 19, 1985, folder "Geneva Memcons (Reagan-Gorbachev Memcons Geneva Meeting 11/19–21, 1985) [1/3]," box 92137, Jack F. Matlock files, Ronald Reagan Library.

100. See Reagan's remarks at the opening tete-a-tete in Geneva, November 19, 1985, Memorandum of Conversation, Morning Tete-a-Tete, November 19, 1985, folder "Geneva Memcons (Reagan-Gorbachev Memcons Geneva Meeting 11/19–21, 1985) [1/3]," box 92137, Jack F. Matlock files, Ronald Reagan Library.

101. For example, see Robert C. McFarlane, Memorandum for the President, "Checklist of US-Soviet Issues: Status and Prospects," February 18, 1984, folder US-USSR Relations [January–April 1984] (1 of 3), box OA 92219, Jack F. Matlock files, Ronald Reagan Library; and Shultz, *Turmoil and Triumph*, 266. Shultz implies that the four-part agenda was adopted in 1983, but McFarlane and Matlock suggest it was adopted in early 1984. See Matlock comments, Brown Conference, transcript, p. 176–177.

102. Robert McFarlane, Brown Conference, transcript, p. 67.

103. Reagan, *An American Life*, 12.

104. Robert McFarlane, Brown Conference, transcript, p. 67.

105. Gorbachev remarks during the opening tete-a-tete in Geneva, November 19, 1985, Memorandum of Conversation, Morning Tete-a-Tete, November 19, 1985, folder "Geneva Memcons (Reagan-Gorbachev Memcons Geneva Meeting 11/19–21, 1985) [1/3]," box 92137, Jack F. Matlock files, Ronald Reagan Library.

106. See the memoranda of conversations from the Geneva meetings, November 19 and 20, 1985, Reagan-Gorbachev Meeting in Geneva, November 19, 1985, folder "Geneva Memcons (Reagan-Gorbachev Memcons Geneva Meeting 11/19–21, 1985) [1/3]," box 92137, Jack F. Matlock files, Ronald Reagan Library.

107. Reagan, *An American Life*, 641.

108. Mikhail Gorbachev, *Memoirs* (London: Doubleday, 1996), 405.

109. Celestine Bohlen, "Gorbachev Discusses 'Lively' Exchanges," *Washington Post*, November 22, 1985.

110. See Gorbachev, *Memoirs*, especially 453.

111. See Shultz, *Turmoil and Triumph*, 526–527. See also NSDD 75, January 1983. Although many suggest that the Reagan Doctrine was global in scope, it applied only to Afghanistan, Cambodia, Angola, Nicaragua, and Mozambique. See James M. Scott, *Deciding to Intervene: The Reagan Doctrine and American Foreign Policy* (Durham, NC: Duke University Press, 1996); Peter W. Rodman, *More Precious than Peace: The Cold War and the Struggle for the Third World* (New York: Scribner's Sons, 1994); Odd Arne Westad, *The Global Cold War* (Cambridge, UK: Cambridge University Press, 2007); and Garthoff, *Great Transition*, 692–715.

112. See Garthoff, *Great Transition*, 696–697.

113. Much of the impetus for this assistance—although not all—came from Congress. In March 1985 the president signed NSDD 166, which called for driving Soviet forces out of Afghanistan "by all means available." See Odd Arne Westad,

"Reagan's Anti-Revolutionary Offensive in the Third World," in Olav Njolstad, ed., *The Last Decade of the Cold War* (London: Frank Cass, 2004), 241–262; and Steve Coll, *Ghost Wars: The Secret Wars of the CIA, Afghanistan, and Bin Laden from the Soviet Invasion to September 10, 2001* (New York: Penguin Books, 2004).

114. Coll, *Ghost Wars,* 11.

115. See James Graham Wilson, *The Triumph of Improvisation: Gorbachev's Adaptability, Reagan's Engagement, and the End of the Cold War* (Ithaca, NY: Cornell University Press, 2014).

116. See Reagan, *An American Life,* 698–701.

117. See Fred Ikle's comments to Paul Lettow in Lettow, *Ronald Reagan and His Quest,* 239. President Bush and National Security Adviser Brent Scowcroft, who took office in January 1989, remained skeptical. "We see the light at the end of the tunnel," Scowcroft famously explained, "We're just not sure if it is an on-coming train." Bush and Scowcroft, *A World Restored,,* 8.

118. Don Oberdorfer, *The Turn,* 299.

119. The five meetings were in Geneva (November 1985), Reykjavik (October 1986), Washington (December 1987), Moscow (May–June 1988), and New York (December 1988).

120. Ronald Reagan, "The US-Soviet Relationship," 3.

2. Reagan's Military Buildup

1. Richard Halloran, "Weinberger Begins Drive for Big Rise in Military Budget," *New York Times,* March 5, 1981; Richard Halloran, "Reagan to Request $38B Increase in Military Outlays," *New York Times,* March 5, 1981; Hedrick Smith, "US Priorities: Basic Reversal," *New York Times,* March 5, 1981.

2. For example, see Andrew E. Busch, "Ronald Reagan and the Defeat of the Soviet Empire," *Presidential Studies Quarterly* 27, no. 3 (Summer 1997): 451–467; and Peter Schweizer, *Victory* (New York: Atlantic Monthly Press, 1994).

3. Richard V. Allen, "The Man Who Won the Cold War," January 30, 2000, Hoover Digest, available at http://www.hoover.org/publications/hoover-digest /article/7398. See also Allen's remarks for the Ronald Reagan Oral History Project, Miller Center of Public Affairs, University of Virginia (hereafter "Miller Center Oral History Project"), May 28, 2002, p. 26, available at http://millercenter.org /president/reagan/oralhistory/richard-allen.

4. In his memoirs Reagan discusses the manner in which his views on the Soviet Union changed during his presidency. See Ronald Reagan, *An American Life* (New York: Pocket Books, 1990), especially 588–590.

5. For Reagan's views before becoming president, see Kiron K. Skinner, Annelise Anderson, and Martin Anderson, eds., *Reagan, in His Own Hand* (New York: Free Press, 2001).

6. Ibid., 12.

7. Ibid., 31.

8. Reagan, "Soviet Workers," May 25, 1977, in ibid., 146–147.

9. Reagan, "Salt II," September 11, 1979, in ibid., 63. Reagan was quoting journalist Ben Stein.

10. Ronald Reagan, Commencement Address at Notre Dame, May 17, 1981, *Weekly Compilation of Presidential Documents, 1981,* vol. 17, p. 532. Note the language: Reagan spoke of "transcending" and "dismissing" communism, not "destroying," "defeating," or "bankrupting" it.

11. Ronald Reagan, news conference, June 16, 1981, ibid., 633.

12. Reagan, *An American Life,* 551–552. See also Ronald Reagan, *The Reagan Diaries,* ed. Douglas Brinkley (New York: HarperCollins, 2007), 75.

13. Ronald Reagan, speech to members of British Parliament, June 8, 1982, *Department of State Bulletin,* July 1982, 27.

14. Shultz quoted in Peter Schweizer, *Victory: The Reagan Administration's Secret Strategy That Hastened the Collapse of the Soviet Union* (New York: Atlantic Monthly Press, 1994), xiii.

15. For example, see National Intelligence Estimate 11-3/8-79, *Soviet Capabilities for Strategic Nuclear Conflict through the 1980s* (March 17, 1980), vol. 1, pp. 3–4. This document was largely written by Stansfield Turner, Director of Central Intelligence (DCI). For an example of the disagreements between the CIA and the Defense Intelligence Agency regarding Soviet military capabilities and intentions, see National Intelligence Estimate 11-3/8-80, *Soviet Capabilities for Strategic Nuclear Conflict through 1990,* (December 16, 1980), p. B-13. This estimate included two different sets of key judgments. By 1982 CIA analysts realized they had been consistently overestimating Soviet military strength. See Raymond L. Garthoff, "Estimating Soviet Intentions and Capabilities," in Gerald K. Haines and Robert E. Leggett, eds., *Watching the Bear: Essays on CIA's Analysis of the Soviet Union* (Washington, DC: Center for the Study of Intelligence, CIA, 2003), available at https://www.cia.gov/library/center -for-the-study-of-intelligence/csi-publications/books-and-monographs/watching -the-bear-essays-on-cias-analysis-of-the-soviet-union/article05.html.

16. See the conclusions of the House Permanent Select Committee on Intelligence—Review Committee (HPSCI Review Committee), *An Evaluation of CIA's Analysis of Soviet Economic Performance 1970–1990,* November 18, 1991, and Douglas J. MacEachin, "CIA Assessments of the Soviet Union: The Record versus the Charges," which originally appeared as an unclassified Intelligence Monograph published by the CIA's Center for the Study of Intelligence (CSI 96–001), May 1996. The article is available at https://www.cia.gov/library/center-for-the-study-of-intelligence /csi-publications/csi-studies/studies/97unclass/soviet.html. Information on the deteriorating Soviet economy was not always reflected in the more formal National Intelligence Estimates. See Garthoff, ""Estimating Soviet Intentions and Capabilities."

17. Douglas J. MacEachin, "CIA Assessments of the Soviet Union: The Record versus the Charges." MacEachin became Special Assistant to the Director of Central Intelligence for Arms Control in March 1989 and served as the Deputy Director for Intelligence at the CIA from March 1993 through June 1995.

18. Stansfield Turner, Joint Economic Committee, *Allocation of Resources in the Soviet Union and China—1980: Hearings before the Subcommittee on Priorities and Economy in Government of the Joint Economic Committee,* Part 3, 95th Cong., June 23, 1977, p. 2, available at https://www.cia.gov/library/center-for-the-study-of-intelligence/csi-publications/books-and-monographs/cia-assessments-of-the-soviet-union-the-record-versus-the-charges/appa.html.

19. National Foreign Assessments Center, Office of Economic Research, *Soviet Economic Problems and Prospects,* ER 77-10436U, July 1977, Records of the Directorate of Intelligence, pp. ii–v, available at https://www.cia.gov/library/center-for-the-study-of-intelligence/csi-publications/books-and-monographs/cia-assessments-of-the-soviet-union-the-record-versus-the-charges/appa.html.

20. Noel E. Firth and James H. Noren, *Soviet Defense Spending: A History of CIA Estimates, 1950–1990* (College Station: Texas A&M University Press, 1998), 75–97. Firth and Noren were longtime Soviet analysts in the CIA. By 1983 CIA analysts had revised their estimates. They believed Soviet defense spending had only been increasing about 1 percent per year during the mid- to late 1970s and early 1980s.

21. Stansfield Turner, Joint Economic Committee, *Allocation of Resources in the Soviet Union and China—1980: Hearings before the Subcommittee on Priorities and Economy in Government of the Joint Economic Committee,* Part 6, 96th Cong., 2nd sess., September 25, 1980, p. 105, available at https://www.cia.gov/library/center-for-the-study-of-intelligence/csi-publications/books-and-monographs/cia-assessments-of-the-soviet-union-the-record-versus-the-charges/appa.html.

22. Directorate of Intelligence, Office of Soviet Analysis, *Soviet Society in the 1980s: Problems and Prospects,* SOV 82-12026X, December 1982, pp. iii–v. Excerpt available at https://www.cia.gov/library/center-for-the-study-of-intelligence/csi-publications/books-and-monographs/cia-assessments-of-the-soviet-union-the-record-versus-the-charges/appa.html.

23. Directorate of Intelligence, Offices of Soviet Analysis, *The Slowdown in Soviet Industry, 1976–82,* SOV 83-10093, June 1983, p. iii, available at https://www.cia.gov/library/center-for-the-study-of-intelligence/csi-publications/books-and-monographs/cia-assessments-of-the-soviet-union-the-record-versus-the-charges/appa.html.

24. MacEachin, "CIA Assessments of the Soviet Union: The Record versus the Charges."

25. Directorate of Intelligence, Office of Soviet Analysis, *Gorbachev's Economic Agenda: Promises, Potentials, and Pitfalls,* SOV 85-10165, September 1985, p. iii, https://www.cia.gov/library/readingroom/docs/19850901.pdf. This paper details the systemic problems with the Soviet economy.

26. Directorate of Intelligence, Office of Soviet Analysis, *Gorbachev's Modernization Program: Implications for Defense,* SOV 86-10015X, March 1986, pp. 9, 10. Excerpt available at https://www.cia.gov/library/center-for-the-study-of-intelligence/csi-publications/books-and-monographs/cia-assessments-of-the-soviet-union-the-record-versus-the-charges/appa.html. In the spring of 1986 the CIA rejected the

DIA's projections for Soviet spending on strategic weapons, stating that they were far too high and therefore incompatible with Gorbachev's plans for modernization. See the memorandum from Douglas J. MacEachin, Director, Office of Soviet Analysis, to the Deputy Director for Intelligence (Richard J. Kerr), "NIE 11-3/8: Force Projections," April 22, 1986, Records of the Directorate of Intelligence, Job 90-60135R, Box 2, Folder 20.

27. Douglas MacEachin in Nina Tannenwald, ed., "Understanding the End of the Cold War, 1980–1987," an oral history conference sponsored by the Watson Institute, Brown University, May 7–10, 1998 (hereafter "Brown Conference"), transcript, p. 180. See also Firth and Noren, *Soviet Defense Spending*, 85–97, 202–204.

28. Gates quoted in Tim Weiner, *Legacy of Ashes: The History of the CIA* (New York: Doubleday, 2007), 382, 376.

29. Lehman quoted in ibid., 379.

30. Douglas MacEachin, Musgrove Conference, in Svetlana Savranskaya, Thomas Blanton, and Vladislav Zubok, eds., *Masterpieces of History: The Peaceful End of the Cold War in Europe, 1989* (New York: Central European University Press, 2010), 182–183. Many Soviet analysts have echoed MacEachin's sentiments. For example, see James Noren, "CIA's Analysis of the Soviet Economy," in Haines and Leggett, *Watching the Bear;* and Garthoff, "Estimating Soviet Intentions and Capabilities." See also Weiner, *Legacy of Ashes*, 375–422.

31. George H. W. Bush quoted in Weiner, *Legacy of Ashes*, 376.

32. Gates quoted in ibid., 379; and Robert M. Gates, *From the Shadows: The Ultimate Insider's Story of Five Presidents and How They Won the Cold War* (New York: Simon and Schuster, 1996), 209, 223–224.

33. Such a process took place after the CIA's Soviet analysts wrote a report concluding that the Soviet Union was not planning to use chemical weapons in Europe. Douglas MacEachin, Musgrove Conference, in Savranskaya et al., *Masterpieces of History*, 182–183.

34. Douglas MacEachin in Brown Conference, transcript, p. 180.

35. Gates, *From the Shadows*, 329.

36. Ibid., 330–334.

37. For example, see *Soviet Defense Spending: Recent Trends and Future Prospects* (written in 1982 but published in July 1983); and CIA, Office of Soviet Analysis, Joint Economic Committee Briefing Paper (September 14, 1983), pp. 8–11, 18. For a discussion about the process of reassessment and its aftermath, see Firth and Noren, *Soviet Defense Spending*,75–97; James Noren, "CIA's Analysis of the Soviet Economy," in Haines and Leggett, *Watching the Bear;* and Raymond L. Garthoff, *The Great Transition* (Washington, DC: Brookings Institution, 1994), 41–42.

38. Firth and Noren, *Soviet Defense Spending*, 77.

39. Ibid., 92; Noren, "CIA's Analysis."

40. A study by the General Accounting Office concluded that during the 1980s the Department of Defense had deliberately exaggerated Soviet military capabilities so as to gain congressional funding for US military programs. See Tim Weiner,

"Military Accused of Lies over Arms," *New York Times,* June 28, 1993, A10; Garthoff, *Great Transition,* 507n10; and Firth and Noren, *Soviet Defense Spending,* 77–93.

41. Douglas MacEachin, Musgrove Conference, in Savranskaya et al., *Masterpieces of History,* 183–184.

42. Douglas MacEachin in Brown Conference, transcript, p. 55 (italics added).

43. Although publication of the revised spending estimates was delayed, pressure from other quarters of the government ultimately forced the information to be released. See Firth and Noren, *Soviet Defense Spending,* 70, 88–92. Gates's recommendation was not wholly without merit: it was notoriously difficult to establish precise figures on Soviet defense spending. Information was sketchy, and the centralized command economy meant that lines between civilian and military expenditures were often blurred. Establishing a conversion rate for the ruble was also difficult, as was determining the cost of specific weapons and projects. Policy makers were usually not familiar with the methodological difficulties in determining these spending estimates and often overlooked the uncertainties surrounding the figures. They misunderstood defense spending estimates to be a concrete measure of Soviet military strength.

44. For example, although Agency experts continued to reaffirm their belief that growth in Soviet procurement of new weapons had stalled in the mid-1970s, an early draft of what came to be NIE 11-3 (1986) predicted a much higher growth in Soviet defense spending than the CIA's Soviet experts were forecasting. In many respects the draft directly contradicted the findings of the Soviet experts in the CIA. As director of the CIA's Soviet analysis section, MacEachin tried to call attention to the inconsistency. He wrote a formal memo to be distributed to the national security community explaining that the projected figures in the draft NIE were based on faulty methodology. This led to estimates of Soviet spending that were considerably higher than what Moscow had traditionally devoted to defense, he pointed out. Such figures were even more circumspect given Gorbachev's economic modernization program, which called for reductions in defense spending. MacEachin's memo, however, barely saw the light of day. Gates saw to it that only a few copies were distributed outside of the Agency. In a "last-ditch attempt" to make the NIE more credible, MacEachin proposed a footnote to the document in which the CIA's reservations could be noted. Gates rejected the idea. Firth and Noren, *Soviet Defense Spending,* 84–86.

45. Ibid., 96. Gates became the Acting DCI after Casey had a seizure in December 1986. He was replaced by William Webster in May 1987.

46. Weiner, *Legacy of Ashes,* 377. See also George P. Shultz, *Turmoil and Triumph: My Years as Secretary of State* (New York: Charles Scribner's Sons, 1993), 507.

47. Shultz quoted in Weiner, *Legacy of Ashes,* 644. In an attempt to get around the problem of politicized and inaccurate intelligence, Shultz began inviting senior Soviet analysts from the CIA to his office so that he could talk directly with them. The secretary used the meetings to probe for information that may have been filtered

out of official briefings. In March 1986 Shultz invited Douglas MacEachin to brief him about Soviet economic difficulties and their potential impact. MacEachin told Shultz that Gorbachev's reforms would probably be insufficient for correcting Soviet economic problems and that by 1987 or 1988 Soviet leaders would have to confront the issue of reducing defense spending. Shultz agreed. See George Shultz, Miller Center Oral History Project, December 18, 2002, p. 27, http://web1.millercenter .org/poh/transcripts/ohp_2002_1218_shultz.pdf; and Douglas MacEachin, Musgrove Conference, in Savranskaya et al., *Masterpieces of History,* 184.

48. Garthoff, "Estimating Soviet Intentions and Capabilities." For similar sentiment by other Soviet experts see the remarks by Abraham Becker, Senior Economist Emeritus at RAND, as paraphrased in James Noren, "CIA's Analysis of the Soviet Economy," in Haines and Leggett, *Watching the Bear.*

49. Douglas MacEachin, Musgrove Conference, in Savranskaya et al., *Masterpieces of History,* 182–183.

50. McFarlane remarks in Brown Conference, transcript, pp. 31–32.

51. "US National Security Strategy," National Security Decision Directive (hereafter NSDD) 32 (May 20, 1982). See also NSDD 75 (January 17, 1983), which states, "The coming 5–10 years will be a period of considerable uncertainty in which the Soviets may test US resolve by continuing the kind of aggressive international behavior which the US finds unacceptable." All NSDDs from the Reagan years are available at www.fas.org/irp/offdocs/nsdd.

52. George Shultz, memorandum to the president, "US-Soviet Relations in 1983," January 19, 1983, in Brown Conference, archival document no. 2.

53. Lawrence Eagleburger, "Review of US Relations with the Soviet Union," February 1, 1983, *American Foreign Policy: Current Documents, 1983* (Washington, DC: Department of State, 1985), 501–502.

54. Douglas MacEachin remarks in Brown Conference, transcript, pp. 12–13.

55. See Ronald Reagan, Address to the Nation on Arms Reduction and Deterrence, November 22, 1982, *Weekly Compilation of Presidential Documents, 1982,* vol. 18, p. 1519; Ronald Reagan, Address to the Nation, March 23, 1983, *Weekly Compilation of Presidential Documents, 1983,* vol. 19, pp. 442–448; Ronald Reagan, "The US-Soviet Relationship," January 16, 1984, *Department of State Bulletin,* February 1984, 2–4; Ronald Reagan, Address to the United Nations General Assembly, September 24, 1984, *American Foreign Policy: Current Documents, 1984* (Washington, DC: Department of State, 1986), 220–227.

56. There were disagreements within the administration as to whether the United States was in the process of falling behind the Soviet Union in the arms race or was already in second place.

57. Reagan, Address to the Nation on Arms Reduction and Deterrence, November 22, 1982.

58. Reagan, "The US-Soviet Relationship," January 16, 1984, 3.

59. George Shultz, "US-Soviet Relations in the Context of US Foreign Policy," remarks before the Senate Foreign Relations Committee, June 15, 1983, *American*

Foreign Policy: Current Documents, 1983 (Washington, DC: Department of State, 1985), 508.

60. Reagan, "The US-Soviet Relationship," January 16, 1984, 1–4.

61. Reagan, Address to the United Nations General Assembly, September 24, 1984, 224.

62. Shultz, "US-Soviet Relations in the Context of US Foreign Policy," June 15, 1983.

63. Jack Matlock remarks in Brown Conference, transcript, p. 272.

64. Douglas MacEachin and Jack Matlock, remarks at Musgrove Conference, in Savranskaya et al., *Masterpieces of History,* 186. See also Matlock remarks in Brown Conference, transcript, pp. 86, 88; and Jack F. Matlock, *Reagan and Gorbachev: How the Cold War Ended* (New York: Random House, 2004), 75–76.

65. Reagan, *An American Life,* 267–268 (italics in original).

66. Matlock remarks in Brown Conference, transcript, pp. 86, 88.

67. "US Relations with the USSR," NSDD 75, January 17, 1983, available at www.fas.org/irp/offdocs/nsdd.

68. Richard Pipes, *Vixi: Memoirs of a Non-Belonger* (New Haven: Yale University Press, 2003), 201–202. See also Paul Lettow, *Ronald Reagan and His Quest to Abolish Nuclear Weapons* (New York: Random House, 2005), 77–78.

69. Richard Halloran, "Pentagon Draws Up First Strategy for Fighting a Long Nuclear War," *New York Times,* May 30, 1982, 12. As Halloran noted, the Fiscal Year 1984–1988 Defense Guidance (approved in March 1982) stated that the United States should develop weapons that were "difficult for the Soviets to counter, impose disproportionate cuts, open up new areas of major military competition and obsolesce previous Soviet investment." For a more detailed discussion about the internal debates surrounding this document see Raymond L. Garthoff, *The Great Transition: American-Soviet Relations and the End of the Cold War* (Washington, DC: Brookings Institution, 1994), 36–39.

70. Tyler Esno has argued that between May and September 1982 there was an "interlude of economic warfare" in which the Reagan administration sought to stress the Soviet economy by attempting to restrict Soviet revenue from the Siberian gas pipeline. This policy caused friction with West European allies and was therefore short-lived. In November 1982 NSDD 66 explicitly rejected the notion of waging economic warfare against the Soviet Union. See Tyler Esno, "Reagan's Economic War on the Soviet Union," *Diplomatic History* 42, no. 2 (2018): 281–304.

71. NSDD 66, November 29, 1982, available at http://www.fas.org/irp/offdocs/nsdd.

72. Caspar Weinberger, November 19, 2002, Miller Center Oral History Project, p. 10, available at http://web1.millercenter.org/poh/transcripts/ohp_2002_1119_weinberger.pdf.

73. Author interview with Caspar Weinberger, July 31, 1995.

74. Carlucci quoted in James Mann, *Rebellion of Ronald Reagan,* (New York: Viking Press, 2009), 251.

75. Lettow, *Ronald Reagan and His Quest,* 55; and Alexander Haig, *Caveat* (New York: Macmillan, 1984), 20–36, 95–116.

76. George P. Shultz, memorandum to the president, "US-Soviet Relations in 1983," January 19, 1983 (italics added), in Brown Conference, archival document no. 2.

77. George Shultz, Miller Center Oral History Project, December 18, 2002, p. 13, http://web1.millercenter.org/poh/transcripts/ohp_2002_1218_shultz.pdf.

78. Eagleburger, "Review of US Relations with the Soviet Union," February 1, 1983, 500.

79. Shultz, Miller Center Oral History Project, December 18, 2002, pp. 18–19.

80. Matlock, *Reagan and Gorbachev,* 75–76.

81. US Policy Guidance, November 19, 1983, in ibid., 76 (boldface in original).

82. Pipes quoted in Lettow, *Ronald Reagan and His Quest,* 78.

83. Jack Matlock, Musgrove Conference, in Savranskaya et al., *Masterpieces of History,* 206.

84. Matlock remarks in Brown Conference, transcript, pp. 86, 88.

85. The precise nature of American vulnerability was murky. Some officials indicated that the United States had already fallen behind, while others suggested the United States would fall behind if current trends continued. See NSDD 12, "Strategic Forces Modernization Program," October 1, 1981; and NSDD 32, "US National Security Strategy," May 20, 1982, available at www.fas.org/irp/offdocs /nsdd. See also Reagan, "Address to the Nation on Arms Reduction and Deterrence," November 22, 1982.

86. Ronald Reagan, "The US-Soviet Relationship," January 16, 1984.

3. The Strategic Defense Initiative

1. George P. Shultz, *Turmoil and Triumph: My Years as Secretary of State* (New York: Charles Scribner's Sons, 1993), 249.

2. Caspar Weinberger, *Fighting for Peace: Seven Critical Years in the Pentagon* (New York: Warner Books, 1990), 306.

3. Shultz, *Turmoil and Triumph,* 250.

4. Weinberger, *Fighting for Peace,* 308.

5. Ronald Reagan, *An American Life* (New York: Pocket Books, 1990), 549 (italics in original). For more on Reagan's antinuclearism see Martin Anderson and Annelise Anderson, *Reagan's Secret War: The Untold Story of His Fight to Save the World from Nuclear Disaster* (New York: Crown Publishers, 2009); Paul Lettow, *Ronald Reagan and His Quest to Abolish Nuclear Weapons* (New York: Random House, 2005); and Beth A. Fischer, *The Reagan Reversal: Foreign Policy and the End of the Cold War* (Columbia: University of Missouri Press, 1997), 77–79, 102–156.

6. Reagan, *An American Life,* 258. See also Reagan, interview with NHK Television, November 11, 1983, *Public Papers of President Ronald Reagan 1983,* 1582, available at www.reaganlibrary.gov/research/speeches/111183c.

7. Reagan, *An American Life,* 550; see also 265.

8. Martin Anderson, *Revolution* (New York: Harcourt Brace Jovanovich, 1987), 72.

9. Edwin Meese III, *With Reagan: The Inside Story* (Washington, DC: Regnery Gateway, 1992), 186–187.

10. Ronald Reagan, "The President's News Conference," January 29, 1981, *Public Papers of President Ronald Reagan, 1981,* 55–62, available at www.reaganlibrary.gov/research/speeches/12981b.

11. Anderson and Anderson, *Reagan's Secret War,* 93–94.

12. Ronald Reagan, Address to the Japanese Diet, November 11, 1983, available at www.reaganlibrary.gov/research/speeches/111183a. Lou Cannon, "President Hails Japan as Partner," *Washington Post,* November 11, 1983. See also Shultz, *Turmoil and Triumph,* 189.

13. Reagan, *An American Life,* 547.

14. Ibid., 13, 547, 550.

15. Ibid., 584.

16. Robert McFarlane in Nina Tannenwald, ed., "Understanding the End of the Cold War, 1980–1987," an oral history conference sponsored by the Watson Institute, Brown University, May 7–10, 1998 (hereafter "Brown Conference"), transcript, p. 144.

17. Reagan, *An American Life,* 548. See also the memoranda of conversations between Reagan and Gorbachev at both the Geneva and Reykjavik summit meetings. Reagan-Gorbachev Meeting in Geneva, folder "Geneva Memcons (Reagan-Gorbachev Memcons Geneva Meeting 11/19–21, 1985) [1/3]," box 92137, Jack F. Matlock files, Ronald Reagan Library, Simi Valley, California.

18. Ronald Reagan, remarks to the Institute for Foreign Policy Analysis, March 14, 1988, available at the American Presidency Project, http://www.presidency.ucsb.edu/ws/?pid=35547#axzz1nhyn0pZ8.

19. The Soviet Union already had a defensive system around Moscow, which it was allowed to retain. The treaty stipulated that the United States would be allowed to field a system of its own, which it did in 1975 around an ICBM site in Grand Forks, North Dakota. The US system was taken out of service after 133 days, however, owing to costs. In October 1985 the Reagan administration reinterpreted the provisions of the ABM Treaty to mean that SDI was allowable, which generated a backlash in the United States. On September 20, 1987, the Senate Foreign Relations Committee issued a report declaring that this interpretation was "the most flagrant abuse of the Constitution's treaty power in 200 years of American history." The Senate subsequently passed a resolution restating its understanding that SDI was not legal under the terms of the ABM Treaty. In 1987 the Senate attached the Byrd Amendment to the INF Treaty, which declared that the United States shall not adopt a treaty interpretation that differs from the common understanding of that treaty shared by the executive and Senate at the time of the Senate's original consent to the treaty. On this debate see Sam Nunn, "Interpreting the ABM Treaty," *Washington Quarterly,* Autumn 1987, 45–57; Abraham D. Sofaer, "The ABM Treaty:

Legal Analysis in the Political Cauldron," *Washington Quarterly,* Autumn 1987, 59–75; and Harold Hongju Koh, *The National Security Constitution: Sharing Power after the Iran-Contra Affair* (New Haven: Yale University Press, 1990), 43.

20. Reagan, *An American Life,* 547.

21. Ibid.

22. George Keyworth, William Clark, and Edwin Meese were among this group. On the genesis of SDI see Frances FitzGerald, *Way Out There in the Blue: Reagan, Star Wars, and the End of the Cold War* (New York: Touchstone, 2000); and Lettow, *Ronald Reagan and His Quest,* among others.

23. Reagan, Address to the Nation on Defense and National Security, March 23, 1983, *Public Papers of President Ronald Reagan, 1983,* available at www.reaganlibrary .gov/research/speeches/32383d.

24. Ibid.

25. Reagan, *An American Life,* 550.

26. For example, see question-and-answer session with reporters, March 29, 1983, *Public Papers of the President, 1983,* 463–470, available at www.reaganlibrary .gov/research/speeches/32983a. See also the transcripts from NSC meetings in Jason Saltoun-Ebin, ed., *The Reagan Files: The Untold Story of Reagan's Top-Secret Efforts to Win the Cold War* (Jason Saltoun-Ebin, 2010), 349–422.

27. Gorbachev remarks, transcript of the afternoon session of the Reykjavik summit, October 11, 1986, Brown Conference, archival document no. 37.

28. Bessmertnykh remarks in "A Retrospective on the End of the Cold War," Oral History Conference sponsored by the Woodrow Wilson School of Public and International Affairs, Princeton University, February 26–27, 1993 (hereafter "Princeton Conference"), Session 2, p. 95.

29. Reagan, *American Life,* 550.

30. Martin Anderson, *Revolution* (New York: Harcourt Brace Jovanovich, 1987), 73.

31. Shultz, *Turmoil and Triumph,* 466, 509.

32. Lou Cannon interview with Frank Carlucci, as recounted in Lou Cannon, *President Reagan: The Role of a Lifetime* (New York: Simon & Schuster, 1991), 291.

33. Haig quoted in ibid., 301.

34. Shultz, *Turmoil and Triumph,* 189.

35. Ibid., 466.

36. For more on officials' reactions to SDI, see ibid., 246–264; Weinberger, *Fighting for Peace,* 291–329; and Martin Anderson, *Revolution,* 80–99.

37. Shultz, *Turmoil and Triumph,* 249–251. The "evil empire" language was removed from the final draft. For more on officials' reactions to SDI and the ensuing internal battles see ibid., 246–264; Weinberger, *Fighting for Peace,* 291–329; and Martin Anderson, *Revolution,* 80–99.

38. Weinberger, *Fighting for Peace,* 291–329.

39. Ibid., 291.

40. Ibid., 300–301.

41. Ibid., 305.

42. Robert McFarlane discussed the military, moral, and economic rationale behind SDI in Brown Conference, transcript, pp. 45–49, 54. See also Robert C. McFarlane, "Consider What Star Wars Accomplished," *New York Times,* August 24, 1993.

43. McFarlane, "Consider What Star Wars Accomplished." See also McFarlane remarks in Brown Conference, transcript, pp. 45–49, 54.

44. McFarlane remarks in Brown Conference, transcript, pp. 45–49, 54.

45. Watkins quoted in Lettow, *Ronald Reagan and His Quest,* 94.

46. As subsequent chapters will detail, Gorbachev eventually reduced his demands, asking Reagan to agree to restrict the program to the laboratory, rather than pledging to deploy any future weapons that might be developed. By 1987 Gorbachev was no longer perturbed by SDI and dropped the matter so as to focus on arms reductions.

47. McFarlane, "Consider What Star Wars Accomplished"; McFarlane remarks in Brown Conference, transcript, pp. 47–48. See also the memo from Thomas Thorne to Secretary Shultz, INR Intelligence Brief, "The Soviet Need for Arms Control: Negative Factors," July 26, 1985, Brown Conference, archival document no. 11. On Reagan officials' views about SDI see Lettow, *Ronald Reagan and His Quest,* especially 145–170.

48. McFarlane remarks in Brown Conference, transcript, pp. 45–49, 54. Paul Nitze, the administration's representative to the INF talks before becoming the special adviser to the president and the secretary of state on arms control, also thought it most useful as a bargaining chip. On Reagan officials' views about SDI see Lettow, *Ronald Reagan and His Quest,* especially 145–170.

49. Weinberger, *Fighting for Peace,* 308, 313.

50. Ibid., 316.

51. McFarlane remarks in Brown Conference, transcript, pp. 45–49, 54.

52. Ibid., pp. 45–49.

53. National Security Council Meeting, February 3, 1987, transcript in Saltoun-Ebin, *The Reagan Files,* 355.

54. National Security Council Meeting, February 10, 1987, transcript in ibid., 366–368.

55. Ronald Reagan, *The Reagan Diaries,* ed. Douglas Brinkley (New York: HarperCollins, 2007), 352.

56. Reagan, *An American Life,* 665–666 (italics in original).

57. Ibid., 547–548.

58. NSC Meeting, February 10, 1987, transcript in Saltoun-Ebin, *The Reagan Files,* 370.

59. Matlock remarks, Princeton Conference, Session 2, pp. 81–82.

60. NSC Meeting, September 8, 1987, transcript in Saltoun-Ebin, *The Reagan Files,* 385–387.

61. Ibid.

62. Carlucci remarks, Princeton Conference, Session 2, p. 54.

63. NSC Meeting on Arms Control and SDI, February 10, 1987, transcript in Saltoun-Ebin, *The Reagan Files,* 366–368, 371.

64. Reagan made similar remarks during a radio address that he wrote himself on October 10, 1978. See "Rostow I," October 10, 1987, in Kiron K. Skinner, Annelise Anderson, and Martin Anderson, eds., *Reagan: In His Own Hand* (New York: Free Press, 2001), 98.

65. NSC Meeting on Arms Control and SDI, February 10, 1987, transcript in Saltoun-Ebin, *The Reagan Files,* 365–372. Nitze's official titles were Chief Negotiator for the Intermediate-Range Nuclear Forces Treaty (1981–1984) and the Special Adviser to the President and the Adviser to the Secretary of States on Arms Control (1984–1989). Rowny was the Chief Strategic Negotiator to the Strategic Arms Reduction Treaty [START] Talks.

66. The Arms Control Support Group (ACSG) conducted a study called THRESHER RAIN, which looked into the idea of transferring SDI to an international body. See Saltoun-Ebin, *The Reagan Files,* 367.

67. Rowny remarks in Brown Conference, transcript, p. 63.

68. McFarlane quoted in Lettow, *Ronald Reagan and His Quest,* 91.

69. Watkins quoted in ibid., 94.

70. CIA, "Possible Soviet Responses to the US Strategic Defense Initiative," September 12, 1983, available at http://www.fas.org/spp/starwars/offdocs/m8310017 .htm. These predictions proved remarkably accurate as subsequent chapters will detail. The CIA also noted that over the long term the Soviets could continue to develop and deploy their own ballistic missile defense (BMD) systems, elements of which the Kremlin would continue to pursue even in the absence of SDI.

71. Shultz, *Turmoil and Triumph,* 189.

72. Reagan, *An American Life,* 550.

4. Soviet New Thinking and the Withdrawal from Afghanistan

1. Rich Lowry, "The Liberal Reagan," *New York Times,* February 18, 2007.

2. Andrew E. Busch, "Ronald Reagan and the Defeat of the Soviet Empire," *Presidential Studies Quarterly* 27, no. 3 (Summer 1997): 451–467.

3. Gorbachev explained New Thinking most comprehensively in his May 23, 1986, address to the Soviet Foreign Ministry and his Address to the United Nations on December 7, 1988. He would bristle when American counterparts referred to "democratic values." He believed it was more correct to call them "universal values."

4. This chapter focuses on New Thinking, while the next chapter focuses on Soviet military doctrine.

5. Gorbachev announced the unilateral suspension of nuclear testing on July 29, 1985. The United States conducted an underground nuclear test on February 3, 1987.

6. The Intermediate Nuclear Forces Treaty was signed in December 1987, while the Strategic Arms Reduction Treaty (START) was signed on July 31, 1991. START came into force on December 5, 1994.

7. Gorbachev made the "bleeding wound" remark in February 1986. See Raymond L. Garthoff, *The Great Transition* (Washington, DC: Brookings Institution, 1994), 727.

8. "Address by Mikhail Gorbachev at the UN General Assembly Session (Excerpts)," December 07, 1988, History and Public Policy Program Digital Archive, CWIHP Archive, http://digitalarchive.wilsoncenter.org/document/116224.

9. Robert Gates, *From the Shadows: The Ultimate Insider's Story of Five Presidents and How They Won the Cold War* (New York: Simon & Schuster, 1996), 290.

10. On the Soviet reform movement, see Robert D. English, *Russia and the Idea of the West: Gorbachev, Intellectuals, and the End of the Cold War* (New York: Columbia University Press, 2000); Andrei Grachev, *Gorbachev's Gamble* (Cambridge, UK: Polity, 2008); Vladislav M. Zubok, *A Failed Empire: The Soviet in the Cold War Union from Stalin to Gorbachev* (Chapel Hill: University of North Carolina Press, 2007); Archie Brown, *Seven Years That Changed the World: Perestroika in Perspective* (Oxford, UK: Oxford University Press, 2007); and Anatoly Chernyaev, *My Six Years with Gorbachev* (University Park: Pennsylvania State University Press, 2000), among others.

11. On the important role that scientific exchanges played in developing new ideas about Soviet security, see Matthew Evangelista, *Unarmed Forces: The Transnational Movement to End the Cold War* (Ithaca, NY: Cornell University Press, 1999); and English, *Russia and the Idea of the West,* 117–158. Not all reformers were Western oriented, however. Some sought to improve socialism, while others focused on modernizing the current Soviet system. See Grachev, *Gorbachev's Gamble,* 30–34.

12. English, *Russia and the Idea of the West,* 117.

13. See National Security Archive, "Alexander Yakovlev and the Roots of Soviet Reforms," National Security Archive Electronic Briefing Book no. 168, October 26, 2005, available at http://www.gwu.edu/~nsarchiv/NSAEBB/NSAEBB168/index.htm.

14. While in Canada Yakovlev developed a close friendship with Prime Minister Pierre Trudeau. Trudeau named his second son, Alexandre, or "Sacha," after Yakovlev.

15. Grachev, *Gorbachev's Gamble,* 35, 24.

16. Vladislav M. Zubok, "Soviet Foreign Policy from Détente to Gorbachev, 1975 to 1985," in Melvyn P. Leffler and Odd Arne Westad, eds., *The Cambridge History of the Cold War,* vol. 3 (Cambridge, UK: Cambridge University Press, 2010), 93.

17. Mikhail Gorbachev, *Memoirs* (New York: Doubleday, 1995), 113–114.

18. Oleg Grinevsky in Nina Tannenwald, ed., "Understanding the End of the Cold War, 1980–1987," an oral history conference sponsored by the Watson Institute, Brown University, May 7–10, 1998 (hereafter "Brown Conference"), transcript, pp. 14–15. For a more complete discussion of the decline of the USSR, see Jack F. Matlock Jr., *Autopsy on an Empire* (New York: Random House, 1995), and Garthoff, *The Great Transition,* among others.

19. Georgy Shakhnazarov in Brown Conference, transcript, pp. 26–27.

20. Oleg Grinevsky in ibid., p. 19. Brezhnev died in November 1982, Andropov died in February 1984, and Chernenko in March 1985.

21. Vladimir Slipchenko in ibid., p. 25.

22. English, *Russia and the Idea of the West*, 147.

23. Oleg Grinevsky in Brown Conference, transcript, p. 16.

24. Ibid., p. 20.

25. Chernyaev's list is found in Grachev, *Gorbachev's Gamble*, 39.

26. Chernyaev, *My Six Years*, 5.

27. For Gorbachev's perspective on new thinking and reform see Gorbachev, *Memoirs;* and Mikhail Gorbachev, *Mandate for Peace* (Toronto: Paperjacks, 1987).

28. English, *Russia and the Idea of the West*, 180–186 (quotation on 180).

29. Yakovlev quoted in English, *Russia and the Idea of the West*, 184.

30. For more on Gorbachev's early years, see Gorbachev, *Memoirs.*

31. Andrei Grachev, *Gorbachev's Gamble*, 46.

32. Gorbachev, *Memoirs*, 401.

33. Mikhail Gorbachev, *Life and Reforms* (Moscow: Novosti, 1995), vol. 1, 334, cited in Zubok, "Soviet Foreign Policy from Détente to Gorbachev," 110; and Grachev, *Gorbachev's Gamble*, 7. Anatoly Chernyaev has claimed that "70 or 80 per cent" of Soviet GNP went to military expenditures in the decades before President Reagan came to office. Chernyaev in Brown conference, transcript, p. 81. Oleg Grinevsky also claims that "80 per cent of [Soviet] industry, either directly or indirectly, was tied into or working for the military-industrial complex." See Brown Conference, transcript, p. 14. Experts on the Soviet economy argue that the issue was so complex we may never know how much the Soviets spent on defense. See Noel E. Firth and James H. Nolan, *Soviet Defense Spending: A History of CIA Estimates, 1950–1990* (College Station: Texas A&M University Press, 1998), 188–190, 196.

34. Slipchenko in Brown Conference, transcript, p. 25.

35. Shakhnazarov in ibid., p. 28.

36. Chernyaev in ibid., pp. 33, 223.

37. The following chapter discusses military policy in more detail. Former Soviet officials contend that there was a secondary reason for wanting to end the arms race: they wanted to repair the image of the USSR. They were concerned that the Soviet Union was viewed internationally as an aggressor that violated human rights. See remarks by Sergei Tarasenko and Anatoly Chernyaev in ibid., pp. 74–80.

38. Gorbachev quoted in Jonathan Schell, "The Gift of Time: The Case for Abolishing Nuclear Weapons," *The Nation*, February 2–9, 1998, available at www.gci.ch/GreenCrossFamily/gorby/newspeeches/interviews/thenation.html.

39. Ibid.

40. Gorbachev quoted in Vladislav M. Zubok, "Gorbachev's Nuclear Learning: How the Soviet Leader Became a Nuclear Abolitionist," *Boston Review*, April–May 2000, available at http://bostonreview.net/BR25.2/zubok.html.

41. Anatoly Chernyaev, Musgrove Conference, in Svetlana Savranskaya, Thomas Blanton, and Vladislav Zubok, eds., *Masterpieces of History: The Peaceful End of the Cold War in Europe, 1989* (New York: Central European University Press, 2010), 188–189.

42. Melvyn P. Leffler, *For the Soul of Mankind* (New York: Hill and Wang, 2007), 376–377.

43. Gorbachev, *Memoirs,* 401.

44. Chernyaev interview with Grachev, in Grachev, *Gorbachev's Gamble,* 55.

45. Gorbachev interview with Grachev, in ibid.

46. Gorbachev, *Memoirs,* 402. In his memoirs Gorbachev summarizes *Perestroika* and provides context about his intentions and hopes for that book.

47. Gorbachev, *Memoirs,* 402–403.

48. Georgy Shakhnazarov, Musgrove Conference, in Savranskaya et al., *Masterpieces of History,* 115.

49. Ibid., 116. Likewise, see Anatoly Chernyaev, Musgrove Conference, in ibid., 113–114.

50. Gorbachev, *Memoirs,* 402.

51. Grachev, *Gorbachev's Gamble,* 55.

52. Anatoly Chernyaev details the opposition to Gorbachev's reforms in *My Six Years.*

53. Kate Connolly, "German Who Flew to Red Square during the Cold War Admits It was Irresponsible," *Guardian,* May 14, 2012, available at http://www.guardian.co.uk /world/2012/may/14/german-red-square-cold-war. Rust, who describes himself as "a bit of an oddball," says he was expressing his frustration over the slow pace of superpower disarmament. He is currently an analyst for a Zurich-based investment bank and is training to be a yoga teacher.

54. See William E. Odom, *The Collapse of the Soviet Military* (New Haven: Yale University Press, 1998); and Zubok, "Gorbachev's Nuclear Learning." Odom notes that the reputational damage to the military provided more leeway for Gorbachev to pursue his reforms.

55. English, *Russia and the Idea of the West,* 215–216.

56. Shevardnadze quoted in ibid., 217.

57. Chernyaev, *My Six Years,* 66.

58. Gorbachev, *Mandate for Peace,* 330.

59. Ibid.

60. Chernyaev, *My Six Years,* 64.

61. Grachev, *Gorbachev's Gamble,* 81.

62. Velikhov quoted in English, *Russia and the Idea of the West,* 217.

63. Grachev, *Gorbachev's Gamble,* 81. Gorbachev then instructed Soviet arms control negotiators to accept American demands for on-site verification of conventional arms agreements, a pathbreaking concession that led the way to the INF Treaty. In September 1986 Gorbachev invited Reagan to a meeting in Reykjavik in the hopes of catalyzing an improvement in relations and a reduction in nuclear

arms. And in January 1987 the Soviet leader called for the global elimination of nuclear weapons by 2000.

64. Akhromeyev quoted in David E. Hoffman, *The Dead Hand: The Untold Story of the Cold War Arms Race and Its Dangerous Legacy* (New York: Anchor Books, 2009), 252.

65. Eduard Shevardnadze, *The Future Belongs to Freedom* (New York: Free Press, 1991), 175.

66. Grachev, *Gorbachev's Gamble*, 22–23.

67. Kirilenko quoted in Odd Arne Westad, *"Concerning the Situation in 'A'*: New Russian Evidence on the Soviet Intervention in Afghanistan," *Cold War International History Project Bulletin,* issue 8–9 (Winter 1996–1997): 129–130. See also Odd Arne Westad, *The Global Cold War* (Cambridge, UK: Cambridge University Press, 2007), 316–330.

68. Transcript of the March 18, 1979, Politburo meeting in *Cold War International History Project Bulletin,* issue 8–9 (Winter 1996–1997): 141–142.

69. Ibid. It is unclear how committed Andropov was to these views and to what extent he was simply going along with what he perceived to be the prevailing view.

70. Ibid.

71. Taraki was killed in October 1979. As head of the KGB Andropov had overseen several unsuccessful attempts to remove Amin from power, including two assassination attempts. When Amin demanded that the Soviet ambassador to Afghanistan be replaced in November, Ustinov and Andropov decided that the only way to resolve the issue was to deploy troops so as to remove Amin. Westad, *"Concerning the situation in 'A,'"* 130.

72. David A. Welch and Odd Arne Westad, eds., *The Intervention in Afghanistan and the Fall of Détente,* Nobel Symposium 95, September 17–20, 1995 (Oslo: The Norwegian Nobel Institute, 1996), 90–93. See also Vladislav M. Zubok, "Soviet Foreign Policy from Détente to Gorbachev, 1975 to 1985," in Leffler and Westad, *The Cambridge History of the Cold War,* vol. 3, 102–104.

73. Grachev, *Gorbachev's Gamble,* 101. Kirilenko had reservations, but ultimately signed the decision to intervene. Kosygin was absent and almost certainly would have opposed the measure.

74. Despite the signing of the SALT II Treaty, the June 1979 superpower summit had yielded few results. Moreover, in the fall NATO had decided to deploy US Pershing II missiles to Western Europe.

75. "New Evidence on the 1978–1979 War in Afghanistan," *Centerpoint: Newsletter from the Woodrow Wilson Center for Scholars,* June 2002, 1–2.

76. Grachev, *Gorbachev's Gamble,* 33. As casualties rose during the early 1980s, domestic opposition to the war increased. Although Moscow had mounted a large-scale propaganda campaign assuring Soviet citizens that all was going well, the increasing number of coffins and wounded soldiers indicated otherwise.

77. The Carter administration had been providing nonlethal aid to the resistance since mid-1979 and began an active program of covert military assistance to

the mujahedin immediately after the Soviets invaded. "New Evidence on the 1978–1979 War in Afghanistan," 2.

78. Zubok, "Soviet Foreign Policy from Détente to Gorbachev," 104.

79. Westad, *"Concerning the Situation in 'A,'"* 132. See also Gates, *From the Shadows,* 319–321; and Steve Coll, *Ghost Wars: The Secret History of the CIA, Afghanistan, and Bin Laden, from the Soviet Invasion to September 10, 2001* (New York: Penguin, 2004).

80. Grinevsky in Brown Conference, transcript, p. 83.

81. Tarasenko in ibid., p. 84.

82. Gorbachev interview with Grachev, *Gorbachev's Gamble,* 48.

83. Gorbachev quoted in Chernyaev, *My Six Years,* 42.

84. Ibid. Karmal refused to believe Gorbachev's warning, however, and continued to pressure Moscow for increased assistance. Gorbachev has indicated that Karmal's resistance, along with the opposition of Soviet military leaders to withdrawal, slowed the process considerably. Grachev, *Gorbachev's Gamble,* 102.

85. Gorbachev, *Memoirs,* 406.

86. George P. Shultz, *Turmoil and Triumph: My Years as Secretary of State* (New York: Charles Scribner's Sons, 1993), 895.

87. Georgy Shakhnazarov, Musgrove Conference, in Savranskaya et al., *Masterpieces of History,* 114.

88. Ibid.

89. Chernyaev in Brown Conference, transcript, p. 81.

90. Arbatov memorandum to Charles W. Kegley Jr., November 7, 1991, quoted in Kegley, "How Did the Cold War Die? Principles for an Autopsy," in *Mershon International Studies Review* 38 (1994): 14–15. See also Slipchenko in Brown Conference, transcript, pp. 264–265.

5. Moscow Calls Off the Arms Race

1. Andrew E. Busch, "Ronald Reagan and the Defeat of the Soviet Empire," *Presidential Studies Quarterly* 27, no. 3 (Summer 1997): 451–467.

2. Ronald Reagan, *An American Life* (New York: Pocket Books, 1990), 548. See also Ronald Reagan, "It Was Star Wars Muscle That Wrestled Arms Race to a Halt," *Los Angeles Times,* July 31, 1991, available at http://articles.latimes.com/1991–07–31 /local/me-16_1_arms-race.

3. Noel E. Firth and James H. Noren, *Soviet Defense Spending: A History of CIA Estimates, 1950–1990* (College Station: Texas A&M University Press, 1998), 75–80, 100–103, 111; Raymond L. Garthoff, *The Great Transition: American-Soviet Relations and the End of the Cold War* (Washington, DC: Brookings Institution, 1994), 505–508; and Matthew Evangelista, *Unarmed Forces: The Transnational Movement to End the Cold War* (Ithaca, NY: Cornell University Press, 1999), 240–245. These trends are based on CIA estimates, which are arguably the most accurate. The

estimates from the Stockholm International Peace Research Institute (SIPRI) were based on Moscow's "official" budget, which was mostly propaganda, as former Soviet officials have acknowledged.

4. Evangelista, *Unarmed Forces,* 291–292, 294.

5. Moreover, part of the increase in the purchase of aircraft and missiles was to offset a decline in the purchase of such weapons between 1975 and 1984. Firth and Noren, *Soviet Defense Spending,* 101.

6. Evangelista, *Unarmed Forces,* 291–292, 294; Firth and Noren, *Soviet Defense Spending,* 100–102, 107–109, 111; and James Noren, "CIA's Analysis of the Soviet Economy," in Gerald K. Haines and Robert E. Leggett, eds., *Watching the Bear: Essays on CIA's Analysis of the Soviet Union* (Washington, DC: Center for the Study of Intelligence, CIA, 2003), available at https://www.cia.gov/library/center-for-the-study-of-intelligence/csi-publications/books-and-monographs/watching-the-bear-essays-on-cias-analysis-of-the-soviet-union/article02.html. The increase in defense spending in 1985–1987 included increased outlays for aircraft and missiles for the war in Afghanistan, but was largely due to an 8.2 percent increase in spending for interceptor and SAM elements. This increase represented a return to historic levels of spending for strategic defense after a decade of decline, and will be discussed further later in the chapter.

7. Determining the exact amount that the Soviet Union spent on defense was—and continues to be—exceedingly difficult. The best explanation of the many challenges of such estimates is given in Firth and Noren, *Soviet Defense Spending.* Soviet officials themselves disagree on how much the USSR spent on its military. Such information was a tightly controlled secret, and Gorbachev recalls that he was not privy to such data until he became general secretary. According to Gorbachev, by the late 1970s total defense-related expenses, including indirect costs, consumed approximately 40 percent of the Soviet budget. Gorbachev's foreign affairs adviser, Anatoly Chernyaev, has placed this figure much higher, claiming that "70 or 80 per cent" of Soviet spending went to military expenditures in the decades before President Reagan came to office. Oleg Grinevsky, the Soviet arms negotiator, has also claimed that "80 percent of [Soviet] industry, either directly or indirectly, was tied into or working for the military-industrial complex." The fact is, the precise amount that Moscow spent on its defense may never be known. See Mikhail Gorbachev, *Life and Reforms* (Moscow: Novosti, 1995), vol. 1, 334, cited in Vladislav M. Zubok, "Soviet Foreign Policy from Détente to Gorbachev, 1975 to 1985" in Melvyn P. Leffler and Odd Arne Westad, eds., *The Cambridge History of the Cold War,* vol. 3 (Cambridge, UK: Cambridge University Press, 2010), 110; Chernyaev in Nina Tannenwald, ed., "Understanding the End of the Cold War, 1980–1987," an oral history conference sponsored by the Watson Institute, Brown University, May 7–10, 1998 (hereafter "Brown Conference"), transcript, p. 81; and Grinevsky in Brown Conference, transcript, p. 14.

8. Soviet military doctrine was a central component of its foreign policy, and really had no direct equivalent among Western states. It was defined by the Party

leadership—not simply the military—and entailed a statement about the political purposes of war and its character, as well as a scientific-technical component regarding how war should be waged, how the armed forces should be organized, and what technical equipment was needed to insure combat readiness. See David Holloway, *The Soviet Union and the Arms Race* (New Haven: Yale University Press, 1985).

9. Yuri Andropov's conviction that the Reagan administration was plotting a nuclear attack is a case in point.

10. See Andrei Grachev, *Gorbachev's Gamble: Soviet Foreign Policy and the End of the Cold* War (Cambridge, UK: Polity, 2008), 34–39. These young reformers were also less inclined to defer uncritically to the demands of the military-industrial complex.

11. At times parity included not only matching US military capabilities, but the broader capabilities of NATO as well.

12. For example, see Aleksei Arbatov, "Parity and Reasonable Sufficiency," *International Affairs* 10 (1988): 75–87; Arbatov, "How Much Defense Is Sufficient?" *International Affairs* 4 (1989): 31–44; and Makhmut Gareyev, "The Revised Soviet Military Doctrine," *Bulletin of the Atomic Scientists* 44, no. 10 (December 1988): 30–34.

13. Gareyev, "The Revised Soviet Military Doctrine," 33.

14. Arbatov, "Parity and Reasonable Sufficiency"; and Arbatov, "How Much Defense Is Sufficient?" Moreover, if the Reagan administration was indeed seeking to entice the USSR into a costly arms race, as some suspected, reducing Soviet defense expenditures would foil its plans.

15. Chernyaev in Brown Conference, transcript, p. 139.

16. Politburo meeting of June 20, 1988, quoted in Grachev, *Gorbachev's Gamble,* 18–19. Gromyko was a central part of the "leadership" to which he referred.

17. Mikhail Gorbachev, *Perestroika: New Thinking for Our Country and the World* (New York: Harper and Row, 1987), 219.

18. Vladimir Slipchenko in Brown Conference, transcript, pp. 137–138.

19. Ibid.

20. Marshal Akhromeyev headed the work on developing this new doctrine and initially encountered resistance within the Ministry of Defense, the General Staff, and the Academy of Defense. By 1986 there was general agreement on the need for the new doctrine. The Warsaw Pact endorsed the doctrine during its May 1987 meeting in Berlin. See remarks by Vladimir Slipchenko in Brown Conference, transcript, pp. 107–108, 171–172, 287–289.

21. As the CIA belatedly discovered, the Soviet Union had not been building up its arsenal at an increasing clip during the late 1970s and 1980s. The rate at which the Kremlin procured new weapons peaked in 1975 and remained stable for the ensuing decade. The CIA also estimated that the growth of Soviet military spending declined between 1970 and 1974 and then decelerated even more sharply between 1975 and 1984. Firth and Noren, *Soviet Defense Spending,* 75–80, 100–103, 111; Garthoff, *The Great Transition,* 505–508; and Evangelista, *Unarmed Forces,* 240–245.

22. Slipchenko in Brown Conference, transcript, pp. 107–108.

23. Robert M. Gates, *From the Shadows: The Ultimate Insider's Story of Five Presidents and How They Won the Cold War* (New York: Simon & Schuster, 1996), 539.

24. Perle quoted in Paul Lettow, *Ronald Reagan and His Quest to Abolish Nuclear Weapons* (New York: Random House, 2005), 215.

25. Kenneth L. Adelman, *The Great Universal Embrace: Arms Summitry—A Skeptic's Account* (New York: Simon & Schuster, 1989), 304.

26. Kenneth L. Adelman, "United States and Soviet Relations: Reagan's Real Role in Winning the Cold War," in Eric J. Schmertz, Natalie Datlof, and Alexej Ugrinsky, eds., *President Reagan and the World* (Westport, CT: Greenwood Press, 1997), 85–86 (italics in original).

27. Roald Z. Sagdeev, *The Making of a Soviet Scientist* (New York: John Wiley & Sons, 1994), especially 123–124; Evangelista, *Unarmed Forces*, 234; and David E. Hoffman, *The Dead Hand: The Untold Story of the Cold War Arms Race and Its Dangerous Legacy* (New York: Anchor Books, 2009), 215–218. The 1972 Anti-Ballistic Missile (ABM) Treaty banned the development, testing, and deployment of ABM systems. The Soviets were allowed to retain their existing ABM system around Moscow and to make minor safety upgrades. In accordance with the treaty, the United States built an ABM system in North Dakota, but shut it down soon after it became operational, owing to costs. For more on the Soviet response to SDI see Evangelista, *Unarmed Forces*, 233–248. In October 1984 a laser from Sary Shagan tracked the US space shuttle *Challenger*, causing temporary systems malfunctions and discomfort for the astronauts. The Soviets said this was in retaliation for the proposed SDI project.

28. Sagdeev, *The Making of a Soviet Scientist*, 123–124, 202–211. See also Evangelista, *Unarmed Forces*, 235–236.

29. Steven J. Zaloga, "Red Star Wars," *Jane's Intelligence Review* 9, no. 5 (May 1, 1997): 205–208. On the Chelomei project see Hoffman, *Dead Hand*, 217–218. The Chelomei proposal was not the first of its kind. In the summer of 1950 Peter Kapitsa, the founder of the Soviet Institute of Physical Problems, had proposed an antiballistic missile system similar to SDI, but based on microwave emissions rather than laser beams. In 1968–1969 Soviet scientists also explored a strategic defense system using particle beam accelerators. Sagdeev, *The Making of a Soviet Scientist*, 96, 99, 123–124.

30. Sagdeev, *The Making of a Soviet Scientist*, 209–211. Deputy Defense Minister General Vitaly Shabanov chaired this commission. See also Anatoly Zak, "The Black Russians and the Black Horses," 2005, available at http://www.thelivingmoon .com/45jack_files/03files/Black_Russian_002.html.

31. Sagdeev, *The Making of a Soviet Scientist*, 273. See also David Reynolds, "Science, Technology, and the Cold War," in Leffler and Westad, *The Cambridge History of the Cold War*, vol. 3, 378–399.

32. Hoffman, *Dead Hand*, 217–218.

33. Slipchenko in Brown Conference, transcript, p. 51.

34. Aleksander Bessmertnykh in "A Retrospective on the End of the Cold War," Oral History Conference sponsored by the Woodrow Wilson School of Public and International Affairs, Princeton University, February 26–27, 1993 (hereafter "Princeton Conference"), Session 2, pp. 22–24.

35. Andropov interview with *Pravda,* March 26, 1983.

36. Rowny and Karpov had been working together for a while and had developed something of a rapport. Rowny was miffed at the outburst and eventually followed Karpov out of the room to continue the discussion. Karpov explained to Rowny that he was under instructions to denounce SDI in the strongest terms. "I did, and now let's go back to our meeting," Karpov added as he walked back to the conference room. Rowny remarks in Brown Conference, transcript, p. 148.

37. Nikolai Detinov in ibid., pp. 37–39. See also Yevgeny Velikhov, Roald Sagdeev, and Andrei Kokoshin, eds., *Weaponry in Space: The Dilemma of Security* (Moscow: Mir, 1986); and Hoffman, *Dead Hand,* 217–218. The Soviet Union had good information on the US Ballistic Missile Defense (BMD) program. Much information about the basic technology was public knowledge or could be discovered through scrutinizing the annual military budgets approved by Congress. In addition, the Soviets learned a fair amount of additional information through espionage. See Evangelista, *Unarmed Forces,* 235.

38. Velikhov quoted in Hoffman, *Dead Hand,* 217–218.

39. Evangelista, *Unarmed Forces,* 239.

40. In fact, the Soviet Union had itself violated the ABM Treaty by building a phased-array radar in Krasnoyarsk, Siberia. Initial Soviet plans for the station were in keeping with the treaty, but in a cost-cutting measure it was moved to a location that was prohibited. Moscow finally admitted to the violation in October 1989.

41. Anatoly Dobrynin, *In Confidence: Moscow's Ambassador to Six Cold War Presidents* (New York: Random House, 1995), 534–5. The Reagan administration had reinterpreted sections of the treaty to mean that SDI was permissible. Both the Soviets and, eventually, the US Senate disagreed with the administration.

42. Detinov remarks in Brown Conference, transcript, p. 38.

43. The Velikhov Committee had acknowledged such a possibility. Nikolai Detinov remarks in Brown Conference, transcript, p. 42. Yuri Andropov and Boris Ponomarev, chief of the International Department, shared these concerns. See Grachev, *Gorbachev's Gamble,* 238n20.

44. Anonymous Soviet official, Princeton Conference, Session 2, p. 63.

45. See remarks of Andrei Gromyko, January 7, 1985, second meeting in Geneva with George Shultz, in Brown Conference, archival document no. 8.

46. Hoffman, *Dead Hand,* 214–215.

47. Grachev, *Gorbachev's Gamble,* 94. Hoffman writes that by the summer of 1985 weapons specialists had drawn up a proposal that included 137 projects in the design and testing phase, 34 scientific research projects, and 115 programs in fundamental science. *Dead Hand,* 215.

48. Slipchenko remarks in Brown Conference, transcript, pp. 51–52. US analysts had reached similar conclusions about the possibility of building a defense system that was 99 percent effective. See Frances FitzGerald, *Way Out There in the Blue: Reagan, Star Wars, and the End of the Cold War* (New York: Touchstone, 2000). Robert McFarlane, President Reagan's National Security Adviser, agreed with Slipchenko's estimates that 60 warheads might find their targets, as well as his argument that it would have been cheaper for the USSR to counter SDI than it would have been for the United States to deploy it. Still, he hoped it might lead to additional costs that would pressure the Soviet system. See Brown Conference, transcript, pp. 53–54.

49. Slipchenko in Brown Conference, transcript, pp. 51–52. Such an "asymmetric response" was an innovation in Soviet foreign policy, as Moscow had typically sought to match or mimic US military capabilities. See Evangelista, *Unarmed Forces,* 238–239, 323.

50. Yakovlev quoted in FitzGerald, *Way Out There in the Blue,* 411.

51. Grinevsky relates that Marshal Akhromeyev called SDI "a chimera." See Brown Conference, transcript, p. 41.

52. Christopher Andrew and Oleg Gordievsky, *Instructions from the Centre: Top Secret Files on KGB Foreign Operations, 1975–1985* (London: Hodder and Stoughton, 1991), 112, 114. For more on the search see ibid., 106–115. Soviet suspicions were not entirely misplaced. In 1993, after an internal investigation, then–Secretary of Defense Les Aspin confirmed that the United States did indeed have a program aimed at deceiving the Kremlin about SDI. The internal investigation determined that during the 1980s the Pentagon developed a deception program designed "to feed the Kremlin half-truths and lies about the project" and to prevent the Soviet Union from obtaining accurate information about SDI research. See Tim Weiner, "Lies and Rigged 'Star Wars' Test Fooled the Kremlin, and Congress," *New York Times,* August 18, 1993, A6; Tim Weiner, "General Details Altered 'Star Wars' Test," *New York Times,* August 27, 1993; Eric Schmitt, "Aspin Disputes Report of 'Star Wars' Rigging," *New York Times,* September 10, 1993; and US General Accounting Office, *Ballistic Missile Defense: Records Indicate Deception Program Did Not Affect 1984 Test Results,* GAO NSIAD-94-219 (Washington, DC: US General Accounting Office, July 1994).

53. See Mikhail Gorbachev, *Memoirs* (New York: Doubleday, 1995), 407; Grachev, *Gorbachev's Gamble,* 94–95.

54. For more details on Velikhov's views, see Hoffman, *Dead Hand,* 219–220; and Sagdeev, *The Making of a Soviet Scientist,* 261, 264–270.

55. The CIA estimated that between 1975 and 1984 spending on strategic defense had been lower than at any time since the 1950s. The Central Committee's July 1985 approval of a missile defense research program restored funding to traditional levels and contributed to a short-term increase in Soviet defense expenditures in the mid-1980s. Gorbachev used both the Chernobyl accident and the Mathias Rust affair as an excuse to purge much of the top echelon of the Soviet military.

Thus, by 1988 he was in a stronger position to implement his plans. Between 1988 and 1990 funding for strategic defense dropped 4.5 percent per year. Hoffman, *Dead Hand,* 215, 219; Firth and Noren, *Soviet Defense Spending,* 108, 111 (Figure 5.5). As with any estimate about Soviet defense spending, these figures are subject to debate. The overall trend, however, appears credible.

56. Sagdeev, *The Making of a Soviet Scientist,* 272.

57. Theodore W. Karasik and Thomas M. Nichols, *Novoe Myshlenie and the Soviet Military: The Impact of Reasonable Sufficiency on the Ministry of Defense* (Santa Monica, CA: RAND Corporation, 1989), https://www.rand.org/pubs/papers/P7521.html.

58. April 7, 1985, and April 17, 1985.

59. Gorbachev letter to President Reagan, September 12, 1985, excerpted in Reagan, *An American Life,* 624.

60. See Mikhail Gorbachev's remarks at the opening tete-a-tete in Geneva, November 19, 1985. Memorandum of Conversation, Morning Tete-a-Tete, November 19, 1985, folder "Geneva Memcons (Reagan-Gorbachev Memcons Geneva Meeting 11/19–21, 1985) [1/3]," box 92137, Jack F. Matlock files, Ronald Reagan Library, Simi Valley, California.

61. Reagan, *An American Life,* 631. Reagan made the diary notation on November 5, after George Shultz relayed the likely Soviet position at the upcoming summit.

62. Gorbachev, *Memoirs,* 406.

63. Ibid., 407.

64. On the origins of this plan see Brown Conference, transcript, pp. 120–125.

65. Anatoly Chernyaev, *My Six Years with Gorbachev* (University Park: Pennsylvania State University Press, 2000), 45–46. The plan to abolish nuclear weapons had originated with Marshal Sergei F. Akhromeyev, the chief of the General Staff of the Soviet Armed Forces, a reformer who would go on to be Gorbachev's personal adviser. Akhromeyev was widely respected within the Soviet military-industrial complex. His support for the general secretary muted criticism within the military, although it did not eliminate it entirely.

66. Jack F. Matlock, *Reagan and Gorbachev: How the Cold War Ended* (New York: Random House, 2004), 178.

67. George P. Shultz, *Turmoil and Triumph: My Years as Secretary of State* (New York: Charles Scribner's Sons, 1993), 699–705; Matlock, *Reagan and Gorbachev,* 177–178. See also Ronald Reagan, *The Reagan Diaries,* ed. Douglas Brinkley (New York: HarperCollins, 2007), 383, 388. On the president's response see Brown Conference, transcript, pp. 128–133.

68. Anatoly Chernyaev's notes from March 24, 1986, Politburo session, Brown Conference, archival document no. 19 (italics in original).

69. Networks of Soviet and American scientists played an important role in keeping the general secretary updated on congressional opponents to SDI. Evangelista, *Unarmed Forces,* 324; see also 322, 325–327.

70. On September 20, 1987, the Senate Foreign Relations Committee released a report declaring that the Reagan administration's reinterpretation of the ABM Treaty was "the most flagrant abuse of the Constitution's treaty power in two hundred years of American history." The Senate also attached the Byrd Amendment to the INF Treaty, which declared that future presidents did not have the right to reinterpret treaties signed before they took office.

71. See the remarks by Nikolai Detinov, Oleg Grinevsky, and Anatoly Chernyaev in Brown Conference, transcript, pp. 37–45.

72. Anatoly Chernyaev's notes from May 5, 1986, Politburo session, Brown Conference, archival document no. 23.

73. Chernyaev, *My Six Years*, 81. On the preparations for the summit see ibid., 78–85. When the two leaders met on October 11, the president was not prepared for a full summit meeting. His delegation had anticipated that the conference would simply lay the groundwork for a future summit.

74. Anatoly Chernyaev's notes from October 4, 1986, and October 8, 1986, Politburo sessions, Brown Conference, archival document nos. 32, 33.

75. Shultz, *Turmoil and Triumph*, 760.

76. Transcript of the afternoon session of the Reykjavik summit, October 11, 1986, Brown Conference, archival document no. 37.

77. Shultz, *Turmoil and Triumph*, 772.

78. Chernyaev in Brown Conference, transcript, pp. 44–45.

79. Ibid.

80. Chernyaev, *My Six Years*, 85.

81. George P. Shultz, December 18, 2002, Ronald Reagan Oral History Project, Miller Center of Public Affairs, University of Virginia, available at http://web1.millercenter.org/poh/transcripts/ohp_2002_1218_shultz.pdf.

82. Chernyaev, *My Six Years*, 32. After twenty-six years in the International Department, Chernyaev became Gorbachev's senior foreign policy adviser in February 1986.

83. Transcripts from Reykjavik summit, October 12, 1986, morning session, Brown Conference, archival document no. 38, p. 8.

84. Palazhchenko, Princeton Conference, Session 2, pp. 95–96.

85. Alexander Yakovlev, Memorandum to Gorbachev, February 25, 1987, http://www.gwu.edu/~nsarchiv/NSAEBB/NSAEBB168/yakovlev03.pdf. The website says the document is "circa December 1986"; but, in a personal e-mail to the author, Svetlana Savranskaya, the translator, noted that the correct date is February 25, 1987.

86. Andrei Sakharov, *Moscow and Beyond* (New York: Knopf, 1999), 21. For an excellent study of this transnational group of scientists see Evangelista, *Unarmed Forces*.

87. The Soviet media covered the speeches closely, indicating both the Kremlin's approval and its commitment to glasnost. The fact that Von Hippel and Stone sat with Gorbachev also underscores the degree to which he agreed with their message.

88. Gorbachev quoted in Evangelista, *Unarmed Forces,* 329.

89. Anatoly Chernyaev's notes from Politburo sessions, February 23 and 26, 1987, Brown Conference, archival document no. 52. Even though Ligachev was a conservative who opposed many of Gorbachev's reforms, he was a strong proponent of disarmament. See Chernyaev's remarks in Brown Conference, transcript, p. 223.

90. Chernyaev's notes from Politburo sessions, February 23 and 26, 1987. Gorbachev dismissed Sokolov on May 30, 1987, in the wake of the Mathias Rust affair.

91. Gorbachev timed this speech to coincide with the Soviet Union's first nuclear test blast since 1985, ending the moratorium he had announced in April 1985. See Chernyaev notes from Politburo sessions on February 23 and 26, 1987.

92. Zubok in Odd Arne Westad, ed., *Reviewing the Cold War: Approaches, Interpretations, Theory* (London: Frank Cass, 2000), 349.

93. Anatoly Chernyaev's notes, October 12, 1986, Brown Conference, archival document no. 40.

94. Shultz, December 18, 2002, Ronald Reagan Oral History Project at Miller Center.

95. Yakovlev quoted in Richard Ned Lebow and Janice Gross Stein, "Reagan and the Russians," *Atlantic Monthly,* February 1994, 36.

96. CIA, "Possible Soviet Responses to the US Strategic Defense Initiative," September 12, 1983, available at http://www.fas.org/spp/starwars/offdocs/m8310017.htm.

97. Anatoly Chernyaev, Musgrove Conference, in Svetlana Savranskaya, Thomas Blanton, and Vladislav Zubok, eds., *Masterpieces of History: The Peaceful End of the Cold War in Europe, 1989* (New York: Central European University Press, 2010), 200.

98. Garthoff, *The Great Transition,* 775.

6. The Triumph of Diplomacy and Leadership

1. Chernyaev interview with Matthew Evangelista, *Unarmed Forces: The Transnational Movement to End the Cold War* (Ithaca, NY: Cornell University Press, 1999), 335.

2. Many Soviet experts believe Gorbachev's attempts at reform caused the USSR to collapse. Absent these reforms, the Soviet Union could have continued a long, slow economic decline. For example, see Douglas MacEachin, "CIA Assessments of the Soviet Union: The Record versus the Charges," *Studies in Intelligence* 1, no. 1 (1997): 57–65.

3. See Paul Lettow, *Ronald Reagan and His Quest to Abolish Nuclear Weapons* (New York: Random House, 2005).

4. Ronald Reagan, *An American Life* (New York: Pocket Books, 1990), 550.

5. For example, see National Security Decision Directive (NSDD) 12, "Strategic Forces Modernization Program" (October 1, 1981), and NSDD-32 "US National Security Strategy," (May 20, 1982), available at www.fas.org/irp/offdocs/nsdd.

6. Ronald Reagan, Remarks to the Institute for Foreign Policy Analysis, March 14, 1988, available at the American Presidency Project, http://www.presidency.ucsb .edu/ws/?pid=35547#axzz1nhyn0pZ8.

7. Ronald Reagan, "The US-Soviet Relationship," January 16, 1984, *Department of State Bulletin,* February 1984, 4.

8. For an interesting discussion about Reagan's communication skills and the effect he may have had on public opinion see Reed L. Welch, "The Great Communicator: Rhetoric, Media, and Leadership Style," in Andrew L. Johns, ed., *A Companion to Ronald Reagan* (New York: Wiley Blackwell, 2015), 74–95.

9. For example, see Kiron K. Skinner, Annelise Anderson, and Martin Anderson, eds., *Reagan, in His Own Hand* (New York: Free Press, 2001).

10. For example, see the NSC meetings on February 10, 1987, and September 8, 1987, on arms control issues in Jason Saltoun-Ebin, ed., *The Reagan Files: The Untold Story of Reagan's Top-Secret Efforts to Win the Cold War* (Jason Saltoun-Ebin, 2010), 365–388. Relations among administration officials had become so tense that Secretary of State George Shultz refused to speak during the latter meeting.

11. Alexander M. Haig Jr., *Caveat: Realism, Reagan, and Foreign Policy* (New York: Macmillan Publishing Co., 1984), 355–356.

12. Reagan, *An American Life,* 269–270.

13. Ibid., 270. In his letter Reagan offered to lift the grain embargo that President Carter had imposed on the USSR after it invaded Afghanistan. Haig was especially opposed to this gesture.

14. Deaver quoted in Lou Cannon, *President Reagan: The Role of a Lifetime* (New York: Simon & Schuster, 1991), 298–300. For copies of both letters see Saltoun-Ebin, *The Reagan Files,* 11–17.

15. Reagan, *An American Life,* 273.

16. Anatoly Dobrynin, *In Confidence* (New York: Times Books, 1995), 605.

17. Ibid., 532–533. Secretary Haig has said that he was at times "astonished" at the difference between Reagan's more hawkish public statements and his private remarks about the need for peace and nuclear disarmament. Jack Matlock has made similar observations, agreeing with Dobrynin that Reagan didn't seem to notice or be perturbed by these inconsistencies. See Cannon, *President Reagan: The Role of a Lifetime,* 301.

18. Anatoly Chernyaev, *My Six Years with Gorbachev* (University Park: Pennsylvania State University Press, 2000), 103–104. The original was in italics to underscore its importance.

19. Gorbachev quoted in Andrei Grachev, *Gorbachev's Gamble* (Cambridge, UK: Polity, 2008), 175.

20. Mikhail Gorbachev, *Memoirs* (New York: Doubleday, 1995), 412–413.

21. Politburo meeting, October 22, 1986, in Nina Tannenwald, ed., "Understanding the End of the Cold War, 1980–1987," an oral history conference sponsored by the Watson Institute, Brown University, Providence, Rhode Island, May 7–10, 1998 (hereafter "Brown Conference"), archival document no. 42.

22. Ibid.

23. Gorbachev quoted in Chernyaev, *My Six Years,* 143.

24. Anatoly Chernyaev, Musgrove Conference, in Svetlana Savranskaya, Thomas Blanton, and Vladislav Zubok, eds., *Masterpieces of History: The Peaceful End of the Cold War in Europe, 1989* (New York: Central European University Press, 2010), 188–189.

25. Gorbachev, *Memoirs,* 402.

26. Jack F. Matlock Jr., "Foreword," in Chernyaev, *My Six Years,* xi. For example, see Mikhail Gorbachev and Zdenek Mlynar, *Conversations with Gorbachev on Perestroika, the Prague Spring, and the Crossroads of Socialism* (New York: Columbia University Press, 2002), 141; Chernyaev, *My Six Years;* and Anatoly Chernyaev remarks in Brown Conference, transcript, pp. 100, 155.

27. For example, see Ronald Reagan, "The US-Soviet Relationship," January 16, 1984, *Department of State Bulletin,* February 1984, 1–4, available at www.reaganlibrary .gov/research/speeches/11684a.

28. For more on the administration's plans to call attention to the president's address see Memorandum from Jack F. Matlock to Robert C. McFarlane, "Action Plan for President's Speech," January 12, 1984, WHORM: Subject File, File Folder SP833 200000-204999, Ronald Reagan Presidential Library, Simi Valley, California.

29. Andrei Grachev, *Gorbachev's Gamble: Soviet Foreign Policy at the End of the Cold War* (Cambridge, UK: Polity Press, 2008), 41.

30. Anatoly S. Chernyaev, Brown Conference, transcript, pp. 65, 80–81. See also Jack Matlock remarks, ibid., pp. 91–92; and Chernyaev, Musgrove Conference, in Savranskaya et al., *Masterpieces of History,* 200; and William D. Jackson, "Soviet Reassessment of Reagan, 1985–1988," *Political Science Quarterly* 113, no. 4 (Winter 1998–1999): 617–644.

31. Reagan, "The US-Soviet Relationship," 4.

32. Anatoly Dobrynin, *In Confidence* (New York: Random House, 1995), 611.

33. Reagan, "The US-Soviet Relationship," 2, 4.

34. Anatoly Chernyaev's notes from April 3, 1986, Politburo session, Brown Conference, archival document no. 20.

35. Chernyaev in Brown Conference, transcript, p. 64.

36. McFarlane in ibid., p. 67. See also Robert C. McFarlane, Memorandum for the President, "Checklist of US-Soviet Issues: Status and Prospects," February 18, 1984, available in Jack F. Matlock papers, US-USSR Relations, January–April 1984, Box 23, Ronald Reagan Presidential Library, Simi Valley, California.

37. McFarlane in Brown Conference, transcript, pp. 66–68.

38. Ibid.

39. Ibid., pp. 67–68. See also Pavel Palazhchenko, *My Years with Gorbachev and Shevardnadze: The Memoir of a Soviet Interpreter* (University Park: Pennsylvania State University Press, 1997). The Reagan administration's decision to focus on topics other than arms reduction frustrated Gorbachev and his aides, however. They

continued to regard arms control as the defining feature of superpower relations. See Gorbachev, *Memoirs,* especially 453.

40. Robert Caro, *The Passage of Power: The Years of Lyndon Johnson* (New York: Knopf, 2012), xiv.

41. Reagan, *An American Life,* 13.

42. Cannon, *President Reagan: The Role of a Lifetime,* 291.

43. George P. Shultz, *Turmoil and Triumph: My Years as Secretary of State* (New York: Charles Scribner's Sons, 1993), 466.

44. As recounted in Chester J. Pach Jr., "Sticking to His Guns: Reagan and National Security," in W. Elliot Brownlee and Hugh Davis Graham, eds., *The Reagan Presidency: Pragmatic Conservatism and Its Legacies*" (Lawrence: University Press of Kansas, 2003), 103.

45. Kenneth Adelman interview, September 30, 2003, Ronald Reagan Oral History Project, Miller Center of Public Affairs, University of Virginia, available at millercenter.org/the-presidency/presidential-oral-histories/kenneth-adelman-oral-history-director-arms-control-and.

46. James Mann, *The Rebellion of Ronald Reagan* (New York: Viking, 2009), 47–51.

47. Richard Nixon and Henry Kissinger, "A Real Peace," *National Review* 39 (May 22, 1987): 32.

48. Shultz, *Turmoil and Triumph,* 509.

49. Kara Goldin, "Great Leaders Take People Where They Might Not Want to Go," *Forbes,* October 1, 2018, available at www.forbes.com/sites/karagoldin/2018/10/01/great-leaders-take-people-where-they-may-not-want-to-go/#70bbdb0b1421.

50. Ronald Reagan, handwritten letter to Mikhail Gorbachev, November 28, 1985, in Saltoun-Ebin, *The Reagan Files,* 286–290. Reagan's determination to abolish nuclear weapons and pursue SDI is even more remarkable given his predilection to avoid conflict within the administration.

51. For example, see globalzero.org.

52. Aleksandr Bessmertnykh in "A Retrospective on the End of the Cold War," Oral History Conference sponsored by the Woodrow Wilson School of Public and International Affairs, Princeton University, February 26–27, 1993, Session 2, pp. 125–127, 160.

Index

administration and, 18; on the
unraveling of the Cold War, 9
McCain, John, 6–7
McFarlane, Robert ("Bud"): appointed
national security adviser in 1983, 18;
on Congress and SDI, 69–70; on Jack
Matlock's reports for Reagan about
Soviet history and culture, 36,
140–141; moderate views in US
foreign policy, 16–17; on the nuclear
arms race, 68; on the objective of SDI,
74; on perceptions of Soviet strength
in the Reagan administration, 50; on
Nancy Reagan as an influence on the
president, 33–34; on Reagan's
opposition to nuclear weapons,
62–63; Reagan's "peace through
strength" policy and, 32–33; Reagan's
speech of January 1984 and, 27, 29
Meese, Edwin, 15, 16, 61, 67
missile defense systems: of the Soviets,
109–110, 179n29. *See also* Strategic
Defense Initiative
Mitterrand, François, 26
Moscow summit (1988), 38
Mulroney, Brian, 60
Muravchik, Joshua, 5
Mutual Assured Destruction (MAD): the
ABM Treaty and, 60, 63; concept of,
59; reactions within the Reagan
administration to Reagan's stance
against, 66–67; Reagan's rejection of
for a nonnuclear world, 142, 143, 145;
SDI and Reagan's opposition to the
concept of, 59, 60, 61–65, 74–75;
Soviet views of the SDI proposal
and, 112

National Association of Evangelicals, 22
National Intelligence Estimates (NIEs),
47, 48–49, 161n15, 164n44
national security advisers, 18, 152n23
National Security Council, 144

National Security Decision Directive 66,
54–55, 166n70
National Security Decision Directive 75,
152n5
National Security Decision Directive
166, 159n113
New Thinking policy: in conventional
accounts of the end of the Cold War,
2–3; development of Gorbachev's
reform views, 85–89; doctrine of
sufficient defense, 107–108;
Gorbachev's implementation of,
77–79, 89–91; growth of reform in the
Soviet Union and, 80–85; impact of
Reagan's hard-line foreign policy on,
100–101; impact of the Chernobyl
nuclear disaster on, 92–94; Soviet
withdrawal from Afghanistan and,
98–99; triumphalism's fallacious view
of Reagan's influence on, 76–77, 79,
99–100, 129–130
NIEs. *See* National Intelligence Estimates
1941 syndrome, 24, 104
Nitze, Paul, 73
Nixon, Richard, 144
nonnuclear world: Sergei Akhromeyev
and, 182n65; Gorbachev's 1986
proposal to eliminate all nuclear
weapons, 117–118; Reagan's and
Gorbachev's common interest in, 139;
Reagan's opposition to nuclear
weapons and MAD, 61–65; Reagan's
vision and leadership for, 8–9,
141–146; Reagan's vision for SDI and,
60, 74–75, 131–132, 142–143;
resistance to in the Reagan
administration, 65–67. *See also*
nuclear arms reduction
North Atlantic Treaty Organization
(NATO): Able Archer 83 and, 24–26,
29, 30; Euromissile crisis, 20–21, 24;
opposition to Reagan's vision of a
nonnuclear world, 145

Studies in Conflict, Diplomacy, and Peace

Series Editors: George C. Herring, Andrew L. Johns,
and Kathryn C. Statler

This series focuses on key moments of conflict, diplomacy, and peace from the eighteenth century to the present to explore their wider significance in the development of U.S. foreign relations. The series editors welcome new research in the form of original monographs, interpretive studies, biographies, and anthologies from historians, political scientists, journalists, and policymakers. A primary goal of the series is to examine the United States' engagement with the world, its evolving role in the international arena, and the ways in which the state, nonstate actors, individuals, and ideas have shaped and continue to influence history, both at home and abroad.

Advisory Board Members

Books in the Series

Lincoln, Seward, and US Foreign Relations in the Civil War Era
Joseph A. Fry

Obama at War: Congress and the Imperial Presidency
Ryan C. Hendrickson

The Cold War at Home and Abroad: Domestic Politics and US Foreign Policy since 1945
Edited by Andrew L. Johns and Mitchell B. Lerner

US Presidential Elections and Foreign Policy: Candidates, Campaigns, and Global Politics from FDR to Bill Clinton
Edited by Andrew Johnstone and Andrew Priest

Paving the Way for Reagan: The Influence of Conservative Media on US Foreign Policy
Laurence R. Jurdem

The Conversion of Senator Arthur H. Vandenberg: From Isolation to International Engagement
Lawrence S. Kaplan

Harold Stassen: Eisenhower, the Cold War, and the Pursuit of Nuclear Disarmament
Lawrence S. Kaplan

JFK and de Gaulle: How America and France Failed in Vietnam, 1961–1963
Sean J. McLaughlin

Nixon's Back Channel to Moscow: Confidential Diplomacy and Détente
Richard A. Moss

Breaking Protocol: America's First Female Ambassadors, 1933–1964
Philip Nash

Peacemakers: American Leadership and the End of Genocide in the Balkans
James W. Pardew

The Currents of War: A New History of American-Japanese Relations, 1899–1941
Sidney Pash